Learning to Be a Man

Learning to Be a Man

Culture, Socialization and Gender Identity in Five Caribbean Communities

Barry Chevannes

THE UNIVERSITY OF THE WEST INDIES PRESS

Barbados • Jamaica • Trinidad and Tobago

The University of the West Indies Press
1A Aqueduct Flats   Mona
Kingston 7   Jamaica   W I

05 04 03 02 01   5 4 3 2

CATALOGUING IN PUBLICATION DATA

Chevannes, Barry.
   Learning to be a man : culture, socialization and gender identity
   in five Caribbean communities / Barry Chevannes.
   p. cm.

   Includes bibliographical references and index.
   ISBN: 976-640-092-X

   1. Men – Caribbean, English-speaking – Socialization.
   2. Gender identity – Caribbean, English-speaking. I. Title.
   HQ1090.7.C3C43 2001   305.331 dc-20

Book design by CAP Designs Ltd.
Cover design by Adlib Studio.
Cover photograph by Suzanne Murphy-Larronde. Reproduced
courtesy of Suzanne Murphy-Larronde and Earthwatch Institute
(www.earthwatch.org).

Printed in Canada.

To Paulette

Contents

Preface

The research on which this monograph is based was carried out by the present writer, then head of the Department of Sociology and Social Work, in association with Mrs Janet Brown, head of the Caribbean Child Development Centre, both departments of the University of the West Indies, Mona, at the request of the UNICEF Caribbean Office, then headed by Mrs Marjorie Newman-Williams. UNICEF's brief for the children of the world has everywhere focused on the female, universally the more disadvantaged, and subject of severe inequalities. But while it is true that here in the Caribbean women lag behind men in such vital areas as overall employment, income, and power, in certain important respects they seem to be doing much better. The female is present in larger numbers at virtually all levels of the education system, with an increasing attrition of males the further up one goes. In a number of anglophone Caribbean countries, on the other hand, a rising crime rate, much of it related to drug trafficking and substance abuse, and including murder, directly involves male adolescents and young men in increasing numbers. The steady reversal in educational performance over the decades led Professor Errol Miller (1986) to develop his well-known, though little understood, thesis that Jamaican men had been marginalized. His work, which he titled *The Marginalization of the Black Male*, has been used by many as scientific validation of the popular perception that women were eclipsing men as the public architects and leaders of society, while the latter seemed bent on the destructive course of anomie.

Quite rightly UNICEF was concerned that its global commitment to bring about greater gender equality, which in effect meant advocacy on behalf of the female, did not forfeit its responsibility towards the male in a region that did not seem in vital aspects to follow the global pattern. The first task was therefore to examine what was taking place in the socialization process to bring about such widening differences in motivation and behaviour between the genders. It is this that constituted the objective of this study. Indeed, Janet Brown and I titled our report, "Why Man Stay So". Our intent here was not to argue that man has an essential and unchanging nature, far from it, but to call attention to what we considered an oft-ignored point, namely that society blames "man" for attitudes and values that society inculcates in "man". In our study, we found a lot of neglect and very harsh and cruel methods of bringing up male children, as will be evident to the reader, making more than a little incongruous our expectation that grown men should be soft and caring. It is important that the discourse on gender behaviours avoids moralism.

Learning to Be a Man is not the final word on male socialization in our region but part of the beginning of our attempts to come to grips with a neglected area of research. Even as I write, there is a proposal developed by the Centre for Gender Development Studies at the University of the West Indies to undertake a comprehensive study of male performance in education, and another being invited from this author. Public anxiety over the declining proportion of males at the University of the West Indies led one daily newspaper in Jamaica to identify, through its editorial, with Chancellor Sir Shridath Ramphal's concern, voiced at the 1998 graduation exercise, that at the Mona campus the proportion of graduating males was under 26 percent, an all-time low.

But as scholars join in the pursuit of knowledge in this area, we have to avoid giving validity to a widely held assumption that the "male problem" is basically a working-class problem. The present study runs this danger by its focus. Scholars in women and gender studies know that this is not the case, that certain male behaviours are problematic at all levels of society. Achieving some balance even from this early stage is necessary if workable solutions are to be found.

Acknowledgments

This work would have been impossible without the foresight and tangible support of Mrs Marjorie Newman-Williams and other members of the UNICEF community, in particular Mrs Eva Richards (Jamaica) and Dr Danielle Brady (Guyana). My colleague and co-investigator, Janet Brown, gave valuable criticism and encouragement, as did other colleagues of the University of the West Indies, who commented on an earlier draft. Among them I must mention Mrs Sian Williams, Dr Patricia Anderson, Mrs Hermione McKenzie, Professor Elsa Leo-Rhynie and Mrs Rose Davies. I owe a special debt of gratitude to the members of the research team: Patrick Phillips, Genevieve Tomlinson, Franklyn Smith and Elaine Nelson (Grannitree); Charles Atkinson, Owen Ellis, Pauline Lawrence-Nattie, Junior Rowe and Jeannette Bartley (Motown); Herbert Gayle, Claudette Richardson-Pious, the late Joe Ruglass and Marcia Higgins (Joetown); Hubert Wong, Roopnarine Tewari, Kamini Persaud, Hardat Singh and Latchman Ganesh (Overflow); and Leo Casimir, Davis Letang, Ava McIntyre, B. Roach, Carole Gallion and Glenroy Toussaint (Riverbreeze). With deep regret, we all mourn the passing of Joe Ruglass, a personal friend, in whose honour we named the inner city community studied.

Professor Jaipaul Roopnarine prepared a literature review prior to the fieldwork, while the following advisors and consultants gave valuable help during the fieldwork: Mrs Edith Bellot, UWI resident tutor, Ms Hyacinth

Elwin, Mr MacDonald Thomas and Mr Francis Severin (Dominica); Dr Janice Jackson, Ms Baswat Shiw Persad, Dr Ivan Henry, Mr Berkeley Steward and Ms Carole Lawes (Guyana); Mr Geof Brown, Mr Clement Branche, Dr Patricia Mohammed and Mrs Monica Robinson (Jamaica).

Thanks also to Linda Craigie-Brown for her tireless commitment in coordinating the administration; Olive Goulbourn for typing the fieldnotes; Marva Campbell, Marilyn Brown, Nehru Hudson, Rhona Jones and Charles Pershad, all staff of the Caribbean Child Development Centre, and Franklyn Wapp, Marlene Smith, Janet Phillips-Higgins and Meloney Lewis, staff of the Department of Sociology and Social Work, for their invaluable administrative support. In putting together the final draft, I received special help from Herbert Gayle on additional bibliographic sources and from Marsha Dennie on general editing.

The hospitality of Joy and Joe James and of Aldine and Conrad Shillingford made the writing and revision of this manuscript a real pleasure. It also would have been impossible without the hundreds of men, women, young people and children, whose trust and cooperation provided us with the information we sought and more. I only hope that the succeeding pages have done justice to their efforts, those of the many others mentioned above and, I cannot omit, the incisive and thoughtful comments of the anonymous readers. As the author I stand alone in accepting responsibility for the final outcome of this work. Finally, for the time and the space I must thank Amba, Abena and Paulette, with love.

1

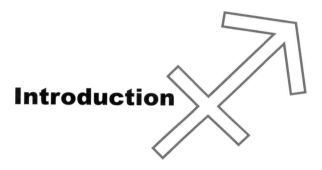

Introduction

In the nearly sixty years of anglophone Caribbean anthropology and sociology, no other institution or aspect of social life has been as researched as the African family. The focus, however, has been on its structure, understandably so, since its complexity was the subject of intense debate. Not surprisingly, therefore, there is little in the literature directly on the socialization of children. An exception was Madeline Kerr's study (1963) of personality formation in Jamaica, which focused on the socialization and education of children. Based on her observations, interviews and tests, Kerr concludes that the Jamaican personality is the product of a cultural split. She identifies five social situations where these are manifest: a split in parental roles between an African matriarchal system continued through slavery and reinforced by present-day economic conditions, on one hand, and a Victorian English model which emphasizes patriarchy, on the other; lack of "culturally directed and approved channels" of socialization (p. 170) resulting in apathy, vagueness and "love of complicated reasoning, or the use of long words and of abstractions" (p. 171); colour problems, engendering feelings of inferiority and powerlessness, which then give rise to compensation through guile and deceit; slavery, from which derives an "extrapunitive attitude"(p.173) and the habit of blaming others; living in a Western technological world, as against living in a world of magic, resulting in the development of conflicting attitudes.

Among the socializing patterns creating this personality type we might mention three. The first is forced weaning, which comes at about two years old. Kerr attributes to this the Jamaican male's strong ambivalence to women, on one hand permanently tied to mother, on the other promiscuous to his spouse. The second is the influence of flogging in producing anxiety. Despite the blood curdling threats, severe beating is seldom applied to the child. It is the fantasy of it that children react to by conforming. This point will bear recalling, for as a method of control the threat of a severe beating to be administered by the father is far more common than the reality. Third, the early socializing of the child into domestic work (indoor for girls, outdoor for boys) combined with their gender-segregated type of play underdevelops the creativity of the child. Once an extroverted and spontaneous person, the child reaches adolescence an introvert, due to "a lack of channels of expression" (Kerr 1963:194).

Outside of this work, information on socialization comes in bits and pieces from the overall studies of the family. Herskovits and Herskovits (1947) were the first and only major scholars to identify the maternal focus as an African tradition in family structure. By two years old children are taught to put things away, and girls will be given small brooms with which to sweep the yard. By the time they reach six years old, girls are helping with household work after school and boys with outdoor work in the vegetable garden, a division that continues right through childhood. Girls play with dolls and housekeeping, boys with marbles, tops, cricket, hunting and fishing. Edith Clarke's study (1957), conducted at the same time as Kerr's, portrayed a pattern of inactive or absent fathers as the framework within which children were brought up by their mothers; hence the title of her study, *My Mother Who Fathered Me*. Mothers were close to the children, gained their cooperation in domestic chores, and flogged and reprimanded them more. The culture produced "reciprocal dependence" between mother and son – he supported her as soon as he began to earn an income, in return for her indulgent growing up. Clarke's focus was on the variation in family structure, as was Simey's (1946) and Henriques' (1953). Henriques found little gender differentiation up to age seven or eight years, but his focus being colour, he found a "general atmosphere of frustration" among Jamaican children, which he attributed to favouritism based on skin colour; conflict with parents over such things as money, job choice, or relations with the opposite sex; or contradictory messages from parents – extreme brutality at one time, excessive kindness the next; or punishment for lying or stealing, but reward for deceiving socially superior people. Raymond Smith (1956) registered a significant, early insight with his emphasis on structure as process. Smith traced the life cycle of the family, from extended to nuclear to extended, highlighting the central role of the mother as nurturer and the special bonds with her son. He used the term *matri-filiation* to describe this central role in intra-familial relationships, and pointed to the opposing marginality of fathers, even though the heads of the households. At the same time the family structure allows for socializing forces other than mother, such as grandmother and aunts. Gender differentiation begins from around eight years old. Boys are considered mature once they begin earning an income, some of which they give to their mothers. Smith was the first, and to my knowledge the only, major scholar to draw attention to the importance of the biological father. It is a very unusual situation for a child not to know who his or her father is, whether or not he is present.

By the time Hyman Rodman (1971) completed his study of Coconut Village in Trinidad and Peter Wilson (1973) his on the tiny island of Providencia, investigators were quite clear about the sex role division of domestic responsibilities: the father, present or not, is the one who *minds* the child, while the mother *cares*. This division remains clearly drawn right up to the studies of the Women in the Caribbean Project (Massiah 1986), which found women the effective managers of the household but deferring to their spouses as heads. Two other important contributions were made by Durant-Gonzalez and by Brown et al. Durant-Gonzalez (1976) showed the domestic restrictions placed on girls, and the role of pregnancy and childbirth as a rite of passage in transforming girls into women. Brown et al. (1993) revealed the importance of fatherhood to men and their conception of their own responsibilities. This study showed that men were more involved in the day to day interaction with and upbringing of their children than generally thought.

By contrast, the Indo-Caribbean family structure presented less of a challenge to anthropology and sociology. The traditional North Indian culture being already well known, the focus of Indo-Caribbean research has been on social and cultural change, and on ethnic identity and race relations. Whatever the area of study, the North Indian culture and indenture provided the backdrop. The pioneering works of R.T. Smith and Jayawardena (1958, 1959, 1996) and of Jayawardena himself (1960, 1963, 1965) remain unsurpassed for the detailed analysis of Indian family patterns in Guyana. Niehoff and Niehoff (1960), Klass (1988), later ethnographies by Nevadomsky (1985), Silverman (1980) and Thakur (1978), along with the demographic work of Roberts and Braithwaite (1962), and the historical study of Bisnaut (1977) all combine to present a picture of continuity and change within the Indo-Caribbean family, some scholars emphasizing more of one than of the other. Continuity in family life may be seen in the ideal of the joint extended family, male dominance in the headship of the family, birth preference, virilocality, and female deference and subordination to males; gender segregation, gender division of labour; Hindu beliefs and practices governing the life cycle rituals. On the side of change, caste as the governing principle of status ascription and social relations has undergone the most radical transformation. Its most far-reaching effect on the family may be felt in inter-caste marriages, where the prestige and social standing of families are no longer based on birth but on principles of achievement, wealth and class being the main ones. Likewise, the status of women has also been undergoing changes, the combined result of the sex ratio in the early years of migration to the Caribbean and of modern education, and itself resulting in new challenges to gender ideology. Segmentation within the joint family, a feature of its life cycle even in India, has become more intense, as the enveloping culture of individualism and personal achievement put greater pressure on male children to establish their own independence. The joint family remains an ideal, however, its jointedness much attenuated and shortlived.

The socialization of the Indo-Caribbean child, then, takes place within an environment that evinces both stability and change. Born into a warm and nurturing environment children are the recipients of attention from close relatives and parents alike, at least until their parents establish their own nuclear units. As in North India, the birth preference is for males, for through them the family line is continued. Gender divisions are clearly demarcated in the division of labour within the household, though, as we shall see, the birth order forces departure from the norms. But generally speaking, boys perform outdoor chores and activities in support of the running of the household and in production alongside their fathers, while girls perform indoor activities under the supervision of their mothers, and in preparation for the roles they are expected later to play come marriage.

Marriage among Caribbean Indians used to take place early, soon after puberty, through arrangements by their families. Western influences, however, have been seeing a decline in arranged marriages and the rise of romantic love, though the respect for kinship involvement and traditional rituals remain. Changes have also been afoot in the pattern of formal education. Well into the twentieth century the clear pattern was to educate boys but keep back girls for marriage. Since the 1950s girls have achieved equal numerical standing with boys in the educational system and have been outdistancing them in numbers and performance. Like his African counterpart, the Indo-Caribbean male faces critical challenges to gender identity.

The relative lack of focus on the socialization of males in the Caribbean and the need to have available more up-to-date knowledge thus provided the rationale for undertaking the present study. Research was already underway when an important study was undertaken by Bailey et al. (1996) on socialization in gender relations. Based on focus group research conducted in Jamaica, Dominica and Barbados among children and community groups, their findings are remarkably similar to our own. Between this study and the present one, we thus have begun to close the gap in our knowledge and to have a better grasp of the current situation in the region.

Objectives

The objective of this work was to study at the community level in a number of Caribbean countries the socialization process, focusing on males. As will be explained presently, the methodologies adopted were qualitative. Specifically and within our short timeframe, the aim was to identify the processes and events through which Caribbean males were imbued with knowledge of the roles they were expected to play as boys and later as men; the process through which they acquired the status of manhood; and the concomitant attitudes and values shaping their conception of themselves and their relations with others, females and males. Because the study of one gender is offset against the other, it was envisaged that this study would also keep within its purview the socialization of females, insofar as it was necessary for our understanding of the males. Thus this was not intended to be a study of the socialization of children in general, but rather a study specifically of our males.

This objective encompassed a *how* and a *what*. We assumed, first, that there was a way, or ways, in which children were trained to be girls and boys, women and men. This could imply some methodology or system. If there were, we wanted to find out what these were. We assumed, secondly, that parents, adults and whoever were the agents of socialization had some fairly definite ideas about gender roles, which they would be seeking to impart. It was important also to get as clear a picture of these as possible.

Our decision to site our study within communities was determined by the methodologies we planned to adopt, namely a combination of ethno-graphic and animation techniques. To be able to observe the interaction between the sexes, on the one hand, and between adults and children, on the other, we saw communities as ideal locations. As *loci* of primary rela-tionships, both in the sense of where families and other primary groups are located as well as in the sense of systems of face-to-face relationships, communities are also tied into the wider social system, through the school, the communications media and other secondary institutions. The commu-nity in this sense is a hub of interpersonal and formal relations.

All the decisions except identification of the communities were made jointly with UNICEF. Limiting the timeframe to only six months and the number of communities to six was determined primarily by the funding available. We felt that six months was the absolute minimum for any mean-ingful ethnographic work, though a year would have been better. And while the funds could permit longer field work in fewer communities, we felt it was important at this exploratory stage to get as wide a cross-cultural com-parison as possible. The reader may judge whether we made an error of judgment. Jamaica was chosen for the acuity of its urban problems, Guyana for its ethnic polarization, which is sharper than in Trinidad, the only other anglophone country with a large Indian population. Determined to include one of the smaller countries, we settled on Dominica, as against any other Windward or Leeward island, primarily for funding reasons.

The Countries

Dominica is a small country in the Windward group of islands with a popu-lation of approximately 70,000. Its Human Development Index (HDI) places it 51st in the world, at a value of 0.819 (UNDP 1993). The HDI is a 0.000 to

1.000 scale used by the United Nations to measure the three most important development indicators combined, namely life expectancy, education and income. With an economy based on export agriculture and agro-industry, Dominica ranks in the high development group. The life expectancy of Dominicans is 76 years, more than eight years above the average for Latin America and the Caribbean and one and a half years more than the average for industrial countries. Spending on education was 5.8 percent of gross national product (GNP), which on a per capita basis was put at US$2,220 in 1990. Although there are no recent estimates of adult literacy, 79 percent of all Dominicans complete primary school. Women make up over 42 percent of the labour force. Over recent years, Dominica's population, more than 90 percent of whom are of African origin, has shown negative growth (minus 0.2), due to out-migration principally to the United States. The country is primarily Roman Catholic. The capital, Roseau, is home to an estimated 22 percent of the total population.

Guyana's HDI ranking is 0.541, or the bottom end of the medium development group. It ranked 105th in the world. Its life expectancy of 64.2 years was slightly below that of the regional Latin America and the Caribbean average of 67.4. Per capita GNP was low, US$380, but its adult literacy high, 96 percent. Of the three countries in the study, Guyana spent the most on education, relative to GNP, 8.8 percent. Its economy also is based on agriculture, the two principal export commodities being sugar and rice. The country, however, is rich in natural resources, large rivers, minerals (bauxite, gold and diamonds) and timber. Guyana's population of 0.8 million comprises two major ethnic groups: the Indians, who make up over 55 percent of the total population; and the Africans, 35 percent. The rest comprise Europeans and Amerindians. The Indians are predominantly agricultural workers and farmers, while the Africans are found predominantly in the service and industrial sectors and the professions. Women accounted for only 21 percent of the total labour force. Georgetown, Guyana's capital, with an estimated 25 percent of the population, has all the features of a Caribbean city: residential stratification, decaying ghettos and a growing crime rate.

Jamaica, largest of the anglophone Caribbean countries, has a population of 2.4 million, 95 percent of whom are of African descent. It ranks 69th in the HDI, with a score of 0.736 which places it near the top end of the medium development group. Life expectancy is 73.1 years, or above the regional average, and its adult literacy rate is 98 percent. Combined primary and secondary enrolment is 80 percent. Per capita GNP was US$1,500, well below the regional average of US$2,130. As a percentage of GNP, Jamaica spent 5.9 percent on education.

Fifty-five percent of Jamaica's population live in urban areas, the largest being metropolitan Kingston, which accounts for nearly 30 percent of the total. Even more than Georgetown, Kingston is residentially stratified, the higher income groups living further and further inland, the lower income groups living along or near the waterfront. The urban ghettos are home to the poor and destitute; there they live in substandard and overcrowded housing. The economy rests primarily on tourism, bauxite, agriculture and light manufacturing. According to the Planning Institute of Jamaica (1998), 16.5 percent of the 1.1 million–strong labour force are unemployed. These represent a formidable army, most of which is distributed in the rural parishes, but with the greatest concentration in Kingston. Forty percent of the lowest income-earning households earned 15.3 percent of the total income (UNDP 1993). The picture is at its worst when viewed from the perspective of the lowest 20 percent; these earned 5.4 percent. The ratio of the highest 20 percent to the lowest 20 percent was 9:1. Up to the mid 1990s Jamaica suffered from high annual inflation rates, 18.3 percent in 1990. A very sizeable informal economy exists, concentrated mainly in Kingston, but also including the city of Montego Bay and the larger towns. Estimates vary as to its size, which is put at between 28 percent and 40 percent of GNP (Witter and Kirton 1990).

Decision on the types of communities to study was also made jointly with our sponsors. We both wished to ensure a rural-urban spread. That done, we were left on our own to identify the particular communities, which we did after extensive local consultation. Only five, however, form the basis of the present study; due to personal misfortune, no ethnographic data were available from the sixth, Williamsfield, an Afro-Guyanese "ghetto" in Georgetown, selected to provide a contrast with the Indo-Guyanese community of Overflow and the inner city Jamaican community of Joetown. Two communities in the study are rural, one suburban, and two urban. The two rural ones are Grannitree in Jamaica and Overflow in Guyana, while the suburban one is Riverbreeze, a working-class community two kilometres from central Roseau, which was settled by people drawn from rural Dominica. The two distinctly urban communities in the study are Motown and Joetown in Kingston. Motown was founded after a major hurricane in 1951, while Joetown lies in that part of Kingston now called the "inner city", a term used to describe the extreme urban decay that is characteristic of similar urban communities across the world.

Research Methods

Our next step was the selection and training of the research team. As this depended very much on the research methodologies we decided to use, it is best to say a few words here. Each team was made up of one male ethnographer and an animation group of three persons, two animators, one male and one female, and a documentalist.

Ethnography is "the art and science of describing a group or culture" (Fetterman 1989:11). To be able to describe, one must first understand, that is to make sense and meaning out of what one observes and hears. To achieve this understanding, the ethnographer must cultivate the trust of the people he or she studies, as a way of getting them to impart knowledge about themselves which is accurate and not misleading. Building trust in a stranger is not accomplished overnight. To help, the ethnographer often relies on a "broker", someone already known to, and trusted by, the community or the group, and, once accepted, he or she adopts the method known as *participant-observation,* a term which "suggests that you are directly involved in community life, observing and talking with people as you learn from them their view of reality" (Agar 1980:114). Participant-observation has the additional advantage of reducing the stranger element which sometimes makes people perform for the observer rather than behave normally. Thus, apart from his or her own observations of what people do and say, the ethnographer asks questions of and converses with just about anyone, but primarily those he or she identifies as knowledgeable and reliable, the "key informants". The ethnographer sees the actions, interactions and products of people, enquires about their beliefs, opinions, attitudes and values, why they do the things they do, what is the meaning of their actions, words, gestures, and in this way tries to arrive at an understanding of the group being studied.

These observations and interviews provide the contents of the ethnographer's fieldnotes; which in turn provide the material on which his or her study is put together. Thus, on top of each ethnographer's observations and interviews comes the writing, the presentation of what the ethnographer understands about the community or culture to the unfamiliar, a process which inevitably involves interpretation. It is here that ethnography has come in for a great deal of introspection and criticism (see Clifford and Marcus 1986). As a text, the ethnographic work is inevitably selective of what it includes and excludes; thus what is presented as a factual portrayal of the way of life of a community is indeed "something made or fashioned" (Clifford 1986:6) by the writer – at best partial truths. As an interpreter of the unknown, the unfamiliar, the ethnographer is like Hermes, who, when he agreed to be "messenger of the gods, he promised Zeus not to lie. He did not promise to tell the whole truth" (Crapanzano 1986:53).

I would have to agree that the profiles and analyses of the males and females whose residence, actions and interactions form the communities we studied are ultimately my own constructs, made even less representational by the fact that they have been reprocessed from the interpretations of our researchers. I have no quarrel with this perspective, insofar as it seeks to expose the inextricably subjective nature of any attempt to know the other and to dethrone the hubris of Western canons of epistemology where *the colonial other* is concerned. But as Comaroff and Comaroff (1992:9) remind us, "Ethnography, in any case, does not speak *for* others, but *about* them. Neither imaginatively nor empirically can it ever 'capture' their reality." The fact that we can never know fully and absolutely does not mean that we cannot and therefore should not attempt to know anything at all.

Supplementing the ethnographic perspective are the data gathered by the animation team. Animation is a reflexive method widely used in development work which utilizes drama, games and other performance techniques to get participants to act out normative patterns of behaviour, to question them in discussion and formulate actions for change (see Kassam and Kemal 1982; Barndt 1981; Slim and Thompson 1993). It was particularly useful in the work of Sistren Theatre Collective (1986) in raising the consciousness of women, and had recently been adopted by Brown, Anderson and Chevannes (1993) in their research project among fathers in rural and urban Jamaica. The animation method begins with an "entry event", a play, or a series of dramatic skits, or a concert, at which the community is informed of the research project, and groups are organized to discuss par-

2

Socialization of the Genders

In its most common usage socialization refers to the process whereby children, from birth through adolescence, are shaped in the values, customs and behavioural norms required to live together with other adult and non-adult members of society. Gender socialization, therefore, refers to the shaping process during which those values, customs and behavioural norms that account for the sexual differentiation in adult personal identity and behaviour are transmitted. A definition like this makes two assumptions. The first is that children are not born with the "values, customs and behavioural norms" requisite for life in society, unlike other primates, though, as we shall see presently, the issue is far from simple. Children learn through a variety of ways: observation, imitation, coercion, persuasion, reward, punishment, instruction, example. Second, the society, meaning the social world of adults, knows what its "values, customs and behavioural norms" are. If it did not, there would be nothing into which children should be socialized. How socialization takes place, what are the socializing ideas creating the identities and separating the behaviour of males different from females? These are questions which the theories of socialization attempt to answer.

scientist needs the cooperation of people. Whereas in the survey method (the most widely used in quantitative social research) cooperation is premised on complete anonymity, in ethnography (the most extensively used in qualitative research) cooperation is personalized and based on trust, on the rapport the researcher is able to establish with the people he or she interacts with. The ethnographic field is therefore narrow in range but intended to be penetrating in depth, as the researcher seeks admittance into people's personal worlds of experience and meaning. Five teams of researchers working each in a different community will produce profiles of varying emphases and quality, for under the constraints of the short time frame some individuals will generate rapport more quickly than others, or display better skills in observation, interviewing, interpretation and writing. The result is an unevenness in the quality of the profiles.

In presenting the findings, the choice lay between a thematic and a community-based approach. I chose the latter so as not to lose the context. of community, which plays a far greater role in shaping our males than is generally thought, and as I hope will become clear. The result is a profile of each community of social relations and culture within which the socialization of our children takes place, and sketches of the personalities and agents effecting that process. The order of presentation is from rural to urban, from Grannitree to Joetown, the general direction of internal migration. The final chapter highlights some of the themes running through the five communities.

3. Gender role expectations and performance by men, as perceived and defined by men and by women.
4. Peer group socialization among children, adolescents and adults.
5. The meanings and expression of love, affection and emotional supports as they differ or are similar, for men and women.
6. The different bases (accorded by men and women) for respecting or rejecting men in society.
7. The behaviours that merit reward and punishment, the means of rewarding and punishing, and the differences in application with respect to gender.
8. The rights adults, adolescents and children perceive adolescents and children to have, at what stages of their development, and the gender differences with respect to these rights.

This being a qualitative research project and not a survey with its carefully designed and tested questionnaire, in which each subject is the anonymous respondent to the specific questions asked, our researchers, particularly those engaged in ethnographic data gathering, were instructed to maintain a degree of flexibility in deciding which of the above concerns to give priority to and when, as well as being "led" by our informants and the field experience.

Fieldnotes were to be written up as soon as possible after the particular engagement (for example, at the end of the day, or first thing in the mornings after activities of the night before), to reduce the loss of important details. These notes were to be turned in to the local coordinators and sent to us to be typed for easier analysis. The research period was to have lasted from February 1995 to July–August 1995.

It would have been a miracle if the project had gone as planned. As it turned out, problems developed in Guyana and Dominica which had serious impact on both the quality and quantity of the ethnographic data, resulting in personnel changes over which we were unable to exercise the kind of control we would have liked. And with time ticking away, we had to make the best of it. It was not until September–October that data gathering, which started late, was everywhere brought to an end.

But even without such unforeseen developments, there was bound to be a certain unevenness. In the quest for new knowledge, every social

ticular issues and questions. These discussion groups are of two sorts: seed groups and core groups, the difference being that seed groups are formed first, and become core with consistency in attendance. Groups may be gender specific or mixed, or organized according to age. The animators' role, as in a focus group, is to lead but not to dominate the discussion, while the documentalist records the data, who says what, along with any relevant observations. Each meeting of the group goes through three phases, a warm-up phase aimed at breaking down inhibitions, the main phase spent exploring the issues, and a cooling-down phase which recalls the evening's conclusions and sets the next agenda. Later the team meets and prepares a summary of the proceedings, in addition to the verbatim notes.

Given our relatively short timeframe, we saw the use of both ethnography and animation as complementary. For the ethnography four students and one social scientist were recruited. For the one Dominican and three Jamaican communities the students were all graduates who had either taken a course or received training in qualitative research. The social scientist was a member of the Faculty of Social Sciences at the University of Guyana, who had himself conducted research using ethnographic methods. Of the ten animators, six were trained social work or dramatic arts graduates, the rest practising dramatists or teachers. The documentalists were drawn from the teaching profession.

A five-day orientation and training programme was then arranged for members of the research teams and the local coordinators, with members of a project advisory committee of academic experts that had been set up in attendance. Apart from the expected introduction of the project's aims and objectives, the researchers were exposed to the general issues by way of expert-led reviews of socialization literature and the problematic position of men in contemporary Caribbean society. One day was devoted to the ethnographic methodology and practice, one to animation techniques, and a third to the key questions for research.

In relation to this last, we formulated eight topics:

1. Gender preferences for offspring, by men and women; the reasons for them, and their practical implications.
2. Gender segregation in household labour, income generation and leisure activities among children, adolescents and adults.

Sociobiological Explanations

Every known society organizes many if not most or all human activities along lines of gender, and orders the relations between males and females in a manner that places females in a position subordinate to males. So universal is this that the question arises whether there is any natural, that is to say biological, explanation for the sexual division of labour and gender identity. The answer is not straightforward. In a reported study in 1972 foetally androgenized females "in later childhood were more tomboyish than controls, expended greater physical energy in their pastimes and showed greater preference for playing with boys" (Hutt 1978:175). In yet another report three androgenized females reared as boys adopted a male gender identity, while four others reared as girls showed preference for traditional boys' toys and activities, none of the seven showing any interest in nurturing activities (Hutt 1978:175–76). And in the opposite disorder, testicular feminizing syndrome, where the target organs are unresponsive to androgen secreted in the testes, the individuals, though males, develop as females. Kagan (1971) found sex differences among children comparable to those among other primates, immature females staying closer to mothers, and younger males engaging in more frequent display of aggression and restlessness. More recently Schlegel and Barry (1991), adopting an ethological approach, have sought to explain sex role differentiation and segregation as an adaptation by human primates to minimize inbreeding. However, Rosenberg and Sutton-Smith (1972), while drawing attention to the traditional view that "the chromosomal-hormonal position is that inherent sexuality provides a built-in bias influencing the way an individual interacts with his environment" (p. 31), nevertheless feel that the role of sex-related behaviour and experience among the higher animals outweighs that of the hormonal and genetic. Quite clearly, then, biology provides some basis for the later development of gender identity and behaviour (Mead 1996:4), but nothing more.

Precisely what that identity and that behaviour consist of is the making of human beings in society. As Ortner and Whitehead (1981:1) put it, "natural features of gender, and natural processes of sex and reproduction, furnish only a suggestive and ambiguous backdrop to the cultural organization of gender and sexuality". Caribbean boys if required will perform every domestic chore except disposing of night soil or one requiring contact with the female underwear. These are learned behaviours, which no biologically based theory can explain. To explain them and other gender-based behaviours, as well as the formation of gender identity, we have to turn for assistance to other disciplines, to the study of personality, society and culture.

The fact, however, that "there is little conclusive evidence on the nature, extent and mechanisms of sex-hormone effects on the development of behavior in man" (Humburg and Lunde 1966:21) is not the end of the matter. The father of psychology and psychoanalysis, one of the most influential thinkers of the late nineteenth and the twentieth centuries, Sigmund Freud, bases his theory of personality on the anatomical differences between male and female. The female child, motivated by penis envy during the phallic stage of development between three and six years old, develops a cross-sex identification with her father, a conflict resolved only much later on when the desire for a child replaces the desire for a penis. The male personality, on the other hand, is formed by fear of loss of the penis, an organ which puts him in competition with his father for the affection of his mother. His cross-sex identification, or the Oedipus complex, is resolved with the development of a strong superego which enables him to break out of his incestuous identification with his mother and identify with his father instead. In these ways both male and female develop different superegos: males become assertive and develop strong consciences, while women, whose superegos are weak, are subject to jealousy, envy and passivity. Despite the male bias in Freudian theory, which it is possible to account for by situating it in its historical context, despite its poor rating as an explanatory model of sex role development (Roopnarine and Mounts 1987:9), Freud's psychoanalytic insights remain powerful enough for contemporary feminists like Chodorow (1971; 1978; 1995) to draw on.

For Erik Erikson (cited in Matteson 1975:18), a woman's "somatic design", by bestowing on her an "inner space" destined to bear offspring, a design denied the male, predisposes in her a "sense of vital inner potential". The womb then becomes "a metaphor for the special emotional creativity he attributes to women . . . and provides them with a special potential for psychological creativity and richness". A man's somatic design, on the other hand, orients him outward. He must seek his sex-role identity outside of himself, a task immensely more difficult than that of his female counterpart. According to Karen Horney (cited in Chodorow 1971:182–83), "the man is actually obliged to go on proving his manhood to the woman. There is no analogous necessity for her: even if she is frigid, she can engage in sexual intercourse and conceive and bear a child. She performs her part by merely *being,* without any *doing* . . . The man on the other hand has to *do* something in order to fulfill himself." This theme finds resonance in Parsons and Bales' (1955) sociological expressive-instrument dichotomy, which I shall later refer to, but as Lindsey (1994:42) reminds us, sociobiological theories are impossible to prove (or disprove) empirically, because "they are based on assumptions of human behavior . . . which may represent cultural stereotypes". If nothing else, however, biological arguments for sex-role identity and behaviour raise questions about "the relationship between individuals, society and nature" (Hart 1989:4). Definitive answers are not easily forthcoming.

Psychological Explanations

Among the other types of psychological explanations may be mentioned social learning, cognitive development and interactionism. *Social learning* theory emphasizes the role of imitation and role-modelling, backed up by reinforcement. According to Mischel (1966) sex typed behaviours are the result of social learning. Deviant behaviour is attributed to the absence of proper role models, as in the case of absent fathers, or to the effectiveness of deviant models. Social learning theory has very wide currency among the general public. Every attribution of criminal behaviour among young males to the lack of good role models, as is quite common in the media, is, without their authors being aware of it, an expression based on social learning theory. However, as Hutt (1978:178) points out, social learning theory is difficult to disconfirm because it assigns the acquisition of sex-typical behaviours *post hoc.*

Cognitive development theory is based on the influential work of Jean Piaget, according to whom a child's conception of self determines how he or she perceives and learns. In other words, the socialization of a child depends on the stage of development of its mind. Gender identity begins to take place from age three and becomes stable by age six. Once this happens behaviour is then organized consistent with this identity (Lindsey

1994:53). Cognitive development theory stresses the active agency of the child in the socialization process; it is "a theory of the individual child's accommodation to an autonomous world", and as such is short on "collective, communal and cultural processes" among children (Corsaro 1992:160).

Interaction theory, as the name suggests, emphasizes the interactional nature of the socializing experience. Every interchange is, as it were, a sort of negotiation between actors that elicit fixed responses or skills. Children are conceived not as receptacles into which adult ideas are poured but as actors in an interactive experience. They test their own perceptions and ideas against those of others and thus develop. It is this interactive experience children have that "shapes their behavioral styles and abilities" (Denzin 1977:21). Interaction theory focuses on language skills as a medium for the shaping of thought, and in this respect shares much in common with cognitive development theory insofar as a child's language competence is acquired over time through the stages of development of the mind. Language "plays a privileged role" in socialization by conveying messages, bridging time past, present and future, and providing an index of "socially constituted categories (e.g. roles, statuses, situations, and events) through the choice of linguistic options" (Miller and Hoogstra 1992:85).

Another important insight of interaction theory lies in the consideration that socialization is a two-way process "in which the child has a substantial role, even as producers of culture", even when the relations are asymmetrical (Miller and Hoogstra 1992:89). Understanding socialization in this way enables one to account for the possibility of children and other young persons still in formation to influence the personal decisions of adults and even to effect changes in the wider society. Advertisers who target children apparently understand this well.

Sociological Explanations

Sociological theories of socialization consider the effect of social institutions in the formation of children's identities. Here the stress is placed on agency. The principal socializing agencies are the primary groups of family and peer group, but school, organized religion and the communications media also play important roles. The family is the first social group a child encounters. The founder of structural-functional theory in sociology, Talcott

Parsons, together with Robert Bales (1955:36–37) liken the newly born child to a pebble thrown into a pond. The point of entrance represents the family of orientation while the widening ripples represent the successive socializing institutions in which he will eventually participate but not before participating in the narrower ones. It is here the child learns very quickly to identify and show affective responses to mother, father and other members of the domestic grouping, whom it begins to distinguish from strangers, and acquires a personal and gender-based identity in affective interaction with them. As it grows it internalizes through imitation and reinforced instruction the values and behaviour of those around it.

Since structural-functionalism has been so influential in sociological thought, it might be useful to trace how, according to Parsons and Bales, the socialization is accomplished. It all depends, in the first place, on the structure of the family, whether nuclear or extended, female-headed or male-headed, small or large, and the functional roles played by its members. Parsons and Bales (1955) explain the process as it takes place in the nuclear family in a three-point argument. First at the structural level they posit a framework for understanding the family as a system comprising two axes. In the hierarchy and power axis, the role of parent is superior to the role of son or daughter, while in the instrumental/expressive axis, the role of the males is oriented "instrumentally" to meeting the needs of the system in relation to goal-objects outside, and that of the females oriented to the expressive, or affective needs of the system. This is a scientific and abstract way of expressing the quite familiar sex-role division by which women are oriented to the internal relations of a family and men to the external. But as a basic structure it allows for the analysis of systems of greater complexity, for example when bifurcated by universalistic versus particularistic orientation. In this case, the universalistic instrumental role of father is as "technical expert", whereas his particularistic instrumental role is that of "executive"; the universalistic expressive role of mother is that of the "virtuoso and 'cultural' expert", whereas her particularistic expressive role is that of charismatic leader.

Since socialization involves in some sense personality formation, the authors focus next on the structure of personality. For them the personality is a "system of action . . . organized about the internalization of systems of social objects which originated as the role-units of the successive series of social systems in which the individual has come to be integrated in the course of his life history" (p. 54). This definition draws attention to a number of ideas. First, a personality cannot be known outside of "social action", by which the authors mean a goal-oriented act (see Parsons 1937); not until a child begins to act, *react* and *interact* does his or her personality become known. Second, "action" derives from internalized "social objects", such as values and behavioural norms. Qualifying the word *objects* with *social* makes it clear that as a process internalization is socially derived. How this is achieved will be explained presently. Third, the internalized "social objects" are themselves systemic in their origin and not random. They are the "role-units" of successive social systems, successive ripples extending from the centre. Parsons and Bales are evidently assuming a society or a social system in equilibrium, in which the subsystems are in coherence with the whole and dissonance totally absent or minimal.

Before going on to the internalization process Parsons and Bales further explain two points. For personality to acquire stability there must be "*some form* of *organization* of the *components* which regulates [ego's] pattern of action in relation to [alter]" (p. 56). This they call "a personality establishment", which though subject to variation and adaptation is able to remain consistent. Second, personality develops primarily not by alteration of the primary drives, but "by a process of differentiation of a very simple internalized object-system . . . into progressively more complex systems" (p. 54). In other words, personality formation primarily derives not from external sources, though these play a part, but through "the process of internal system-differentiation" (p. 55). These two points would help to explain how one's basic personality structure retains consistency but at the same time is subject to socialization by the different social systems one comes in contact with.

We come finally to the issue of internalization, a central point, since on this rests the socialization of a person. The authors offer a surprisingly simple explanation, drawn from analysis of social control processes. In these the agents of control are forced to play a dual role. On one hand they must to some limited extent participate with the deviant "on his own terms", be part of the deviant subsystem of interaction, but at the same time, on the other hand, be also authentically part of the wider system relative to which the subsystem is defined as deviant. In such a position the agents of control are able to effect the transformation from deviance to conformity. "Very generally we may say that the socializing agent uses his interaction in the subordinate subsystem role to motivate the child by forming an attachment to him. He then uses his other role as in some sense defining a 'model' for the child to emulate and as a basis of 'leverage' " (p. 59).

We now see why the family is singled out for the role it plays in socialization. It is the most important primary group for the child, one that structures its life, provides nurture and affective development and mediates with the environment. It is through the resulting bonding from face-to-face interaction that the exercise of superordinate power of mother and father is accepted and internalized. As the first socializing agent, the family is the site where a child's personality begins to develop, where a gender identity consistent with the wider social system is acquired. In the pre-Oedipal stages of a child's life, Parsons and Bales argue, the mother by virtue of her daily interaction with the child assumes the instrumental role which in later life is transferred onto the father, in addition to her expressive role.

As I have already indicated, the assumption here is that one is dealing with the nuclear family. As a neat if complex way of explaining its role in socialization, structural-functionalist emphasis on the family can be used to mislead. As Leichter (1974:42) warns, "when the family is studied with the goal of finding solutions to social problems, the tendency to overstate the impact of family relationships is much in evidence". Ogbu (1982:253) also attacks what he calls a "process-product paradigm", which is based on some assumed causal relationship between family processes, especially parent-child interaction, and child-rearing product or outcome. Intervention strategies based on such assumptions will clearly fail. Instead, he calls for a *cultural-ecological* approach which would seek first to fit child-rearing practices within the competencies, or adult personal qualities, required by a particular society.

A more recent sociological theory, the *interpretive approach*, has evolved out of an attempt to understand the peer group, the next most important primary group in the socialization process, but a neglected one in sociological literature. William Corsaro (1992), the founder of the interpretive approach, emphasizes the cultural character of children's discovery and interpretation of a world endowed with meaning, which they reproduce and build on through various other stages of the process. Interacting interpretively with the environment they create their own "peer cultures" as soon as they come in contact with others their age, thus shifting the socialization process from the asymmetrical adult-child pattern to one of mutual socialization. To understand how mutual socialization takes place Corsaro draws on four concepts:

Routines. Routines are "recurrent and predictable activities that are basic to day-to-day social life" (Corsaro 1992:163). The quality of predictability allows routines to become arenas for making the unfamiliar familiar, or to "serve as anchors that allow us to deal with ambiguities, the unexpected, the problematic while comfortably within the friendly confines of everyday life" (p. 163). Routines are collectively produced through public negotiations. In these negotiations, social actors link shared knowledge of various symbolic models with specific situations to generate meanings while simultaneously using the same shared knowledge as a resource for making novel contributions to the culture and for pursuing a range of individual goals" (p. 164).

Primary frameworks. Drawing on Erving Goffman's concept of frame, Corsaro sees primary frameworks as "the underlying knowledge of the event structures of cultural routines" (p. 164), which allow for their interpretation. When children in role-play identify certain objects and relate them to their use function (bed we sleep in; oven we cook in), they activate cultural frameworks of family routines, thus establishing "frames of interpretation" and producing cultural routines.

Contextualization. Without context primary frameworks could not be interpreted since it signals the nature of the cultural routine. Paying credit to Gumperz, Corsaro stresses "the identification of actors' use of clusters or constellations of contextualization cues to general specific cultural routines" (p. 165) as an indispensable tool of analysis in the interpretive approach. Contextualization cues include both verbal and nonverbal features.

Transformation. In transformation the actors transform a given activity that already has meaning within a primary framework into something else, such as when children's play patterns adult routines. This type of transformation, following Goffman, is called *keying*. *Embellishment*, the "intensification or magnification of the meaning of certain elements of (or of entire) primary frameworks" (Corsaro 1992:165), is another type of transformation, the difference being that in embellishment the primary framework remains the same. Repetition, exaggeration and highlighting are all forms of embellishment, through which children create their own meaning even while reproducing the primary framework.

Interpretivists (see Corsaro and Miller 1992) owe much to Geertz, Goffman and Gumperz for their conceptual building blocks. A key premise is the centrality of culture, which, following Geertz (1973), they define as "webs of significance" residing not in people's heads but in their negotiated and public actions. By privileging culture they locate the study of socialization within a given time and place, insightfully emphasizing the active participation of children in the production of meaning. From the interpretive point of view, as children acquire social skills and knowledge, creatively contributing to the production of cultural routines, they "unwittingly support the reproduction of (and in some cases extend) the wider adult culture" (Corsaro and Rosier 1992:69). One implication of this perspective, according to Gaskins et al. (1992:11), is the room it allows for "individual variation in the meanings that children create out of cultural resources".

The Role of Culture

The role of culture in the socialization of children has had a long pedigree, dating from Margaret Mead's classic ethnographic study, *Coming of Age in Samoa*. Through its ethnographic method anthropology has made major contributions to the study of socialization, providing rich data on the process among different cultures and peoples and, on that basis, enabling cross-cultural comparisons. *Coming of Age in Samoa* (1961, first published in 1928) was written with the problems of American childhood and adolescence in mind, and in presenting her observations in Samoa Mead wanted to show that the stress and neurosis of adolescence in the West was not a universal phenomenon. Samoan children pass from adolescence to adulthood without the anxiety that attend their counterparts in the West. Their sexuality, for example, is free of the moral taboos and double standards confusing the Western adolescent, and is a matter for indulgence, except where the social status of a chief's family is at risk. Mead offers two explanations for these differences, one social – as an advanced civilization, the West presents the adolescent with a wide, and often conflicting, range of choices, whereas the simple, homogeneous Samoan civilization does not;

the other cultural –Samoans emphasize balance, devalue individualism, and adopt a permissive non-neurotic approach to sex, the very opposite of the values rated in the West. They have a "quiet acceptance of the physical facts of life" (Mead 1961:221) – intercourse, pregnancy, birth, death, which they make no attempt to shield children from, as is the practice in the West. Samoans' transition to adulthood is smooth and non-traumatic, that of Americans marked by abrupt reconditioning, as Ruth Benedict (1934) also pointed out (Jensen 1985:48–49).

Culture, sex role differentiation and identity

Every known society, consistent with the reproductive role of a woman, assigns every newborn infant to its lactating mother for its nourishment. This is not to say there are not instances of women breast-feeding other women's children, but these are more the exceptions than the rule. In most societies mothers suckle their babies, sleep with them and, until they gain locomotive ability and even after, carry them around while they work. In many cultures such children are weaned between two and three years old, or when the mothers become pregnant again. The resulting bond from this intense and prolonged contact is universal to all societies. It develops in the child a strong sense of identity with mother. For girls, this is not a problem. For boys it is.

Under the influence of Freud, and drawing on her rich cross-cultural work, Mead (1996) developed a culturally constructed model of gender identity, using an early-middle-late childhood schema as her frame, early childhood being equivalent to the Oedipal/Electra phase of development, middle childhood to prepubescence, and late childhood to puberty or adolescence. A girl's gender identity in early childhood bestows on her a sense of security arising from the similarity between her body and her mother's, but in the ensuing phase, when gender differentiation and segregation begin to take place, a sense of insecurity. This insecurity is the result of what Freud called the penis envy. At this stage she takes her female identity on faith only, but as soon as she begins to develop breasts and to menstruate, she develops a sense of security in the latent power of motherhood. The movement of a boy through the same phases is in counterpoint to the girl's. From an insecurity arising from his realization of his cross-sex identification with his mother, he achieves security in the consciousness of his phallus as a source of identification with his father, but lapses once more into insecurity on finding that this does not *ipso facto* qualify him to enter the world of men. What makes him a man is his achievement of what each culture decides he needs to do. "If men are . . . ever certain that their lives have been lived as they were meant to be, they must have, in addition to paternity, culturally elaborated forms of expression that are lasting and sure" (p. 160). All a woman needs for her identity as a woman is to fulfil *her* biological role. But for a man, his paternity is not enough. He must *learn* to be a man, which for most cultures, says Mead, means providing food for some female and her young. The form of doing this may be specific to each culture – providing for his sister's children, in matrilineal societies, or for his own in patrilineal nuclear households, but the pattern is universal.

Both male and female children share virtually the same nurturing experiences in their earliest years, but soon enough, a separation ensues and boys and girls begin to be trained to assume different roles. Barry, Bacon and Child (1957) reviewed the socialization of boys and girls in 110 cultures and made ratings on two aspects of the process: first, "attention and indulgence towards infants", and second, the "strength of socialization from age four or five years until shortly before puberty", with respect to training in (a) responsibility or dutifulness; (b) nurturing younger siblings and other dependent people; (c) obedience; (d) self-reliance; and (e) achievement. The authors found that in 85 or 92 percent of the 96 cultures for which they had relevant ethnographic data there were no sex differences in infancy, that is up to age four or five years. However, with respect to childhood socialization, in most cultures it is the girls who are targeted for training in responsibility and nurturance, and the boys who are targeted for training in achievement and self-reliance. Obedience training is directed to girls in 35 percent of cultures and to boys in 3 percent; 62 percent showed no gender difference.

Barry, Bacon and Child went further. Classifying their sample according to whether these had large or small sex differences in socialization, they correlated them with forty aspects of culture covering "type of economy, residence pattern, marriage and incest rules, political integration, and social organization" (Barry, Bacon and Child 1957:330). They discovered statistically significant relations for six aspects of culture, from which they drew the conclusion that an association exists between a large sex difference in socialization, on one hand, and on the other an economy in which male strength is valued at a high premium, as well as a society that values "a large family group with high cooperative interaction". In a later paper (Barry, Child and Bacon 1959), they modified their argument somewhat. Here, they found correlations between the type of training and the type of economy: societies with very high accumulation of food resources exert greater pressure towards responsibility and obedience and lower pressure towards achievement, self-reliance and independence. Both genders are trained in the same way, but obedience and responsibility are emphasized more in the training of girls than boys in high accumulation societies, whereas achievement, self-reliance and independence are emphasized more in the training of boys in low accumulation societies.

If boys and girls initially share the same nurturing environment, and the same kind of bonding with their mothers, the question of how the change is effected among boys is apropos. Again, through the use of cross-cultural comparisons, Burton and Whiting (1961) tested a cross-sex identity and initiation hypothesis, namely that "where a boy initially sleeps exclusively with his mother and where the domestic unit is patrilocal and hence controlled by men, there will be initiation rites at puberty which function to resolve this conflict in identity". They distinguish three kinds of identity: they call the status a person is assigned *attributed identity*, the status a person sees himself or herself as occupying *subjective identity*, and the status a person wishes he or she could occupy, but is disbarred from, *optative identity*. The aim of socialization, they argue, is to produce adults whose attributed, subjective and optative identity are isomorphic. In patrilocal societies, the male problem is essentially his optative identity. In such societies, a boy would have grown up with a strong cross-sex identification, due to the early nurturing and childhood sleeping arrangements with his mother, but would have *status envy* of his father, whose status is higher but whose sleeping arrangements and domestic interaction are more with the members of his patrikin than with the boy's mother. Thus, cross-sex identity in a boy combined with patrilocal residence produces an identity conflict, which, according to their hypothesis, can only be resolved by male initiation rites. From a sample of sixty-four societies they found twelve with both exclusive mother-child sleeping arrangements and patrilocal residence. All had elaborate initiation rites: "hazing, sleeplessness, tests of manhood, and painful genital operation, together with promise of high status – that of being a man if the tests are successfully passed" (Burton and Whiting 1961:75). These rites serve the function of brainwashing their primary feminine identity and establishing their secondary male identity. Harrington (1968), however, qualifies this conclusion with his finding of statistically significant relations between the high degree of sex differentiation and circumcision proper, rather than supercision. Supercision societies have even lower sexual differentiation than societies practising neither form of mutilation. He therefore upholds the view that circumcision as part of male puberty rites is intended to resolve cross-sex identification by replacing it with "proper masculine identity and role behavior" (p. 954).

Initiation itself is an event with a beginning and end that may span days, or weeks, or even months. It is clear that societies do not depend on these rituals to fix the way boys and girls should behave. Puberty rituals effect a change of status, but they complete the training of a child for adulthood. How is this training organized, and what is its content? Whiting and Edwards (1988) provide one answer. In their cross-cultural study involving six cultures: India, Kenya, Philippines, Okinawa, Mexico and the New England part of the United States, they argue that cultural forces combine with "parental pressure, behavioral dispositions and developmental processes to program the daily lives of individuals, to map the settings they frequent, and to provide the rules of behavior governing the actors who share each setting" (p. 17). In some settings, as far as the children are concerned, the principal persons they interact with are parents, particularly mothers, in other settings older caretaker siblings, and in still others the peer group. Whiting and Edwards distinguish five types of interaction: nurturance, training, control, sociability (teasing, talking to, laughing with, touching, etc.) and responsiveness to the child's requests. Generally speaking, in Kenya the most frequent type of interaction was in training, the second most frequent being control. In the other five cultures, the order is reversed: control ranks highest, followed by training. Training increases with age and its content changes. For younger children the focus is on such things as manners and hygiene, while for older children the focus is on chores and socially useful activities. Girls receive more maternal training than boys, boys receive more maternal control than girls. The most frequent type of interaction among lap children (up to a year old) and knee children (two to three years old), not surprisingly, is nurturance, no matter who the principal actors of the settings are, whether mother or older siblings. For yard children, however, that is children between four and five years old, the principal type of interaction is control; and for school age children, from six to ten years old, the emphasis is on training.

Gender identity formation begins with the yard children. Girls at this age are in the presence of their mothers significantly more than boys of the same age. At this age both boys and girls were observed to select same-sex companions when choice was possible, and boys observed at greater distance from home when not involved in assigned tasks. Among school age children this sex differentiation becomes even more pronounced. The authors call this low frequency of cross-sex peer interaction their "most dramatic finding" (Whiting and Edwards 1988:256).

Whiting and Edwards' findings do suggest cross-cultural regularities, but were this their main contribution they would have added little new. What is new is their idea of a *setting*, which becomes the focus for the actual transmission of the cultural values, beliefs and behavioural norms of any particular society. Harkness and Super (1983) use a similar idea, a *niche*, to highlight the mode of a child's acquisition of culture.

By way of concluding this section on the role of culture in socialization, I call attention to an observation first made by Mead (1996:159–60), namely that men's gender identity "is tied up with their right, or ability, to practise some activity that women are not allowed to practise", with "a need for prestige that will outstrip the prestige which is accorded to any woman". The concept of prestige relations, along with kinship and marriage, Ortner and Whitehead (1981) argue, provide an explanatory framework for the production and reproduction of cultural notions of gender and sexuality.

Prestige, which derives from the command over resources and connections to resources, and may be ascribed or achieved, is always supported by, or appears as an expression of an ideology: "definite beliefs and symbolic associations that make sensible and compelling the ordering of human relations into patterns of deference and condescension, respect and disregard, and in many cases command and obedience" (Ortner and Whitehead 1981:14). Three points are germane to gender. A gender system is a prestige system first and foremost. Concepts that differentiate men from women are often used to grade individuals of the same gender, while prestige positions outside gender are often rendered in gender terms. It follows, secondly, that prestige structures tend toward symbolic consistency. Third, gender concepts like marriage, consanguinity and the sexual division of labour are a function of male prestige. As proof of this, whereas men are defined according to various role categories (warrior, elder, statesman, etc.), women are defined largely in terms of their cross-sex relations – wives, mothers, and so forth. Thus, "the primary categories of maleness are not simply from the 'public' domain in general, but specifically from the sphere of prestige relations" (Ortner and Whitehead 1981:19). For most societies, marriage is the cross-sex bond that carries the greatest prestige. Where the cross-sex bond most emphasized in certain cultures is a woman's affinal role (wife, mother-in-law, etc.), women in such cultures are the object of far less respect than in cultures in which woman's kinship role (mother, sister, etc.) is the point of emphasis. We do well to bear this point in mind when discussing gender relations among anglophone Afro-Caribbean peoples, where both systems of prestige may be found.

The above theoretical perspectives and reported findings on sex-role differentiation and identity would indicate that there is no one angle that might provide a comprehensive explanatory model of socialization, and it is not my intention to attempt one here. We are dealing with an issue of great complexity. Since socialization does concern the raising of even a single child, there is much to be gained from looking at the processes surrounding the individual organism and personality. But, then, because we are social beings, we immediately find it necessary to consider the social (group and society) contexts, and to follow the paths we construct to give order and meaning to our lives. Not everyone, however, internalizes the ordered paths of meaning, not in exactly the same way or to the same degree. In everyday social intercourse, some men are described as more masculine than others, or some men as acting more like women, and in similar vein among women. Implicit in such statements, whatever their intent, is the acknowledgement that the socialization process may not everywhere produce the same effect. I would therefore argue that any good theory of gender socialization has to fill two conditions: it has to be multidisciplinary and it must be able to offer insights into the construction of difference.

That a full view of the socialization process must incorporate several disciplines is recognized by most scholars, who only vary in the extent to which they are able to make this explicit while focusing on their particular perspective. We have seen the sociologists Parsons and Bales venturing into a theory of personality, Corsaro crossing social psychology and cultural theory, and Margaret Mead the anthropologist drawing on Freudian psychology. A number of feminist theorists have been making considerable strides in understanding the construction of gender identity, precisely by taking a multidisciplinary approach.

Phyllis Katz (1986), for example, presents a concise and very useful summary, based on available literature and her own work, of the process of formation of a gender identity. Although heavily psychological, it is forced to incorporate sociological and cultural postulates. Gender identity, which for Katz is "a psychological construct, referring to an individual's phenomenological experience of being masculine and/or feminine" (p. 23), is shaped on one hand by "developmental antecedents". These are a number of *cultural, sociological* and *biological* factors, which, except the biological, are themselves subject to the personality's own actions, whether in terms of reinforcement or modification. Gender identity thus formed is shaped on the other hand by its own "behavioral consequences", verbal and behavioural acts which not only are the ways whereby gender identity expresses and thereby manifests itself, but which also provide "interactive feedback" that may reinforce or modify the internal awareness and experience which constitutes gender identity.

In Katz's view gender identity is being constructed at every developmental stage of the life cycle, from infancy right through to late adulthood, as the developmental antecedents and behavioural consequences interact with the personality. In relation to adolescence and adulthood, she makes two useful distinctions that are often glossed over. One is between *early adolescence,* when the child must adjust to the physiological changes of increasing sexual maturity, a task which is more stressful for girls than boys, but which for both involves the new ways of relating to the opposite sex; and *later adolescence,* when the concerns with heterosexual relations and life goals become more acute. The other distinction is between *young* and *later adulthood.* In young adulthood marriage, parenthood and occupation are the main axes around which gender identity is being constructed, as against later adulthood when women must adjust to the end of child-rearing responsibilities and to the menopause, both men and women adjust to ageing, and men to their waning sexuality. Thus, "one's gender identity, while basic in one sense, is also in continual transition throughout one's life" (p. 51).

But a gender identity need not be constructed around the bipolarity of masculinity and femininity. Here Katz briefly discusses the various forms of *berdache*, or transsexual behaviours such as homosexuality and transvestism, and androgyny. This latter, which, as some scholars use it, is a form of orientation combining both masculine and feminine behaviours, or as others define it, refers to behaviours and roles in which a gender schema is not relevant, poses theoretically challenging questions for our understanding of gender identity insofar as it is used self-descriptively by individuals.

One of the most notable feminist scholars writing on androgyny, Sandra Bem, is also one who consciously seeks to incorporate multidisciplinary perspectives into her gender-lens theory of the construction of gender identity. "Each of these . . . perspectives has something profound to say about the process whereby male and female infants are transformed into the kinds of masculine and feminine adults who willingly accept the different – and unequal – roles assigned to them in an androcentric and gender-polarizing society" (1993:137). Her theory builds on these insights to develop an understanding of how society transfers its gendered way of looking, classifying and orienting behaviour to a child and transforms that child into a male or female adult.

Gender as a bipolar and androcentric way of schematizing the world, Bem reiterates, is embedded in *culture and social practices,* and it is this schema (or lenses) that society passes on to children, who once they have put on the lenses, so to speak, are predisposed "to construct an identity that is consistent with them" (p. 139). But how does all this take place? How is the transference made? Her answer is twofold: by "[p]reprogramming an individual's daily experience into the default options of a particular culture" (p. 139), that is by structuring the daily lives of children – a point noted by anthropologists Whiting and Edwards (1988), as the reader will recall, and by "the less visible process of tacitly communicating what lenses the culture uses to organize reality" (p. 140), nonconsciously. Nonconscious transference takes place not only by "a kind of subliminal pedagogy" (p. 141), by means of which *metamessages* are also sent (from seeing others wear a wristwatch a child would learn that it is possible to tell the time to the nearest minute, but would also learn the metamessage "that time must be quantified precisely and that human behavior must be scheduled precisely" [p. 141]); but also in a meaning-construction sort of way, "more a matter of picking up information than transmitting it; in this case, the culture itself is more a text to be read – and read by an active, meaning-constructing reader – than a lesson to be taught" (p. 141). It is particularly through metamessages, the metamessages transmitted by language and social practice, that androcentrism is internalized and reproduced. Once internalized, the polarized and androcentric lenses structure a person's idea of reality, guide his or her choices, and construct the self, all in such a way that the effect seems as much a force of social structure and culture as it is of personal choice.

This process, argues Bem, holds true as a general but not an absolute pattern. Not everyone is so preprogrammed. There are in every society and culture mismatches whose bodies are of one sex and their psyches of the other. They develop their own gender identity by looking *at* rather than *through* the lenses. Far from being unnatural, such phenomena are part of the diversity of nature interacting with culture, very much, she says, like the diversity of food preferences: the natural desire for food does not in itself determine what is acceptable food in one culture as against the next, or what one person will prefer as against another within the same culture.

This possibility for otherness and difference from the normative is an understanding shared also by Nancy Chodorow. In a recent article (1995) she presents a number of clinical cases drawn from her psychoanalytic practice to substantiate her claim that "people recreate and charge recognizable cultural meanings in ways that emotionally, often conflictually, through unconscious and conscious fantasy, construct their own sense of personal gender" (p. 525). Basing her argument on the premise that human beings have the innate power to create personal meaning, and further that they invest cultural meanings with affect, or "personal animation", Chodorow argues that "[b]oth an individual, intrapsychic animation and a putting together of cultural categories (themselves emotionally laden and embedded) create the meaning of gender and gender identity for any individual" (p. 521). One's gender identity is one's personal creation, constructed by processing culturally loaded gender meaning through one's own subjective fantasies, feelings and emotions. What this means is that there is not one masculinity or femininity but many.

What we see here, then, with Katz, Bem and Chodorow is the openness to incorporate a multidisciplinary approach in trying to account for the construction and reproduction of gender identity. From their psychological or psychoanalytic points of view, they draw on the understanding of culture as a shared system of meaning, an approach that finds common ground with the interpretivists. The intellectual influence of Clifford Geertz (1973; 1983) is unmistakable, and it also opens up a way for them to account for difference. For if meaning is central to the understanding of culture, then interpretations based on individuals' internal biological as well as external social experiences will inevitably exhibit variations. How such variations are dealt with is itself a matter of cultural practice. As Leo-Rhynie (1998:241) sums it up, the lesson from her theoretical review is that the cultural context, the family, the social environment, and the interactive role of the subjects themselves all contribute to the development of gender identity.

In many societies, including the West, gender is understood as an expression of opposites, variations from which are considered and treated as deviant. Kimmel (1996) treats the history of masculinity in the United States as one of hegemony. He identifies two models of male identity in the late eighteenth century: the "Genteel Patriarch", whose identity was built up around landownership; and the "Heroic Artisan" whose was built up around "physical strength and republican virtue"; and a third early in the nineteenth century which he called "Marketplace Manhood", "a manhood that required the acquisition of tangible goods as evidence of success", which has now reconstituted itself in contemporary culture as "American Everyman", excluding women, non-white, non-native born and homosexual men. Hegemonic concepts of manhood act as standards against which all men are supposed to measure themselves and are measured.

But as Nanda (1990) shows, not only are deviants from normative heterosexual practice in North India tolerated but a cultural niche is, as it were, found for them. Hijras are cultural performers who are called upon to bless by their dancing and ritual performances the most significant events in the life of a family, namely the birth of a male child and marriage. This is their cultural role. But hijras are all male transvestites, who include eunuchs, hermaphrodites and homosexuals, with some even supplementing their living by functioning as male prostitutes. Culturally, the hijras are considered neither male nor female. Their existence as sexual deviants is possible, Nanda explains, because of Hindu philosophic tolerance of difference.

Understanding *what* gender means and does not mean among a given people is thus an imperative in any effort to see *how* such a people construct their sense of being male or female, whom they incorporate, whom they exclude. This study of male gender socialization among Caribbean peoples is therefore as much a study of their meaning of gender as it is a study of the way they construct it.

3

Grannitree

Grannitree is a farming community in the rural parish of St Mary, forty kilometres from downtown Kingston. Like so many other villages all over the island, it conforms to the spatially dispersed settlement pattern described by M. G. Smith (1965) some forty years ago, along a roadway. Houses are spaced at shouting distances on both sides. The road to Grannitree describes an unpaved crescent off one of the main arteries connecting Kingston to the north coast, up a promontory, through the small farming settlement known as Peace, around the side of an inner valley, on through Grannitree, down through Sink Hole and once more on to the main road – a detour of not more than six kilometres through fertile sandy loam deposits from which trickle forth a half-dozen underground springs that provide drinking and domestic water as they find their way to the northbound Wag Water River. But the steep lay of the land makes it susceptible to slippage after protracted rainfall.

Yams, sweet potatoes, coco, dasheen are some of the ground provisions grown in Grannitree, both for consumption and for sale in the markets of Kingston. In the entire district we found only one farmer who grew vegetables. But a most important tree crop is "chocolate", as the cocoa plant is called. The beans are collected by incoming agents and sold to the chocolate factory in Highgate, a town situated on a plateau twenty kilometres to the northwest. In

Grannitree, as in other parts of rural Jamaica, a small farmer's farm is called his "field" or "bush", and is generally a piece of land separate and apart from his "yard", the plot on which he and his family reside.

Grannitree residents however, are not only farmers. As Lambros Comitas (1970) long ago pointed out, occupational multiplicity is the norm in peasant communities. Here in Grannitree and its surrounding districts farmers are also artisans and entrepreneurs. They are not only attuned intimately to the soil, but they are also expert masons, carpenters, woodworkers, mechanics, and small businessmen.

It was 9:15 a.m. There were several women and young boys trekking to and from the stand pipe and springs with buckets of water balanced on their heads with the cushion known as a *kata*, and small farmers going to or coming from their farms. According to Mr Mitchell "di yam head-dem start grow, so is time for dem to plant". The typical farmer is dressed in rough-looking material – khaki, denim or corduroy. His footwear is a pair of hardy rubber water-boots, such as Ironman™, his tool always a cutlass, and sometimes a hoe or a fork as well. Mr Watson, for his part, was coming *from*, rather than going to, his field. He had left early, so he said, to "tie out di cow", that is put the cow to graze in fresh grass. He said he also cut some potato slips to plant in freshly prepared mounds.

A group of men was standing at the shop corner, poking fun at one other. They appeared to be farmers, clad in their rough clothes and armed with cutlasses, but they weren't on the way to their fields. Instead they were there waiting to complete work on a retaining wall they had started. A group of youths, including some teenagers, had left on a truck to bring back sand, stones and gravel. Actually, the wall was already built, but they were planning to use the material to fill the side of the road to bring it in line with the wall.

Their conversation shifted to a discussion on the virtues of different organic manure, some arguing that chicken manure had more chemicals and was therefore stronger, others that cow dung was better for the plants. At this point the member of Parliament waved as he drove past. One of the men complained that he did not stop to come out and talk. When the truck with the material arrived, both young and older men got together as a team to unload the vehicle and fill the gap in the road. In the main, though, the packing of the stones was done by the older men.

Farming alone is insufficient to produce a livelihood in Grannitree, although for some members of the community it provided a start in their upward mobility. Apart from artisan skills such as those described above, many men and women commute to and from Kingston to work. As we shall see later, Kingston rides the consciousness of many of the youths as the place to go, either to learn a skill or to find employment.

Socialization

Durant-Gonzalez (1976) in her ethnographic study of "St Mary District", a community not far from the site of the present study, informs us that up to age four little distinction is made between male and female children; they are cuddled, carried, protected, trained and treated in the same manner by both men and women. However, "[a]s the child advances in age and leaves the toddler stage, younger boys begin to follow and mimic older boys at play and in carrying out agricultural chores", while "[s]mall girls of the same age are directed toward domestic activities and are found following and mimicking the activities and behavior of their mothers and older girls" (p. 32). From this early age, parents make a greater effort to place limits on the physical whereabouts of girls than of boys; to teach girls "proper sex behavior and modesty" (p. 33) and boys how to suppress reaction to pain. The sexual division of labour becomes acute around the onset of puberty. The movements and activities of girls are curtailed and their activities focus on "woman's work" around the house, while boys engage in "man's work", that is "economic production-cultivation tasks" (p. 34), though sometimes girls are found performing agricultural activities and boys domestic activities, depending on the composition of the household.

The same pattern is observed in Grannitree, whereby children are subtly socialized by being integrated into the activities of adults and older siblings. Explaining how a woman learns to become a higgler, Durant-Gonzalez describes what she calls a "Phasing-in Stage", in which the socialization is first of all informal and "emerges simply as an outgrowth of daily life" (1976:141), for example taking the child to gather the fruits to be sold in the market, or sending the child to fetch the cord to tie the sack filled with fruits. This informal participation may become formal later on, when the child is relied on directly for its labour and may even be remunerated in cash or kind. However, the point I wish to make here is that an important aspect of the socialization process in Grannitree takes place informally, by way of integration into adult activities. In the above example the men involved in repairing the road included teenagers, while in the examples which now follow children, especially boys, are part of the household economy.

I met Calder and a girl who attended Kingston Secondary. There were several children, boys and girls, with loads on their heads, heading in the direction of the bus stop on the main. They were transporting provisions for their mothers and guardians who sold in the Kingston markets, mainly the Constant Spring and Coronation Markets. We passed a group of ten boys playing cricket in the road, using a piece of zinc for the wicket, a tough young orange for a ball and a piece of board for the bat. They stopped to let us through. I stopped at Mr Francis's grocery. In addition to his shopkeeping, Mr Francis reared chickens and ducks. When I expressed surprise that there were so many boys playing cricket at that hour of the day, he informed me that some of them had been stopped from school in order to help their parents get things out for the market.

I paid a visit to the playing field where a number of boys were playing cricket, most of them still clad in their school uniforms, an indication that they had not yet reached home from school. They were using the cricket gear the adult team practised with. I asked one of the few not in uniform why he had not gone to school. His mother, he said, refused to send him back to school for the rest of the week, since he did not go the Monday before. Because he had no writing in his book to show, she said she was not going to send him for the week. Harry is in Grade 2, only eight years old. He told me he had two goats, which his mother gave him to take care of. He also has, so he says, a lot of eggs from his chickens, some of which he eats, the rest he sells.

At eight years old, Harry already knows the value of livestock and the importance of work caring for them. This training gives him a window into the adult world. For boys like Harry – and we encountered several – school is less important than the world of work. By stopping them from school in order to assist in household production and marketing, parents, wittingly or not, give them a sense of their future direction. Durant-Gonzalez (1976:142–43) did observe, however, that children are kept from school to participate formally in economic activities only when their parents' network of mutual aid within the wider community is limited. Though we did observe some girls carrying loads to the bus stop, the tendency was to pull the boy child into economic and productive activity but expose the girl child more to education. For this, as Mr Watson confirms in the case of his own twelve year-old son, *"Boy or man must not sleep in bed late; it mek dem lazy. A man mus' come out early so dat dew water wet dem. Girls can stay an help their mother look after breakfas' an' fetch water."*

This integration into the adult world of work, but at the same time in a gender-segregated way, is not confined to production and marketing. Once, after some very heavy showers, we came upon a group cleaning up Mother Nation's Revival church. It included a number of men and women, three girls and four boys aged from eight to fifteen years old. A noticeable gender division of labour confined the women and girls to sweeping and cleaning the church gate, armed with brooms and buckets, while both boys and men handled the machetes and forks, trimming the passageway to the church, bushing the overgrown grass and breaking the soil. The point is that by integrating children in their own purposeful activities adults convey clear ideas on expected adult, and in this case gender-sensitive, behaviour. To be sure, by incorporating children in their activities these rural parents are able at the same time to control them. But while this may well be so, the same pattern was observed in the cricketing activities. Many times we observed adults and children playing together in mixed teams, and once came upon members of the Grannitree cricket team coaching a number of boys in batting technique. At the same time, of course, boys play their own games by themselves, sometimes on the public road, sometimes on the school playing field; if the latter, they make use of the gears of the team, apparently with impunity.

What such integrative opportunities provide is the context for children to learn by example in morally sanctioned formal ways. But there are informal ways also. Indeed, a great deal of, if not most, socialization takes place informally. For example, both boys and girls apparently learn how to make a *kata* by imitating adults or older young people. There is no need, here, for formal instruction. Again, on numerous occasions we observed males bathing in the open by a standpipe or a stream along the road, and occasionally females in streams away from the road. Particularly with the males, there is no sense of shame where the exposure of the sexual organs in the act of bathing is concerned, even in the presence of a stranger.

One very important informal socializing agent in Grannitree is the bar. In Grannitree there are nine of them, but the two most popular are the ones operated by Biiti and by Fern, both women. A number of factors account for their popularity. Like bars everywhere they allow men to meet and talk, on their way home from the field or after dinner. Most bars are extensions of small groceries, so that they are integrated parts of the local retail trade. Besides, both Biiti and Fern are young, both have personalities that the men find warm. In addition, both bars accommodate gambling.

It was not until about 12:30 p.m. that I arrived in the community. There were several young men at Fern's bar. Some were playing the usual game of dominoes, amidst the usual smoking, both ganja and cigarettes. Four of them were gambling in one corner of the shop, using a pack of cards, each hand for $2. I left to interview Brother and Sister West. Three hours later when I returned the group had grown considerably, and with it the gambling. The mood was jovial. They had received a bonus for the cocoa supplied to the Highgate factory.

But for the free spending made possible by the cocoa bonus, a scene like this is quite regular. Bars are the main places where men socialize with one another, and therefore places where male points of view on wide-ranging issues are expressed, fought for, reinforced. They are very much like the Paramaribo winkel, "a neighborhood waystation for lower-class men, the one neutral and accessible point in space where men . . . can congregate and interact" (Brana-Shute 1979:v). Being public, bars are open to any adult. By law they do not admit children. However, boys are frequently present, lurking in the margins, watching and listening to the proceedings, without any effort to remove them. In this way they are exposed to ideas, habits and activities they may later choose to practise.

The chief purpose of my visit today was to meet with the members of the Grannitree Cricket Team, who were planning a match with an adjacent community. On the way up from the bus stop I had a lively conversation with two young women on a return visit to the community they had left some years before, and Chuli, who worked as a security guard at Half Way Tree in Kingston. On arrival at the Grannitree square I found two men and two women playing dominoes in the room adjoining the bar, five other young men standing around watching the game, two of them members of the cricket team, and four small boys. I joined the audience. The women were paired against the men. They were actually gambling, each at $2 a game.

A little while later, another two young men joined our observer group, one of whom smoked and passed a ganja spliff to the other. Altogether the spliff passed between four men. Into the back room where the dominoes were being played came an eleven-year-old boy selling ripe bananas. He was, so he told me, trying to earn money for school. The bananas were from his father's cultivation, but he had cut and ripened them, and with his mother's permission was selling them. He claims that he turns over the proceeds to his mother, who then doles it out *"likl-likl"* (little by little).

A quarrel between the losing side of women and the victorious men brought the round of dominoes abruptly to an end, but it was quickly quashed by some of the observers, reasoning that the argument *"don't call fa"* (was unnecessary). Not being in the room when it broke out, I could not tell what had actually transpired. But apparently, Janice had accused Boloman of cheating. However, one of the observers called on her to apologize to Boloman. She retorted that she did not apologize to anybody, *"especially man! Unu man wan' uman fi bow to unu!"* (You men want women to bow to you.) Instead, it was Boloman who should apologize; he had started cursing badword. *"Unu man wan' tell uman anyting an' when dem tell unu back, unu seh dem facety. No man naa keep mi down or trample pa mi!"* I was drawn into replacing the two women, with another observer as partner. The winners warned us that they were *"domino chemists"* whom nobody could beat. We played four rounds of six games, managing to save one from the chemists.

We do not know if at the time the quarrel broke out the boys were still around. What is clear is that nothing prevented them from moving around and among the young men and women. And throughout the fieldwork we encountered many examples like the above. Boys thus become exposed informally to many ideas, values, opinions, practices.

One practice they soon adopt, which the older folk bemoan, is the badword vocabulary. In Jamaica, most if not all badwords refer either to the sexual organs and sexual activity, or to the anal organ and excretal activity. This may be the case in most societies, but, in addition, words derivative of the female menses are common in Jamaica. One of the most common badwords is *raas* (from *your ass*), along with other related anal expressions, *raas klaat* (ass cloth) and *raas uol* (ass hole); but the most offensive is bombo, the female genitalia, and the related *bombo klaat, blood klaat,* and *pussy klaat.* Words like *fuck, shit* and *shit house* figure less prominently, but are nonetheless considered indecent. Despite the female bias in badwords, they are used indiscriminately by men as well as women.

Children learn the full range of badwords, their weight, the contexts of their usage, which, besides anger, includes the expression of surprise, shock and even joy. We found many parents and teachers concerned about children using badwords. Some blamed this on those parents who used badwords when reprimanding their own children, while others blamed it on the malformation of today's young people. But badwords, while common, are not expected to be used by children, and the children know this. They know further that it represents gross disrespect to use it in the presence of "big people" or adults. On one occasion we came upon a group of boys playing on the road. One of them in a sudden burst of anger uttered a badword and immediately one of his peers said to him, *"Yu no see big people!"*, meaning that he should show me respect by controlling himself. I was only passing by.

Similar patterns of restraint are shown by adults in the presence of people holding higher status. If a badword is spontaneously used the offender will often apologize afterwards to such persons present; if used in a premeditated way, the badword will be prefaced by "Excuse me!". Janice's refusal to apologize was in part hardened by this culturally understood code. For her to have apologized to one whom she accused of first disrespecting her with its use, would, as she saw quite clearly, have meant admitting her subordinate place. And since as players they were equals, the only basis on which an apology could have been warranted was gender. Thus, what children, particularly boys, learn is not only that it is wrong to use badwords, but also that it is wrong to use it in the presence of anyone claiming seniority, whether by age or social status. They internalize the "frames of interpretation" and contextual usage, becoming, in effect "a part of adult culture . . . through their negotiations with adults and their creative production of a series of peer cultures with other children" (Corsaro 1992:169).

Young boys learning to play cricket from young men learn not only cricket but the ways peculiar to young men. Smoking is held as a sign of manhood. Only adults can smoke cigarettes publicly, without sanction, and this they do at the bars and shops and on the cricket field. Boys learn to smoke secretly among themselves, in private imitation of what they see big men do in public. There is also high consumption of ganja by the young men. But where a young man sent in to bat may hand over his cigarette to a younger boy, he will avoid giving him his spliff. Before he can smoke a ganja spliff, a boy must "graduate"; he must establish himself as a man in the eyes of other young men.

So far I have been explaining the informal, face-to-face channels of communication and activity through which children learn to be children and learn, as well, to prepare themselves for adulthood. These take place inside as well as outside the yard. It is in the domain outside the yard that boys are allowed the freedom to move about, and although parents cannot avoid sending girls out of the yard, on errands, to church, to school, they would much prefer to have them remain at home. We frequently find boys playing on the road through Grannitree, and on the playing field, or hanging about in the village square or near the bars. In what follows I focus on the ideal roles, behaviour, and values which are transmitted. In particular I examine sex roles and gender ideals, sexuality and maturity, and morality.

Sex Roles and Gender Ideals

A sharp gender division of labour prevails in Grannitree, at least in the ideal, almost with the strength of ideology. In this division, a woman's role is ideally that of housewife and a man's that of provider working outside the confines of the house. In reality, many men report taking part in household activities and many boys are trained to undertake chores ideally reserved for girls; and conversely, as the reader may have already observed, many girls are often drawn into helping in productive activity outside the household. In such departures from the ideal, where children are concerned, a lot depends on the personal ideas of the parents, the changing cultural environment, as well as on the birth order within a family. But as an ideal, we were told repeatedly by Grannitree and Sink Hole residents that young girls are expected to receive their training on the instruction and by the example of their mothers, around the house, while boys are expected to receive theirs helping their fathers in the field. Mothers should train girls, fathers train boys. This gender role division finds coherence in the view that boys should be grown tough, while girls should be protected, and in the semiotic life of the community, in which the male-female dichotomy is represented in an opposition between *"out a road"* and *yard*. The road, which includes the village square, represents a domain frequented and controlled by the male, the yard a domain governed by the female. As Durant-Gonzalez (1976:39) observes in relation to the latter, a yard is always identified in the female, as in "Miss Verne's yard" and not "Mass Josiah's yard".

The sex role divisions, according to Mr Wilson, start when, "after they reach a certain age", mother controls the girls and father the boys. His own daughters spend most of their time with their mother performing household chores, while his sons are for the most part with him outdoors. He remembers as a small boy wanting to do things in the house, but his father insisting that he work outside taking care of the animals.

What this "certain age" is Mr Wilson does not say. Whatever that age, when a boy reaches it he begins to undertake simple outdoor chores, such as fetching water at the pipe, or learning to be responsible for his own chickens. He learns also that taking out the chamber pot is a girl's chore, though if he has no sister he may well be called upon to do so, along with other household tasks.

Chanette:	My brother have fi carry water, tie the goat, and me have to wash the plate and sometimes spread di bed and sometimes clean the house, and so on. Sometimes mi breda don't do nothing. Me have fi do everything. Me and him fight.
Animator:	Why?
Chanette:	Because sometimes when my mada tell him to sweep di yard, him chat bout "Make Chanette do it!"
Animator:	Is he older?
Chanette:	No. I am older [he is eleven, she fifteen], but sometimes him go on like *him* bigger than me.
Animator:	Have you ever done his work around the yard?
Chanette:	I always do his work. Because I like to tie goat, him always beg me, "Chanette, go tie di goat fi me!" When me beg *him*, *"Tony, go sweep out di verandah fi me!"* him naa go sweep di veranda. Me have fi go tie the goat *and* sweep di verandah.

Animator: So what about your bigger brothers? What do they say when he says that?

Chanette: Dem laugh. Dem say dem pass through that age already and dem not doing it again!

Animator: Where did he learn that certain work is for girl, since all of his brothers before him did it?

Chanette: Him hear him friend-dem with it: "Girl pikni fi take out chimmy; girl pikni fi dust; girl pikni fi do all di housework!"

Annette: Most of the boys, if clothes on the line to take up . . .

Natalie: Yes! True! (General laughter and agreement.)

Annette: . . . dem no take up brassiere, panty and slip and those things.

Chanette: One day I wasn't home, and my mother wasn't home, and one of my brother was there. An' when we come back dem take up everything and leave the brassiere, the panty and the slip. One day I see my likl breda use a bamboo stick take up a panty (general laughter).

Animator: Whose panty?

Chanette: My own.

Annette: When mummy wash clothes and tell Alton to take them up because him come from school earlier than me and Sandra, him take up everything and leave the brassiere.

(At this point Alton appeared at the church door.)

Animator: We have been hearing that you do not take up panties and brassieres from the line. Why?

Alton: Girls must do that!

Annette: So who take up your brief? Suppose you grow big and your wife sick, wouldn't you take up her panty?

Alton: I would get a helper.

Annette: Nowadays helpers don't wash your underwear for you.

Clinton: Not sure [if I would take it up from off the line].

Animator: So when the rain falls and you are the only one at home, what do you do?

Clinton: I take up the boys' own and leave the rest.

Annette: Why?

Clinton: That's female work!

Annette: Suppose when you grow big and have a wife, and you wife sick and you have to wash your wife's panty, you wouldn't wash it?

Clinton: Yeah!

Girls: Oh! Oh! (applause)

Animator: Who taught us, the young men, that the young men must not take up panties and must not take out chimmy?

Chanette: They say is only maamaman alone take up panty and wash their wives panty, and so on. So they say, "I am no maamaman, so I not taking up no panty!"

Mavis (very quietly): A maamaman is somebody who take bati!

(At this point Tony enters. One of the animators asks him why he refuses to help in the housework.)

Tony (very confident): Only when uman sick man fi clean house!

Animator: Who says so?

Tony: Me say so!

Animator: Yes, but where did you get it from?

Tony: I was only talking.

Animator: What do you mean?

Tony: When uman hearty, dem fi do everything, but from dem sick, you [man] have fi do everything.

Chanette: Whether you sick yes or no, Tony tell you him naa tidy no house! If mi mada tell him to take up di plate, him say: "Mek Chanette or mummy do it, man, dem a gyal pikni!" Everything, "Mek Chanette or mummy do it!" One time I go spend holiday, you hear the first thing him say [when I came back]? "Chanette, me naa take out no chimmy, 'cause when you gone, is me take out di chimmy!" (Laughter)

Annette: [Taking out the chimmy] is notn! Cause you pee-pee in it. If it underneath the bed, you have fi draw it out!

Chanette: But you see Tony? Tony don't take up di chimmy and hold it, y'know! Him make it stay far and pee-pee in it!

The context of this exchange was a mixed group discussion of teenagers thirteen to eighteen years old, but the majority female. There were three animators, two females and one male. The discussion defines the normative boundaries of male gender roles.

The taboo against males touching women's underwear can be broken under the special condition of no other female being available. Boys do take out the chimmy, boys do pick up female underwear, males may wash women's underwear. But these must never become habitual, otherwise one becomes a maamaman, a derogatory term for a man who by assuming the female role inverts the gender divisions. Another term, used in an adult male group discussion to describe a man who would accept household money from, rather than give household money to, his woman, was *man-uman*. A *maamaman* is a tamed and domesticated man, bossed by his spouse. There is even the view that his inversion might be sexual as well – hence Mavis' muffled remark that a *maamaman* is also one who *"take bati"*, that is a homosexual. Thus, although circumstances may require a boy to undertake chores he believes are specifically female, he will make every effort to relinquish them as soon as a sister, or his mother, is available. No such taboo exists in the opposite direction. By pointing this out, pointing to the lack of symmetry in this level of gender relations, the girls show that they contest their assigned roles. To be socialized does not mean to be submissive.

By the time a boy reaches nine or ten, he is forced to get up before daylight, *"mek dew water wet him"*, to tie out animals or accompany his father to the field. This is a toughening-up process believed to be enhanced by early-morning exposure to the cool mountain air and wetness of the bush. Thereafter he is closely supervised by his father.

Mr Maxwell is a farmer. He owns and drives his own truck, which he uses to transport goods and people to and from the area. He has six children, four sons and two daughters, the oldest being twenty-six-year-old Melvin. He hasn't yet bothered to teach any of them to drive, out of fear of accidents and damages, which he can ill afford. It was hard enough to find a bank to lend him money to repair the vehicle. But one day he will eventually teach his boys, not his girls, to drive. Driving a truck is a man's job. In America, it is possible for a woman to drive a big truck, because the roads are good; in Jamaica the roads are very bad, creating too many accidents. In any case, a father's or a male guardian's duty is to supervise and train his sons, while most of a girl's training should come from her mother.

It took me an hour to get a bus from Half Way Tree and another to reach the community. It was 11:00 a.m. On the way up from the bus stop I joined Manley. He is fifteen years old. A former pupil of Sink Hole All-Age school, he was removed by his mother and sent to Tarrant Secondary near Half Way Tree in Kingston, because she felt he was not learning enough. There he is now studying electrical installation and is glad to be doing this practical area. He lives with both parents, two brothers and a sister. Manley still goes to the field with his father, but there are times when his mother objects, feeling that farming is not prosperous. She is more interested in him fixing televisions and radios. But still he cultivates his own little garden, planting yams and other ground provisions, which the family eats. Sometimes he sells his yams to the local shops. His father, too, cultivates yams, but these he takes to the market himself.

Manley's sister spends most of her time with their mother, while he and his brothers spend most of theirs with their father. She helps her mother prepare the meals and keep the house neat and clean, while they are encouraged to do "rough" work such as gathering firewood, taking care of the animals and fetching water.

Manley's mother would like his sister to be a nurse or a teacher, but his father doesn't really express any particular desire about his children's future. He does not smile or talk much, is very strict and works continuously. Manley normally comes home early on Fridays to help him take his produce down to the bus stop, to be transported to the Annotto Bay market.

In the life of this fifteen-year-old boy and his siblings are reproduced the gender role divisions his parents probably grew up with. Males take care of the outdoor work, the rough and tough of the field and the animals. Digging yam hills is rigorous work, requiring the use of a fork and a machete, reaping them even more so. From his father Manley would have learned the full routine of yam culture: how to separate and store the yam head from the rest of the yam, how to sun and store yams for future, long-term use, the planting time, how to make the mounds, called yam hills, how and when to cut the bamboo and other saplings to make yam stick for the vines to run on, when to reap, and how to reap without the machete perforating the soft texture. He would have learned as much by instruction as by observation.

But at the same time, Manley's mother has other plans for him. Acquiring a vocation holds out a more promising future than cultivating the field. His mother reflects a strong current we encountered in Grannitree, by which boys are siphoned off into vocational subjects or apprenticed to learn trades, while the girls continue in school. The conflict between Manley's parents is of a non-contradictory sort, for by pushing him to learn a trade, his mother is ensuring her son's occupational multiplicity, a regular feature of the men in his community.

Once, at Biiti's bar, when Everton declared that he wanted his younger brother to become a soldier or teacher we asked him why not a farmer. It depends, he replied with a sense of pragmatism, on whether the boy could make money from farming. Just then, Floyd, who was part of the discussion, called out to Biiti: "Biiti, when Donald grow big, yu wouldn't want im turn farmer?" Biiti laughed and said, "I'd want im to be a suoja [soldier]! Don't yu see dat me a suoja a'ready!" In this play on the word *"suoja"*, she meant both that *she* preferred him being a soldier rather than a farmer and that she wanted him to be trained to rough it and have survival skills.

At one discussion planned by our team of animators, a group of young men expressed the idea that the expectation that, as soon as they begin courting girls, males should shoulder the financial responsibilities is one of the main reasons why boys leave school early *"fi go look money fi tek care o' uman"*. When to that is added the stoppage from school to attend to the field and the animals and to follow parents to market, males end up less educated.

Girls, meanwhile, are sent regularly to school and given special attention. This is strikingly evident from even the basic school level. The basic school housed in the Seventh Day Adventist church had, on one of our visits, thirty children in attendance, but only ten of them were males. The teacher pointed to the school fee as a problem for many parents, but drew attention to the fancy hairstyles and clothes worn by the girls. This pattern continues through to the higher levels of the education system, and is observed at the primary and two all-age schools in the district. Research currently undertaken by Errol Miller in the causes of functional illiteracy as manifest in a reading problem confirms that this pattern is widespread. All the incoming Grade 7 students of a mix of six comprehensive high, new secondary, and all-age schools were tested for their reading ability, and those proving to be functionally illiterate carefully examined for family background, health and attendance record in Grade 1 through to Grade 6. Miller found strong correlation between illiteracy and attendance at the Grade 1 and Grade 2 levels, grades in which the fundamentals of reading are taught. Two-thirds of the functionally illiterate subset are males (Errol Miller, personal communication, 22 July 1998). The thinking behind giving the girl child the chance over the boy was expressed in the following way in one of the mixed discussion groups (eight men and four women, including the pastor and his wife):

BJ: Some parents, say [for example], dem have four, five children, an' dem never have it fi spen' pon all, dem more spen' it pon de girl child!

Animator: Why?

BJ: Well, dem say di bwaai kyan work pon construction work [laughter and hand clapping in agreement], an' di girl now fi go up iina university or some big job or sopm [something], but di bwaai kyan run up and dong, fight fi imself.

Fioni: Is not all parents! If di bwaai show more interes' in school and di girl not . . .

Animator: I don't think he was saying all parents. I think he was saying those parents that found themselves in a situation where things were tight.

Fioni: Well, my parents did have six o' we, and me never see dem put out effort pon neither three a di bwaawi nor none a di girl. Dem never even help one of us!

BJ: Anyhow yu don't have it and yu have fi spen' di likl wha' yu have pon all a di children, non a dem naa go work out to be notn. Yu have fi spen' pon di one dem who yu see sopm iina dem – spen' pon those!

This kind of gender selection operates in situations of relative deprivation, where parents' ability to support the children in school, all at the same time, is limited. Parents apply their own gender privileging, making girls better prepared and boys less prepared to perform in schools (Figueroa 1997). Following the logic of BJ's argument, the choice of the girl child is due to the greater interest in education shown by the girl.

Luce:	You see di difference? The girl-dem more ambitious!
Pastor:	Ambitious!
Luce:	Dem step out more. Is not dat di parents would'n try wid di bwaai-dem. Lemme tell yu sop'm: whether di bwaai or di girl, anyone put out interest and ready fi go ahead, the parents are ready wid dem.
BJ:	Even with the teacher iina school, dem always take tender care wid di girl pikni-dem more than wid di bwaai pikni-dem.
Luce:	No! No! [then agreeing afterwards] Yu know why it look like it is the girl? Sometimes it is the girls who are the ones showing interest. So the teacher get to love dem and put out more interest on dem. The bwaai-dem, as dem 'quint, dem out a door, and dem naa pay no interest. So [the teachers] dem just no bother wid dem. Dem start help who trying to help demself.
BJ:	Is not dat! Is just because is uman! Uman put more interest iina uman!
Luce:	Man-teacher do it too, and do it to girl!
Mervin:	I think it is just a matter of potential and interest. This is not to say that potentially the boys are not as good as the girls, but the girls seem to be more interested. What the boys need is motivation and financial backing.

At this point the discussants suggest that boys are more easily distracted, by the wider culture, DJ music, gun toting, drugs and so on. But the general consensus was that in education the greater emphasis was placed on the girls, and that this was due to their greater interest in learning.

If girls are socialized to be more interested in education, what are the boys socialized to be interested in? Uppermost in a boy's mind, once he attains a sense of being male, is the need to earn and control money.

In an informal interview Calder sought to explain the reasons behind the men's claim that in their community they were the ones who were progressive, despite the lesser access to schooling and other types of exposure. From early, he explained, older males, especially fathers tell them that " 'we as a man must go out there and find food, because it does not matter what we have, that's the job for the man. Man must go out there, go struggle and find food'. From I hear that, I just know that whether we have an education or whether we don't have an education, that's our job ."

But finding food is not all. It is man's job to find money in order to assume responsibility for woman. In one of our discussion groups, Shinehead claimed that this was a teaching of his parents. And when he asked his father, "Why don't you send the girl to the bush to tie out the goat?" he told him, "You cannot do like the girl, because what girl sell is it you have to buy!" "[That's why] I started chasing money. I couldn't go to school!"

Training in responsibility to have access to money explains why some mothers, like Manley's, discourage their sons from concentrating on becoming farmers and encourage them instead to take up skills training. In choosing practical skills, such as electrical installation and auto-mechanics, as young men they will be able to command reasonable incomes that can be supplemented by farming. Leo-Rhynie (1989:87) presents data that confirm the orientation of boys to industrial and technical vocations such as metalwork, woodwork, general electricity and technical drawing, while girls select secretarial and home economics courses such as clothing and textiles, home management, shorthand and typing, food and nutrition. The greater selection by girls of liberal arts subjects, such as languages, gives them a preparatory edge into many of the professions. So, if Manley's mother has her way, her daughter will become a secretary, nurse or a teacher, a professional.

Yet, Grannitree youths point out, it is the males who end up better off in the long run, for while the girls have their CXC and GCE passes to show for their years of schooling, they often fail to get a job. The boys, however, having acquired a skill, get employed or start their own work and end up taking these same females as wives and girlfriends. Interestingly, the same point is also made by Joetown youths in Kingston, as we shall see later in Chapter 7. In a tracer study of secondary school graduates Brown (1994:138) discovered that, indeed, male graduates who one year after graduation were own-account workers or blue-collar workers had higher mean weekly incomes than their female counterparts. But he also found that the mean weekly income of female graduates employed as white-collar workers was higher than their male counterparts in similar white-collar jobs. Evidently, this fact is already well known by Jamaican youths.

In the idea that it is the role of a young boy a-courting to be responsible for his girl is the germ of the notion of the male as provider. There are certain fixed notions about what is expected from a male. Assuming the financial burden is one of them, and taking the initiative in male-female relationships is another.

I visited the Sink Hole All-Age School. Some children were playing ring games. I decided to join them when they started "The Farmer in the Dell". My participation did make a few of them shy. After a while I noticed that the "farmer" they selected was always a boy, and the "farmer's wife" always a girl. The "nurse" was always a girl, the "cat" always a boy, while the "rat" was always a girl and the "cheese" always a boy. This "cheese" would subsequently stay in the ring to become the "farmer" in the next round, and the sequence continue. Much to everyone's amusement, children and teachers looking on from the windows, I started playing the "farmer". Then when my round was over, I suggested reorganizing the sequence to make a girl the "farmer". Amusement turned to hilarity. Why did they find it funny, I asked, when there are female farmers in the community? They didn't reply but soon had a problem singing, *the farmer takes a husband*. It was then they pointed out that it sounded "funny" and did not fit the rhythm and beat of the tune. One of the boys shouted out: "Sir, a no uman choose man, a man choose uman!" "Who told you that?" I asked. "Is so it go! Then yu don't know that already, sir?" As it turned out, my female "farmer" proved very reluctant in choosing a husband.

Finally, when that round was over, and they reverted to a regular male "farmer", I suggested a boy as choice for a "farmer's wife". The laughter greeting this suggestion was uncontrollable. They all pulled away hands, breaking up the circle, and with it the game, and ran laughing in all directions.

I tackled my "man choose uman" friend. Nobody told him that, he said, one just knows it. He closed the argument with: "Any uman who look man is not a good uman!" I then spoke with one of the girls in the game, thirteen years old. She would never "look a guy". Even if she saw one and liked him, she would keep away from him and not let him know. When you let boys know that you like them, they take advantage of you.

The average age of these children was about twelve years, just around puberty. They have already been prepared to reproduce the idea that in sexual approaches the initiative lies with the male, not the female. A female who initiates sexual overtures is without respect, or, as Benji remarked at the discussion meeting, echoing the words of a popular song, a girl "cannot do what the men do and still be a lady".

Sexuality and Maturity

Male-female relationships have other markers of inequalities, and it is in these inequalities that boys mature into men and girls into women. For girls, as Durant-Gonzalez (1974:34–38) points out, the transition from "gal pickney" to woman begins with child bearing, which, not uncommonly, takes place during adolescence, and ends with the acquisition of "a sufficient level of social maturity" brought on gradually by the assumption of the mother role in the household.

In Grannitree, once they reach puberty girls are routinely told to be wary of boys and men, out of the fear of pregnancy, while parents turn a blind eye to their boys' sexual adventures outside the yard. Every parent is bent on guarding daughters against neighbours' sons. The result is, as a female discussant puts it, "You would like your son to get meat from my daughter and my son must get no meat from your daughter!"

Inevitably, once they are known to be sexually active, girls run into conflict with their parents. In the following case, no pregnancy resulted, but Carlene's parents did not wait for one to punish her.

Maas Rupert had invited me to come with him to his vegetable garden. I arrived in Grannitree too late. He could not wait, but left his cousin, Vibert, to guide me to his bush. Vibert is only twenty-three years old. He left school at fifteen, having completed the all-age school. He started doing job work for farmers, clearing land by the slash-and-burn method or "billing" the weeds with a machete. There were two methods of payment, one by the day's work, at a rate of $250 with lunch, or $300 without; the other by task. He preferred the latter, for once the farmer agreed on his estimate of how long it would take to clear the land, and paid down one-third of the money, he'd bring in others to help him and shorten the time. Of late, he works only for himself, growing sweet potato, though there is not much in farming. Vibert has no children, but he has a girlfriend, Carlene. They have been friends for over five years, from the time she was fifteen years old and he eighteen. Carlene's parents found out about the relationship and her mother gave her a sound beating. She cursed and quarrelled that Carlene would soon get pregnant and stop from schoool. Her father also quarrelled and stopped talking to Vibert. But neither beating nor quarrels could douse the relationship. Sometimes she would leave school early to stay with him before going home. He tried his best not to get her pregnant. Although he found condoms distasteful at first, he never failed to use them. She had a special love for him, he believes, because he was her first. She was not his first, though; by age fifteen he had had three.

Virbert says that as soon as he "set up himself" he is going to get married. Marriage is the best thing for a young man. Carlene's parents' attitude towards him has changed over the five years they have been together. Her father now talks to him and they have even asked him to do jobs for them. He no longer lives with his parents but with his cousin, Maas Rupert. His father did not approve of him moving out, because he wanted Vibert to stay and work with him, as his first born. They are still not on good terms. But Vibert felt that he had to "face life" for himself, and besides, his father was too strict. As soon as he saves enough money he is going to "raise up a house", so Carlene can come live with him. As we went through Maas Rupert's vegetable patch, Vibert said that although there is a lot of joy seeing one's crops grow, he could not spend his life as a farmer; there is no money in it. While hoping his big brother (on his mother's side) will send for him as soon as he straightens out his illegal status in the United States, he plans to set up a business. He is a good cook, a skill he learned in school.

By Grannitree and Jamaican standards (see Chevannes 1992), Vibert's and Carlene's early sexuality is normal, his earlier than hers. Most people think seventeen or eighteen years old is about the right time for girls, but acknowledge the reality is as early as fourteen. Carlene was lucky not to have got pregnant, and only the discovery of her secret affair and her parents' violent reaction forced the two lovers into using a contraceptive. Contraceptives make it easier for girls to fulfil their sexuality without their parents finding out. This was a strongly held view among young men in the community. Nevertheless, the availability of these technologies does not make parents any less apprehensive about their daughters getting pregnant, bringing shame on the family and damaging their chances of a good education. But a son impregnating a girl carries no such apprehension, because, it would seem, his chances of making money to support woman and child are not entirely dependent on the education system. And he does not carry around a pregnancy. Hence the unequal treatment.

Another example of the inequality between genders, this time between sexually mature men and women, is ability, if not the right, of man physically to discipline woman, without social sanction. Boys do not have this right. When they do, it is a sign of having made the transition to men. The following discussion highlights a number of themes already discussed, for example the informality of the socialization process. But it is the topic of woman-beating that animated the group of young men.

I arrived in the community at about 11:00 a.m. On the way I passed several children carrying water on their heads – none was a girl – and several men bathing in the stream nearby where the boys were fetching water. In the square were four other boys between eight and eleven years old, racing on bicycles, and several others sitting down watching another group kick a football improvised from rags. Floyd, Everton and some other young men were at Biiti's bar and snack shop – actually, they were on the street nearby. On seeing me, Floyd remarked that the animation meeting the previous Sunday was "nice" and asked whether another one was scheduled. He found the discussion on whether women should get beaten exciting. Using this entree I asked the young men, none of whom was at the meeting, for their opinion. Floyd was first to begin. He restated his position: he would never beat his girlfriend, because he did not want anybody to hit him or his sister or his mother, and he prayed that his relationship did not reach the stage where he had to hit anybody, meaning of course his girlfriend. "Suppose she hit yu?" someone asked. He would hit her back, he replied, because he was a man and no woman should beat a man. However, no woman would try to beat him. Sixteen-year-old Everton interjected, "Some uman wi lick yu iina yu bombo klaat! A wha' yu a talk bout?" This elicited from Floyd the concession that the situation requiring a man to beat a woman was easy to come about, for he and his girlfriend got into a fight. She told him a big badword and he hit her. Still, he ended, some men "sof", meaning that there are some who would not have retaliated. Everton was emphatic: he definitely would not hesitate to beat a woman. "If she do di ting dat I don' like, she ha fi get lick!" Mainly at my doing, the discussion shifted on to boys like Everton who had to leave school early and grow "like Ragamuffin", crude and rough, while girls continue in school or get pregnant. But the shift was not for long. Blakey had joined the gathering, so Floyd asked him: "Why man beat uman?" "Uman fi get lick!" he answered.

"A so me a say, too!" interjected Everton, going on to explain that if he caught a man in his house with his woman, he was going to beat both man and woman. The hypothetical situation drew Biiti. While she objected to woman-beating as a general right for men, she agreed that cheating made the situation different. If the woman did the "wrong ting" she should get "brush up". "Suppose," I asked, "a man bring in di uman?" Biiti laughed, "Im fi dead, im fi get beatin' too." But, she went on, if she caught her man with a woman, she would simply pack her things and leave. Blakey offered his position. If he caught another man in his own house, he would not beat man or woman, but ask both of them to leave. "Yu a mad man!" exploded Everton. No, Blakey explained, if he got caught in another man's yard, he would not want the man to cut him up. After all, no man would be caught in a house if he was not taken there by the woman. What would cause him to beat her was if when he asked her to leave she refused. And if the man tried to intervene, he would have to "dust" him, too. Every man, he concluded, took chances, and if he took a chance and went to a woman's house, he would not want the man to hurt him.

The discussion, although stimulated by our presence, possessed all the spontaneity of the village square. And in that public atmosphere created in the middle of the day by a group of young men, there was no guardedness about keeping certain things from the ears of boys. The boys did not park their bicycles or abandon their football game to listen, but some of them could have heard, and probably did hear, the opinions expressed. However, the points which bear fuller discussion are becoming a man and the issue of wife-beating.

At sixteen years old, Everton was quite at home in the company. He was already a man. A number of developments mark the transition to manhood in Grannitree. First is the ability to make income earning the principal activity. Everton was already out of school, forced by economic conditions. Floyd had explained that Everton had stopped "because di yout' didn' have any pants, shoes or shirt". Now, although he had ambitions to be a soldier, policeman or security guard while he was a student, and had also liked woodwork, Everton was currently working as a higgler. This is exactly as Maas James, a mature farmer, was to say, in another discussion in the square later that same month. Maas James and his other friends were asked when did a boy become a man. His reply was as soon as boys started earning their own money and taking care of themselves. Milverton, his friend, introduced a qualification and second point, namely that the boy must also be assuming responsibility, that is having someone dependent on him. This, according to Juki, a third member of the group, meant having a girlfriend, disobeying one's parents and coming home late. Everton was not interviewed to find out whether he had a girlfriend to support, but the chances were quite slim that he did not.

These two requirements, economic independence and sexual responsibility, have to be taken together. The first without the second begs questions about a young man's sexual orientation, the second without the first leaves him still dependent on his parents, and therefore still a child subject to parental disposition. Thus, becoming a man in Grannitree, in the final analysis, has less to do with one's age and more to do with one's activities. As long as one remains a student, one remains a boy. School and the activities associated with it keep a male a boy. As soon as he completes the transition to the world of work, he becomes a man. For, as inferred from an earlier discussion, the preparation for manhood begins early. At ten or eleven years old, boys are ushered into this world by parents, who begin to train them in income earning activity, whether negotiating the sale of ripe bananas or looking after their own livestock. How long the transition lasts will depend on how long it takes to be fully self-sufficient. Manley, at fifteen years old, had still some years to go, although he was already selling yams to the local shops. If what Mrs Royes, the vice-principal of one of the all-age schools, told us is correct, Manley is representative. According to her, at about fifteen years old, boys are sent to Kingston to learn a trade, while girls, either at the 11-plus exams or later at the Grade 9 achievement test go on to further academic work, as a result of performing better than the boys. Thus, Everton at sixteen is a man, but for most Grannitree boys the transition is accomplished somewhat later.

Becoming a woman is a somewhat more complex process in Grannitree. Because more is expended on keeping girls in school, when they drop out there is a greater sense of disappointment. Mr Patterson is very disappointed in his eighteen-year-old granddaughter, Dorothy, for getting pregnant while at school, far more than her own mother and grandmother. He wanted to put her out of the house but his wife intervened, straining their relationship. He accused her of *"keeping up slackness"*, in accepting the pregnancy.

Now a mother herself, Dorothy joins hands with her mother and sends things to sell in the market; in this way they both support their children. She is therefore a woman, because she is a mother and is now responsible for herself. Had she returned to school, she would have remained a girl.

For a large number of Jamaican females, the transformation of a girl into a woman is accomplished through child bearing, and although, as Durant-Gonzalez correctly points out, the transformation is complete only when she assumes the role commensurate with the status of mother, the acts of pregnancy and child bearing serve as a rite of passage. Rites of passage, as Van Gennep (1960) identified, entail first a separation, then a period of liminality, and finally a reintegration. In a study of several hundred women who became adolescent mothers, all were shown to have undergone very painful psychological and sometimes physical separation from their families, which was brought on by the announcement of the pregnancy; a period of liminality, marked by confusion, depression, low self-esteem and suicidal tendencies and lasting months, sometimes the entire duration of the pregnancy; and finally a reintegration with their families, with whom, especially their own mothers, they report an even better relationship than they had before getting pregnant in the first place (Chevannes 1996).

For the male adolescent there is no ritualized status change. There are no physiological changes announcing paternity comparable to pregnancy. Manhood is, as Chodorow (1971) says, achieved by doing, not by being. For this reason, the *nouveaux hommes* like Everton are more doers than their more experienced colleagues. Everton's vehemence on woman-beating represents more fully than those of the other participants the prevailing ideology governing man-woman relationships. It is expressed in its ideal form: a man has the right to beat a woman if she transgresses.

Biiti's position is more subtle. It reflects both the influence of the dominant ideology as well as the position of a potential victim. It is true that, as a bar and snack shop owner, she would not want to alienate her customers, but we do not think she was dissimulating when she conceded that a woman should be beaten for taking an outside man home to have sex. For she not only voiced her objection to the general ideal, but tried to focus on the offence itself rather than on the gender of the offender, calling for equal punishment, though somewhat half-heartedly. She knew quite well that no man was going to allow his woman to beat him, so she personalizes the point by explaining that were she to discover her man with another woman in her house she would simply pack up and leave. The point is she says nothing that differs sharply with the men, unlike the confrontationist position adopted by Janice in the face of her *domino chemist* opponents. Biiti's view is more the norm.

Floyd's and Blakey's positions, however, are not the same as Everton's. They are tempered by experience. In Floyd's case, the use of a badword by his girlfriend to show her disrespect for him was what precipitated his physical retaliation. But by expressing his prayer that his relationship would never deteriorate to that level, he showed that he valued it remaining harmonious. In other words, a man had the right to beat his woman, but he wished he did not have to exercise it.

Blakey's position also is contextualized by experience. *Uman fi get lick* expresses an ideological thesis, a general, taken-for-granted, obvious and unquestioned "truism". In real life, however, one of the most dishonourable of offences, namely an illicit sexual affair in the confines of a man's yard, ought not in his eyes to merit beating the offending woman. Blakey puts himself in the position of the male participant in an outside affair. Every man takes chances, he says, thinking of himself, thinking also of the norm among young men that a man should not confine himself to one woman but should "look others". Taking a chance refers not to the sexual intercourse, per se, but to invading another man's home. Because *man choose uman*, and not *uman choose man*, it is more the expected norm for the man to check the woman at her yard than for her to check him at his. This expectation, in Blakey's eyes, gives men common cause. No need therefore for physical force. Despite the nuances, all these different views have the same common point of view, namely that women are subject to being beaten by men.

Male-gendered views in Grannitree are reinforced by the gender-segregated activities that tend to bond males together. Games like domino and cricket, certain types of productive work, like clearing and planting the land, and leisure activities centred around the village square or the sound system, are routine. They follow daily, weekly and seasonal patterns. But there are the occasional times when the young men string up the sound system, build a fire, roast yams and breadfruits, barbecue chicken, play games and have their own fun day, usually not without the presence and assistance of the women. At the one that took place during our field trip, tug-o'-war between opposing groups of men was the main mass sport, but there were also Ludo, dominoes and cards. The children present were mostly boys, including eleven-year-old Donald, who had stolen away from home without completing his chores. His mother, Sandra, who had come looking for him, was not amused. She exploded some badwords at him, grabbed him by the collar and shook him. Donald headed home at once.

Moral Values

A recurrent theme in the reminiscences of the older members of Grannitree is the present day deterioration in the behaviour of children, so different from in days gone by.

I set out to Grannitree to conduct an interview with Mrs Patti Francis, the wife of the pastor of the Church of God branch in the community. She was busily sweeping the yard with a bunch of wild shrubs which when tied together made an excellent broom. Pastor had gone to his field to plant yams. Orrett, their eleven year old grandson, had just arrived home from school. She ordered him to "take off your clothes and go over to Miss Agnes and tell her to send the thing come". "The thing" was Miss Agnes' paadna hand (savings club contribution). Mrs Francis was the banker. Born in 1922 in Sink Hole, Miss Patti married Pastor forty years ago. But before that, she got pregnant at twenty years old for a man who "deceived" her and she had her first son, followed by a daughter two years later. As a result of the first pregnancy she had to leave the church. She bore Pastor six children.

Her secret for a successful marriage was to respect herself and her partner, and then "leave it in the hands of God". She remembers her first three headmasters at school: Mr Watson, who was very strict, and after him Mr Thomas, whom the children nicknamed "Col' Soup", and then Teacher Spencer. Now when Teacher Spencer flogged a child, you dare not go home and tell your parents, like what is happening now. Nowadays, when teacher scolds a child, parents go and curse off teacher. She could never go home and tell her parents she was punished at school, for her parents would give her a flogging. Today, boys are more preoccupied with sports, and they all give in to pleasure. As soon as they reach thirteen or fourteen years old, they feel they are big men who have nothing to do with school. Sometimes, she says, some of the fathers encourage this, and cites the case of a woman who tearfully pleaded with her to speak to her husband to help send their seven children to school. Miss Patti says she told the husband that "children have long memory and if you don't treat them good, later you may not be able to find someone to give you water". But the man was adamant. He showed her a large sum of money, declaring he would give them none of it, because all they went to school for was to learn to curse badword.

Then she took off on the matter of indiscipline. Children, when they reach a certain age, lose interest in school and become indisciplined. Calling one of the man's daughters to encourage her to go to school, she found that the girl already had a boyfriend and had stopped from school as a result. She was only thirteen. According to Miss Patti, having a boyfriend at thirteen was nothing new, for when she was growing up she saw twelve-year-olds having babies. But it was definitely more prevalent today. Discipline started to deteriorate with the introduction of the sound system, causing children to stay out late and exposing them to outrageous behaviour. She herself did not go much to sound systems and clubs, because her father was very strict. When she did get permission it was from her mother, who was very tender-hearted. Father, however, was like a rock. When he said "No!" he meant no.

In a family, concludes Miss Patti from her own experience, there has to be some balance, one parent being strict, the other comforting. It is usually the mothers who provide the comfort. Growing up in her days, children had to go to bed early. If any of her siblings came in late, her father would administer a sound whipping with his "sibljak". This, she said, induced fear and respect in the children, making them accountable for their actions. Whether girl or boy her siblings were all treated in the same manner. They did not find real love in their father. He might have been loving, but he never showed it; mother was always affectionate. This did not mean she did not punish. The last time Miss Patti got a whipping from her was at age nineteen. With every lash around the legs, her mother repeated "Manners were made to be used!" This line Miss Patti used in raising her eight children. Patti Francis said she grew her children to be disciplined and to have manners to parents and elders. "Elders" included older siblings. Thus, among her two sisters and five brothers, the older ones had the right to discipline the younger ones. When her sons got to be thirteen or fourteen and she could not hold them to administer a flogging, she used to tie them to the bedpost as their form of punishment. They even had to eat meals there. The girls, however, she could still hold and flog. Once, her first daughter, married and living with her husband, came to visit her and made a rude remark. Miss Patti flogged her. Her daughter's only comment was, "Is because you know I am not going to lick you back." Nowadays? Children are using badwords to parents. The reason, in her opinion, is that the parents first use them. They use the rod, but they also use a lot of curse words, so their children grow up losing respect for them. Miss Patti says she notices that the government is saying that children should not get flogging in school, but this is the reason why the society is the way it is. Children must get spanking. If she were principal of a school, they would have to have manners and respect. As soon as they start getting rude she would suspend and expel them.

At seventy-two years old, Mrs Patti Francis is a woman one would call one of the pillars of the community, the wife of a successful preacher, the mother of eight fully grown children, the trusted banker of a paadna. She represents continuity with the past as well as embodying the well-known disconcerting frustrations felt by an older generation helplessly watching what it regards as a deterioration in moral standards, marked by the waywardness of the young and the demoralization of parents who have sunk to the level of their errant children. Mr Patterson, the Watsons, Mother Nation, Maas James, the school principals, virtually all the older citizens, compare the present day upbringing of children unfavourably with their own.

Mr Maxwell was the only one we met who betrayed any sense of sympathy for the *children of today*, pointing out to us that they faced greater problems and temptations than he did. Whereas in his day the only waywardness of a boy was *"to hide and go river go ketch fish, play cricket, play marble, ketch bird"*, for which he might escape a flogging by taking home a *"pretty mango for yu mada"*, nowadays children are exposed to drugs, violence, sex and diseases. He even found parents today more open to explaining sex to their children, and justified the earlier sexual experience of boys over girls by explaining that they needed to learn how to handle themselves for the time when they would take a partner. But his views are those of a minority of the older heads. In the views of most older folk, what the children of today lack are discipline and manners.

We can deduce from Mrs Francis's complaints and from her recounting of the offences that merited punishment what older heads like her mean by discipline. She first focuses on the concept by observing that nowadays children leave school prematurely and become indisciplined. What she seems to intend is not so much the origin of the word in *disciplina* (learning), but the departure by children from the paths laid down for them by parents. But parents too can induce indiscipline in their children by their own example, a view which suggests that beyond parents there are social values held by the community which parents are expected to transmit to children. Thus, ultimately, by discipline is meant conformity to the values of the community or society.

In that regard, one of the values the older heads believe to be losing its weight is "manners", a concept that covers a wide range of proper behaviour, from eye avoidance to forms of greeting, from terms of address to forms of deference, the common thread linking them being the social presentation and conduct of self. "To have manners" is to observe all the norms of right intercourse, to perform all the rituals of social grace. Underlying these norms is the notion of respect. A child who has "no manners" is a child who does not show respect to those who deserve respect. We have seen the examples of boys reprimanding one another for using badword in the presence of an adult stranger, a "big man". The age factor is the operative principle here. In Grannitree, age demands respect from those lacking age. The way Mrs Francis was grown required younger to show deference and obedience to older siblings. It is this principle which enables older siblings, particularly the girls, to become surrogate parents over younger ones. Age invests them with authority.

But besides age there is another ascribed status relationship. Miss Patti's daughter's rude remark was rude only because she used it in the presence or hearing of her own mother. She had violated a norm of right intercourse, not because the offended person was older, but because she was her mother. She violated the status relationship between parent and child. These are permanent states, which give parents authority over children, and children the obligation of deference and respect. Several of our Grannitree informants made it quite clear that a child always remains a child to them for as long as that child remains under their roof, or, as one of them put it: "when im turn im own key". In this sense, having manners also means not challenging the authority of a parent within one's parental home.

Some status relationships are achieved, and they too require good conduct. In Grannitree, teachers were another group that decried the lack of discipline. Discipline was the main topic of discussion at a Grannitree All-Age Parent-Teacher Association (PTA) meeting in May: girls flaunting the dress codes, especially on Fridays, and chewing gum, boys carrying pocketknives to school.

The normal method of enforcing discipline and manners in children is flogging or beating. One of the complaints of the older heads is that the failure to flog and, in the case of many parents, resorting to verbal abuse and defending the waywardness of their children, are contributing to children becoming worse nowadays. Modern society is to blame, Mr Watson told us. *"First ting dem say* [is] *dat di teacher mus' not flog di children when di children rude. Dat mean di chil' can go to school an' tell di teacher anyting. When children come home an' complain dat teacher punish dem at school, di parents may go to teacher an' curse di teacher."*

Parents are under the impression that flogging is forbidden in schools. Actually, the regulations permit flogging but only by designated persons, such as the principal or vice-principal, and even so under certain conditions. Gone, then, are the days when every teacher, by virtue of being one, carried his or her own strap or cane. This, the older heads complain, has given free rein for indiscipline to go unchecked.

What is more, both older heads and teachers complain, some parents defend the indiscipline of their children. At the Grannitree All-Age PTA meeting, the principal begged parents to come and see him when their children report problems with their teachers, rather than go directly to the teachers. "Don't come and call any teacher or child from out of the class," he said. Parents should tell the children that if they have a problem at school they should talk to the teacher or the principal. "Don't let them run come home to you." As soon as they run come [home], you see the parents coming like any bad bull and making up all kinds of noise." At this the parents applauded and one of them shouted, "Gangalii!" (a term of unsure derivation, but meaning virago, a self-proclaimed street fighter).

There were twenty-seven mothers and three fathers present. The cheering was in disapproval of the practice by some parents of rushing to school like some big gangster to defend their children's wrongdoing. The parents present saw the need to give teachers the scope to discipline errant children and would probably support the older heads like Mr Watson and Mrs Francis in their contention that many parents are to blame for their children's indiscipline. Mrs Francis was therefore right.

There are some who resort to using badwords to get children to conform. This, Mrs Francis maintains, is like trying to win respect with disrespect. Children learn to show disrespect to others through the use of badwords, from being themselves disrespected by parents. These complaints from the older informants are not baseless. Parents, like Sandra, have no scruple cursing their children. One day we did overhear Mrs Banfield cursing and threatening one of her children: *"A gwain brok yu up. A don' know why when people sen' yu out yu don' run go an' come! Yu have fi play an min' yu own business!"*

Using the expression *"A gwain brok yu up"* to reprimand her son for being dilatory on an errand, she could easily have said, *"A gwain brok up yu raas"*, as is the commonly understood expression. Such an expression is sometimes more hurtful to the child than flogging, which could be one of the reasons for resorting to it.

Flogging, when it is carried out, is generally done by the mother, if she is able to manage it. When, however, boys get older, and therefore stronger and more firmly set in their ways, it is the father who *"drop di lick"*. Grannitree men seldom beat their daughters. This they leave to their wives and babymothers.

The association of discipline with control opens up an aspect of community life in Grannitree to reveal, from the point of view of parents, an underlying tension between the yard itself, which they control, and the informal and unregulated life outside of it, which they do not. This tension is one of the themes which link this and all the other communities of this study.

Conclusion

In this rural community, the gender socialization of children takes place for the most part informally, in the context of everyday life, when the culturally rooted behavioural norms and the values underlying them are acted out or expressed. Activities are coded with gendered values and these are quickly learned by children and reproduced among themselves. Preparation for gendered life begins fairly early, after the toddler stage when the child begins to show acquisition of cognitive awareness. Males begin learning their role expectations: toughness, survival, economic responsibility. They learn in context. Here in this rural community, the contexts are the backdrop of female behavioural norms and values, against which and in relation to which male role expectation and performance are played out. Thus, by the time they are ready to complete the transition to full manhood, the parameters would have already been set and understood.

4

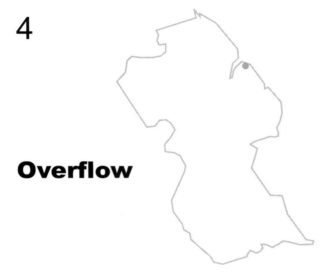

Overflow

Overflow, Guyana, is a composite of three contiguous villages, with a total population of approximately, 15,000, an estimated 90 percent of whom are Indo-Guyanese, the rest being Afro-Guyanese. (Population estimates are based on a registered school population of 2,400, and is in keeping with estimates derived from the Bureau of Statistics.)

Overflow had its beginnings more than forty years ago when the sugar estate resettled some of its workforce, a circumstance that makes the community somewhat different from other similar Indian settlements. Indian villages either grew up around rice farming or "were the residue of abandoned sugar plantations" (Smith 1996:112), in either case maintaining some degree of economic independence. Unlike these, Overflow is still dependent on the sugar estate, where many men find work as cane cutters and skilled labourers. A significant number of the younger people are salaried and wage workers in both public and private sectors in the capital, Georgetown, six miles away. There is also a thriving micro-enterprise sector, focused around transport, fishing, cattle rearing, gardening, woodworking, mechanics, and retail trading. Occupational multiplicity is normal (Comitas 1970; Silverman 1980; Williams 1991:49), as most male estate workers turn to their gardens in the crop-over time.

There are two all-age and one secondary school catering to the educational needs of the community. Even so, many parents opt to send their children to school in the city, some out of the widely held feeling that city schools are "good schools" and the local schools "bad schools", others because they themselves work there. The good-bad distinction between schools based in Georgetown and those based in the rural areas is common all over Guyana. Since most schools are outside of Georgetown and since not every child can go there, the "extra lesson" phenomenon has become an informal adjunct to the formal educational system. Many Overflow parents pay for extra lessons, some of which are taken in areas as far away as Georgetown.

The three schools aside, there are no state-run institutions within Overflow. The nearest health centre is between two and three miles away, depending on which end of the community one calculates from. However, there are two private doctors who actually reside and practise in Overflow. The government school also runs a monthly clinic for the children. There is no police station within Overflow. The community does its own voluntary policing as the need arises, which is not very great, since the main crimes are petty larceny, occasional housebreaking and wounding generally arising from domestic disputes. Overflow is not without its quota of sports clubs – cricket, domino, bridge. Its only community centre has been in a state of disrepair ever since the nationalization of the sugar industry in the 1970s; before that, the estate maintained the centre.

Indian Background

The overwhelming majority of Overflow citizens are Hindu. Together with a minority of Muslims and converted Christians, they are the descendants of those of the 240,000 Indian indentured labourers (Roberts 1979:128) recruited between 1841 and 1917 who chose to remain in the British colony, and the heirs of a cultural heritage which, though of Indian origin, has been shaped by the experience of colonial and postcolonial Guyana.

At the core of Indian culture and social structure was (and still is) caste, a system of social organization based on hereditary specializations called *jatis*. *Jatis* are grouped into a system of four orders or *varnas*, ranked in descending order of purity and prestige from *Brahmin* (priest), *Kshatriya* (warrior), *Vaisya* (trader), and *Sudra* (menial servant/artisan). Outside of these four orders and below even the *Sudra* are the Untouchables, indigenous tribes, who were thought to be so unclean as not to be fit enough to live within the village proper (Bailey 1960; Tyler 1986:82). The first three orders are considered twice-born, and therefore pure, while the *Sudra* and *Outcastes* are polluting. These orders maintain a relationship of interdependence, called *jajmani,* which because it is governed by principles of purity and pollution, produces asymmetry rather than reciprocity in social relations. For example, the Brahmin accepts food from no one but his own caste, but he may give food to all other castes, while the Untouchable may give food or water to no one, but receive from all.

Family and kinship relations are also governed by caste. One may marry only within one's caste. This caste endogamy is balanced by village exogamy, that is, by the need to find one's spouse outside one's village. The family structure itself is strongly patriarchal, with the ideal being a joint extended family. As the head and supreme authority, the male's main responsibility is to provide for his wife and children. His duty is to bring in the money, while that of his wife is to wash, cook, take care of the children and see to the general upkeep of the house, including responsibility for the purchase of food and other necessities. As his children get old enough, his sons bring in their wives to live, while his married daughters go off to live in their fathers-in-law's homes. His authority extends over his sons and their families as well. When he dies, his eldest son becomes head of the family. Having a son is important in other respects: he ensures the performance of ritual obligations as chief mourner at his father's death and, of course, the continuity of the paternal line. As a virtual stranger joining her husband's family, a wife's status and relations with her in-laws immediately improves with the birth of her first male child. "The comparative desirability of male children is reflected not only in their joyous reception but in differential mortality rates as well. Almost twice as many female children die as infants" (Tyler 1986:132). Socialization of children is the responsibility of all the adults and senior siblings within the structure of the joint family, under whose care they learn respect for authority; the codes of deference, younger to older, females to males, lower status groups to higher; the value of cooperation between members of the family; religious beliefs and observances; and so on.

Indenture and Creolization

As a device to meet a need for labour, indenture itself, coupled with the framework of an entirely different social structure, influenced a number of changes in the reproduction of Indian culture in British Guiana, particularly the caste system. All the *varnas* were represented in the recruitment, though there was a bias against the nonagricultural groups (Smith and Jayawardena 1996:113–14). Under indenture caste observances were impossible to maintain.

Conditions in the ships during the long voyage to the West Indies had made caste avoidance impossible. Absence of segregation was perpetuated in the plantations, where the laborers were housed in barracks partitioned into rooms, one to a family. Here members of different castes lived in close proximity, sharing the same water supply, latrines, and sometimes even kitchens (Smith and Jayawardena 1996:115).

Moreover, two demographic features of the whole recruitment process severely influenced changes. One was the small representation of some castes which made them not viable as endogamous units (Smith and Jayawardena 1996:114). The other was by far the more significant, namely the acute shortage of females. Between 1838 and 1868, the average number of women per 100 men was 32.2 (Moore 1984:1), and although this ratio improved as the years went by, 58 females per 100 males by 1891, at no time throughout the period of the indentureship system did it approximate equity. The result was inter-caste marriages and an assertion of female independence, including polyandry during the latter half of the nineteenth century (Moore 1984:5). The breakdown of caste observances was further deepened by the system of ascription governing social relations on the plantations and within the wider society. The assignment of occupations was determined not by caste but by aptitude and qualification, with the result that men of lower castes came to occupy positions of authority and prestige over men of higher castes. Thus, in their survey of Blairmont estate Smith and Jayawardena (1996:125–26) found 62 percent of Brahmin and Kshatriya men in low status, unskilled jobs, and over 10 percent of low caste men in high status, junior staff jobs. On Port Mourant estate, the proportion of high caste men in low status jobs was 85 percent, while that of low caste men in higher status positions was 2.56 percent in the junior staff category and 14 percent among the skilled labourers.

Inter-caste marriages on the two estates were more frequent than intra-caste marriages, 54.4 percent compared to 45.6 percent. On Blairmont estate, for example, 22 percent of low caste men had married high caste women, while 40 percent of high caste men had married women of lower castes. "A *Brahmin* will be reluctant to marry his daughter to a *Sudra*, but even these scruples may be overcome if the young man is very wealthy or has a profession" (Smith and Jayawardena 1958:179).

The virtual disappearance of caste as a social divider also had an impact on the articulation of Hindu religion. The form practised by the Brahmins, the orthodox *Sanatan Dharma*, became common to all Indians except Muslims and Christians, as the lower castes could now participate. Hitherto, the lower castes practised blood sacrifice and spirit possession, practices taboo to higher castes. Now the Brahmins "performed ceremonies for all castes, touching and intermingling with all their clients. Gradually they came to accept food and water from the lowest castes" (Jayawardena 1965:229).

Marriage is a most important social institution among Indians, for through marriage kinship and affinal ties are extended, the continuity of the male line is provided for and the family's social standing maintained or improved. Up to the 1950s most marriages were arranged, and followed orthodox Hindu practices (Smith and Jayawardena 1958). However, Silverman (1980:210) presents data which show a steady decline in the proportion of arranged marriages in the village of *Rajghar* from the mid 1940s, and a corresponding increase of "partially arranged" marriages and marriages by elopement. "Partially arranged" marriages are those in which the decision to marry is made by the couple, but with the subsequent consent and involvement of the families. From 1961 to 1965 a third of marriages were arranged, while from 1966 to 1970, 42 percent. In his random sample of Crabwood Creek fourth generation boys and girls, aged from fourteen to nineteen years old, Rauf (1974:79) reported that 78 percent of the boys and 92 percent of the girls preferred marriage by mutual selection over marriage by parental arrangement.

The wedding ceremony itself has undergone significant changes. Since it is regarded as an opportunity to display social standing, many of the symbols of wealth and prestige common to the wider social structure are incorporated, for example, in addition to the lavishness of the gifts and feasting, the use of knives and forks for guests of high social class (Smith and Jayawardena 1959:364–65), or the departure of the bride in an expensive white wedding gown instead of the traditional *sari*. Here, class status ranks over religious and other traditional requirements (Williams1991:226–36).

The Family

The large joint extended family headed by a male remains the ideal family structure, as in India. In actual practice, while the normative head of household is male, the family is joint extended only in a minority of cases. In the community studied by Thakur (1978) 40 percent of households were nuclear, while 23.7 percent were extended. In Rajghar, nuclear households accounted for more than three-quarters of households, with only 13 percent extended (Silverman 1980:209). In and of itself the presence of a significant number of nuclear households does not necessarily imply the decline of the extended family, since segmentation seems a necessary part of the life cycle of the joint family even in India (Tyler 1986:134). But as Smith and Jayawardena (1959) point out, social and economic factors make the joint family in Guyana short-lived, and no deeper than three generations. Among the contributing factors may be the lack of physical space or property to accommodate sons and their families, values of independence and individual achievement, and "the fact that the kinship principle is subordinate to other criteria of status and group membership" (p. 371). Thus, families with property are more likely to remain extended families for longer periods than those without property. Poorer families are able to approximate the ideal for a shorter period of time, if at all, and sometimes prepare for the inevitable segmentation by securing plots for their sons even before marriage. But whether of short or long duration, the extended family functions as a unit of cooperation and affective ties centred around the male head.

Fazzad is a sixty-three-year old Muslim and the father of six children, three boys and three girls. He is the head of an extended family of fifteen others: his wife, Fatima, their two married sons, the latter's wives and nine children, and an unmarried son. His unmarried daughter lives abroad. All four of his children's marriages were arranged. In her early years as a wife, Fatima used to work as a domestic, but because Fazzad felt strongly that a wife should not work, he taught Fatima his own tailoring skill, so she could stay at home and sew. Neither daughter-in-law works outside. Despite expressing liberal views on religious tolerance, even suggesting that he would not object to his grandchildren attending Christian churches, he feels strongly that wives should adopt the religion of their husbands. One of his daughters-in-law, a Hindu, had to adopt Islam as a condition for the marriage. Fazzad's position on the matter derives in part from his role as a Muslim priest. Decisions in the family, he says, should be made *"fifty-fifty"*, implying equality between men and women, but he makes no bones about the fact that his views as head are above the views of all others.

Ideally, most men would prefer if their wives did not have to work, but in actual fact many women do work, either as domestics and labourers or as self-employed, working out of home or in the market. Self-employment that keeps women in the home is preferred to employment outside.

The Indian family is also patrilineal in descent. Having a male child is considered a necessity; without a son, not only will one's blood line disappear, but there will be no one to defend a mother and her daughters against "eye pass". Jayawardena (1963:72) defines "eye pass" as "[a]n offence against the egalitarian norms . . . To *eye-pass* someone is to offend his *amour propre*, to belittle and humiliate him, to ignore his rights and claims". Disputes arising from eye-pass are always conducted in public and the insults traded often attack the honour and name of a wife or daughter.

Sons also strengthen the family by themselves becoming sources of labour power and economic well-being by their own presence and by providing additional labour through marriage. They are also needed to perform the burial rites of their parents. Where one is lacking, the role has to be performed by some other male, perhaps an uncle or cousin. Girls marry out, but they contribute to the family through the development of a network of affinal relationships that may bring honour and privilege. These expectations tend to shape the gender preferences at birth and govern the way children are brought up and prepared for adulthood.

Roop is a thirty-year-old married man, the father of two sons. During his wife's first pregnancy, he prayed for a boy, because *"I want my name to live on."* The daughter, he said, could come afterward, for the boy *"will have to look after his sister, to take all protection for her, to see she is no trouble in society"*. When the child was born, he was so anxious that he left work to see the baby, but the nurse objected, reminding him of the Hindu custom whereby a father *"ain't suppose to see a child unless they go and open a book"*. So, the following day Roop went off to a priest, who opened the Patra, found a name for the child and *"checked to see if the child born in any planet"*. He was born under *"a slight moon*". The Pandit then told Roop to take an offering of peas, rice, onions, potatoes and a towel and *ouche* the child seven times, that is, to pass it over the child in a circular motion and donate it as a gift to the Pandit. He was then allowed to look upon the child on the third day. Had the child been "*born under a moon, right, I couldn't have seen him until twenty-one days, according to the Pandit*".

Strictly speaking, it should not matter in what order a male child is born, if the reason is to ensure continuity of the male line. But the ideal is to have the male child first, so that he "*may look after his sister*", by becoming an additional source of protection from other men.

Nine days after the birth a *ninth day* celebration is held. It begins first with a puja, or service of prayer, followed by a feast. Roop said he shaved his head for the occasion.

This account compares in some respects with similar practices in Trinidad, where, according to Klass (1988:118–20), the Pandit consults the horoscope to find a name, referred to as a "planet name" or "pandit name", but a name which is kept secret by the family, lest it be used by evil persons to harm the child. There is no mention of the *ouche*, but a feast is held after the purification of mother and child on the sixth day.

Shivnarine, the captain of a fishing trawler, with three daughters already, badly wanted a son. Certain that the fourth child was one, he began planning a big "nine-day" even before his wife took in. They had another daughter. He showed great displeasure initially, but eventually got over the disappointment. Nevertheless, he conveniently arranged a trip at sea and absented himself. The "nine-day" was reduced to a simple puja with a little food, without music and drinking. His friends and workers were disappointed, but not nearly as much as he – they for the cancellation of the merriment, he for the threat to his lineage.

Once the cultural imperative of having sons is met, according to our Overflow informants, having a girl child next becomes a very important ideal. A man is not yet fully a man until this is done. The explanation is that a girl child enables him to fulfil his social role as one who gives to others, and not just receives from others. Giving is a way of displaying social status. The ideal is to have a boy first and then a daughter. Brackette Williams (1991:56–57) describes the distinction residents of the Guyanese village of Cockalorum make between *making a living* and *making life*.

Making a living refers to the work one puts out to earn a livelihood. Making life, however, refers to a person's interest in others. By giving birth to a boy one is guaranteed the receipt of a daughter-in-law, and through her the continuity of one's name; giving birth to a girl ensures that one is able to "make life" by marrying her to someone else's son. As one of our Overflow informants expressed it, "You are not a man until you have a girl." Of course, it could also be said that "You are not a man until you have a son", which is probably how Shivnarine felt.

Division of Labour

Outdoor economic and domestic activities are generally performed by males, though women participate in the labour force also as traders in the market and wage-earners in the city. Ideally, most men and women prefer women staying at home to take care of children and manage the home and home-based economic activities such as dressmaking, hairdressing and retailing, but economic realities dictate otherwise.

From an early age, Indo-Guyanese children are socialized into a division of labour along gender lines. There was ample evidence of this. However, the actual process of training involves deviation from the gender ideals, depending on the number and birth order of boys and girls, in such a way as to allow cross-gender domestic work. But such gender crossing is neutralized by the wider social norms and cultural values.

Following is a short list of the domestic chores according to the gender of the child from as early as age six:

Boys	Girls
fetching water	washing clothes
watering plants	cooking
collecting cow dung	daubing with cow dung
cleaning up the yard	sweeping and cleaning the house
collecting firewood	
weeding and gardening	

A boy's domestic chores mainly fall outdoors, a girl's indoors. Girls can help to do the above outdoor chores, but boys rarely help in their sisters' chores. There were many examples of girls fetching water along-side boys, but none of boys performing girls' chores. Roop, however, said that with only one sister amidst five boys, he and his brothers *"had to help out. I had to wipe steps and daub bottom house. My mother was very strict. I didn't regret anything. I learnt something, keep the place clean and tidy. But my mother she never encourages us to wash our clothes; that was the girl chores."*

With the recent addition, he himself now has two children, both boys. The bigger one has little choice but to help with the sweeping, because *"he will grow up in a clean environment [and] know to keep his surroundings clean"*.

Thus, in cases where certain roles cannot be fulfilled because of a gender deficiency, gender ideology is observed in the breach. It is some-times rationalized by saying that training boys in the performance of female chores equips them after they get married to monitor their wives. Such cross-gender roles, however, cease at around the time of puberty. Somewhere between twelve and fourteen years old, according to Roop, *"a girl should have a different aspect of job to do, as well as boys"*. By *"a different aspect"* he means a clear gender-based division of labour more in line with what is the norm in adult life. From this time on, he contin-ues, *"girls [do jobs] like wiping, sweeping out the house and washing clothes, even cooking and things. The boys start looking at the poultry stocks; he would have to assist in weeding, planting and doing some kitchen gardening actually"*.

Girls help in the maintenance of the home, and thus learn skills that they will use as adults. The ideal, for both men and some women, is to confine a woman's productive activity to the household, to take care of the family's domestic needs. As another informant puts it, *"The women who goes out to work soon gets into trouble by themselves, or other people mouth put them in."* The home is safer. Men as breadwinners and women as housewives is the ideal arrangement expressed by both males and females and sought after by many.

The Abdullahs are a working-class family. Dadoo is a forty-three-year-old labourer on the estate. Miriam, his wife, is three years younger. They have four children, all boys. The oldest one, Zamani, is twenty years old, the last one six. Economically, they would classify as low-income earners.

Their house has none of the modern amenities that Miriam enjoyed before their marriage: refrigerator, gas stove, running water, concrete floor. Though the property on which they live once belonged to Dadoo's now deceased parents, conflict with hostile relatives gives the family a single-minded goal: to establish their own home. Father, mother and eldest son fantasize openly about their dream home – the number of rooms, the amenities, the kitchen utensils, yet they are nowhere near their goal. Where Miriam could help by taking on work, as she is eager to do but has not done since the birth of their second child, there is pressure from Dadoo and Zamani that she remain at home. *"She could work if she want to,"* Dadoo explains, *"but the children don' wan' deh mother work."* But he too is unwilling to allow her to work after all these years. He feels a great sense of pride that he can afford to keep his wife at home, and is prepared to endure any hardship to increase his earnings. Besides his cane-cutting, he acts as a watchman at the home of one of his relatives, and rears his own cattle. During crop-over time he does odd jobs like cleaning trenches and fishing. Zamani is more blunt: he does not want his mother to work; she should be at home. He contributes $200 of his weekly income to the home. Although a job would bring the dream of their own home closer to reality, for *"we gettin' old"*, Miriam shares the conviction that a wife must be at home when her husband returns from work and her children return from school; she *"mus' try to keep di husband and di children together as a happy family"*. Young men like Zamani are required to render support in the income earning and subsistence activities of the family. If his mother is a trader, a boy has to help her to transport the goods. In Overflow it is the women who engage in trading, both the buying of stock and retailing of it in the market. Husbands help their wives with the transport, but if they have a son old enough he replaces his father.

Cooperation

One of the values Overflow residents try to instil in their children is cooperation among male siblings. Rivalry and fighting, even for simple things like pillows, are suppressed by corporal punishment. Informants, who in recounting their early life mention sibling rivalry, always add that they had to keep knowledge of it from their parents. When Ravi's two eldest boys were seventeen and eighteen, respectively, they got into a heated argument during his absence. He neither flogged nor scolded them. All he said to them was, "I leave you in the hands of the Lord!" Then together with his wife he began to pray and meditate. "God answered my prayers and changed one of them", the elder boy, who became a convert to the Church of God. The tension between them eased. During the interview with Ravi, the two sons, now in their twenties, were outside lining up the yard for a survey.

Cooperation is the ideal of the Indo-Guyanese joint family. As a value, it explains joint venture operations between father and sons, as in house construction and rice farming, and sibling substitution, as in the case of Krishna, who substituted his brother on the minibus he operates, in order, so he said, to find more time for his family.

Education and Work

Two factors exerting influence on the way adolescents are prepared for the world of adults are the education system and the economy. Formerly, the tendency in Overflow was (and still is, among those living at the southern end) to place little value on education, an unnecessary hangover from the past. Up to the 1930s there were more East Indians outside of primary school than in it, and the higher up the primary school system they went the higher was their drop out rate (Bacchus 1970). Attempting to explain this apparent devaluation of education, Bacchus (pp. 14–25) points to the difficulties Indians experienced in moving up the social ladder, as well as their distrust of Western values, and to the substitution by most of them of wealth accumulation. In remedying this apparent neglect, many families adopted a selection strategy, selecting one son to be educated and focusing the resources of the family on him (Cross 1980:7). In this way, while a majority of the Indian population remained illiterate, the ratio of Indian lawyers and doctors increased steadily, so that by the 1940s and early 1950s Indians were in a majority in these professions, though in later years this proportion was to even out. By then enrolment in primary schools had begun to reflect their demographic position in the population as a whole, and enrolment in secondary schools show increasing representation.

Examination of Indian gender representation in education reveals that dramatic progress in the education of girls at the primary level was made between

1925 and 1954, when the enrolment ratio of Indian boys to girls decreased from 3:1 to almost 1:1 (see Bacchus 1970:11, 25). The progress for girls at the secondary level, however, was not as rapid, since their further education often came in conflict with the institutionalized need to marry early. All that has changed, as the situation in Overflow reflects. The Overflow Secondary School reports a 3:2 enrolment ratio of girls to boys. Early marriages are no longer the prevailing practice, and parents now recognize that girls ought to be as fully educated as boys. According to the headmaster, *"The girls are much more serious-minded than the boys; they tend to take education more seriously."*

Overflow parents value education, for both boys and girls, and many will pay for it, if necessary. A good education for a girl betters her chances of a good match for marriage, while a good education for a boy increases his earning power, his family's income, and his ability to build his own house and attract a desirable wife. However, the Guyanese economy, by placing greater pressure for survival on families, drives many boys into the labour force at an earlier age than their parents would like, for, married or not, sons are expected to contribute to the household economy.

But economic conditions are not the only factor pulling youths out of school and into work. Many lack sufficient personal motivation to resist the pull of the peer group, especially where the group's interests are in conflict with the routine of school. Male bonding is a powerful social force in Overflow. Beginning during adolescence and continuing right through life, it is reinforced by cultural practices separating the genders, for example rites of passage and forms of social cooperation.

While waiting for the core group to assemble for our discussion, we walked across the road to a shed where six young men were chatting. Over the past month I had observed them gathering there about 5:00 p.m. each day and playing dominoes. They were in their early twenties. All of them had dropped out of school. They worked as manual labourers, some part-time, some full-time. They meet in the shed, because *"we want somewhere to relax after work. We used to play ball in the school ground, but we get problems with the watchman. We used to keep vigilante here, but after the t'iefing stop, the group brok up."* One of them admitted that he had work to do at home but, *"After work you want to relax. We don't have yard space. My mother does ask me to paint, but I want some free time."* The group used to meet on a bridge across the road but shifted to the shed when the bridge broke. They drink regularly every Sunday and on their birthdays, with whatever money they have after handing over some to their parents. They told us they and not their parents decided how much to contribute to the household. Average wage was $450 a day (a little more than US$3). Economic factors, they said, influenced their dropping out of school, but they also wanted "to play big". Now, they find themselves in a dilemma. High costs do not allow them to propose marriage – $40,000 for the bride's dress alone, plus $100,000 for the feast – yet they would all like to get married. *"Right now, I want a better job."* Sanath expressed the hope that his two younger brothers would complete primary school. His greatest mistake, he said, was running from school.

On a previous occasion, Sanath had told us that not even the public humiliation and punishment by his mother were strong enough to prevent him from missing school to be with his friends. At present, his friends are important to him; that's why he drinks. *"You need company, so you tek a drink sometimes."* If you don't take a drink, or, worse, if you *"don't give a raise to buy a drink"*, they avoid your company. This male group plays together, drinks together, and participates in community activities together.

The fact that increasingly parents are spending more on private "extra lessons" is an indication of their conviction that education enhances the ability of a child, male or female, to earn more in the long run. However, Overflow parents weigh the cost-benefit of an education, since this constitutes an important avenue both for economic stability as well as for social standing. It becomes important, then, to monitor children and gauge their potential and performance, in order to decide whether and to what extent they should push them into the labour force, as against encouraging them through the education system. Roop is already quite clear that as his son grows older, *"he will have more school work and I don't want to take him off to sweep and wipe"*. If the boy turns out to be bright, Roop will require less of him around the household; if he turns out average or below, chances are that he could find himself spending less time in school and more on helping his parents. Soon enough, by age fourteen, he will drop out to herd cattle or to look for a job. This is more or less what happens to many boys, like Sanath and his friends, or like Tiger, an eighteen-year-old whom we interviewed. No amount of beating by his father could get Tiger to attend school. He dropped out during second form, when he was fourteen. Now he works at any odd job, on land or sea.

According to informants, no more than 25 percent of adolescents not attending school and young adults below twenty-five years old are working on the estate. A few lucky ones find employment in the six woodwork establishments operating in Overflow. The rest simply join the ranks of the unskilled, underemployed labourers and handymen who, while waiting on the odd job, hang out on the corners and at rum shops.

The twin problem of dropping out of school and unemployment is most chronic among those residing at the southern end of Overflow, where on any school day one may find many children at home. Excuses offered by mothers are generally the lack of clothing and lunch. According to informants, very few students from this end of Overflow have ever completed secondary school, and none has ever gone to training college or university. *"Close of play score is primary school for most of them!"* The high concentration of poverty and unemployment contributes to behaviour one informant calls *"Warrish! Tell dem people anything, and they start 'busing you down and run for cutlass!"* A magistrate serving the community once characterized this part of Overflow as "The lawless republic!"

If Overflow citizens regard education as a means to achievement, higher education also weakens the hold of tradition. Sabhu and Indira were students attending different schools when they met and fell in love. She came from a wealthy west coast family, he from a poor Overflow family, his mother widowed while Sabhu and his brother were young. The young couple sought but were denied parental approval, both for essentially the same reason, namely the mismatch. Neither her father nor his mother would relent. So, they decided to provoke a crisis. One day when Sabhu's mother was absent, he went and brought Indira home. His mother was furious when she returned, but not as angry as her father when the family discovered her whereabouts. Using his influence and power, he had the police lock up Sabhu for kidnapping. Indira threatened to commit suicide, by no means an idle threat, should her father force her to return. In stepped her uncle and, aided by good counsel from the police, persuaded her father to accept the wishes of his daughter. The young couple duly got married, taking care until then, Sabhu insisted, to protect Indira's virginity. Today, Indira's father is very proud of his son-in-law who teaches at a tertiary institution.

The fear that the older generations of Indians felt towards the education system as an agency of socialization in Western values and away from "Indian" traditions is realized when pubescent and fully mature boys and girls meet as a result of being in school together. Education at the secondary and postsecondary levels is the site of a clash of values. On one hand are the demands of the family and kinship system requiring early marriage and childbearing by women, and on the other values of the wider society which encourage women's achievement through education and equality of status with men. This conflict is clearly not new, as is reflected in the preferential education of boys throughout the first half of the twentieth century. But as the frontiers of conservatism are pushed back, it is the lower levels that yield before the higher. Primary levels are integrated before secondary, secondary before tertiary. Thus, according to 1990–91 census figures for the highest level of education ever attained by Guyana's population of over 700,000, the proportion of males to females is marginally lower at the primary and secondary levels, more or less in keeping with their respective size in the population overall, but higher at the postsecondary and university levels, where males represent 52.6 percent and 66 percent, respectively (CARICOM 1997). While the data was not disaggregated for race and ethnicity, interviews with staff and students of the University of Guyana confirm that Indians represent only a small fraction of the already small number of women studying for undergraduate and graduate degrees.

Sex, Marriage and the Life Cycle

Marriage marks a decisive turning point in the life cycle of the individual, male or female, and in the development of the family. To the Overflow community, it is the gateway to legitimate sexual relationship, and it is presumed that until they are married a couple have never had sexual intercourse, that the girl is a virgin. To behave otherwise is to bring shame on the family, especially the girl's. This is the point Sabhu was making with his declaration of Indira's virginity, and is in marked contrast to the African tradition, as exemplified in the Grannitree data, where the fear of teenage pregnancy is motivated not so much by the shame of sexual indulgence as by the prospect of girls dropping out of school.

As soon as a young man signals his intention of getting married, his family meets with the bride's family both to get to know each other and to plan the wedding. Weddings are important social occasions, requiring a reciprocity of gift giving, and a lot of food, music and drinking. In the back of everyone's mind is the effect on the social standing of the respective family. No other event is as significant to the family's status and prestige (Smith and Jayawardena 1960:356, 363–67; Williams 1991:226–36). The pandit is consulted to determine the most auspicious day for the wedding, and as big a feast as possible is planned. As an occasion for displaying wealth and prestige, Indira's wedding must have been a disappointment to her father, who was called on to sanction a marriage that brought his family neither wealth nor addition to its reputation. Sabhu's mother's objection was probably based on the embarrassment she could foresee in the lopsidedness of the exchange of gifts, which, according to Smith and Jayawardena (1958:193) are not only elaborate, but tend to balance out. Thus, the complaint by Sanath and his peers that their unemployed status puts them at risk of not being able to marry is not an idle one. To be sure, poverty had not prevented the arrangement of marriages in the past, nor was it likely to prevent young men getting married in the present, though it certainly would affect the elaborateness of the outlay and the nature of the subsequently extended paternal household. The complaint, rather, is about the ideal of a very large, prestigious and festive event marking the assumption of Indian males to a role of responsibility for a family.

In light of these social and cultural necessities that attend marriage, common-law relationships are discouraged. They are seen as lowering social status and immoral; they bring shame on the family. At twenty-five years old and a medical doctor working in the state sector, Ahmed feels that, as the Bible says, "A man should leave his parents and cling to his wife." He therefore wants to own his own home. But the costs for both a wedding and a house are so prohibitive that he finds his dream of a happy family fading. He paints a dismal picture for the society, projecting an increase in common-law arrangements and in children born out of wedlock, a break down of the extended family and general moral decay. The following case shows that his fears are not unrealistic.

Mr Gopaul is a sixty-four-year-old man who lives with his wife and their thirty-four-year-old son, Prakas. Prakas is the second of four sons and the fifth of seven children. All his other siblings are now resident in the United States. He is the only one that has come to nought, and the family misses no opportunity to remind him of it. Gopaul was disappointed that his first child was not a son.

"I wanted a boy!" he said. *"And when he get di boy,"* interjected Laksmi, his wife, *"he sorry na been a wan neda gal!"* She did not explain then and there, but it was an obvious reference to Prakas. The children grew up sharing household chores, everybody helping in the garden, but only the girls were required to cook and wash. When they did well, they would be rewarded with playthings and toys at Christmas time, but when they did wrong, *"they get licks!"* Prakas used to get plenty. Any adult, mother, father or grandmother, was entitled to beat, but Gopaul never beat his daughters; Laksmi did that, when she had to, which was rare. She much preferred talking to them. The Gopauls raised their children to have manners. They learned the morning greeting, *"Morning!"* or *"Ram! Ram!"* to invoke God's blessing. All the decisions – what to do today, what tomorrow – were taken by Gopaul and his wife. Only when the children got married were they thought big enough to make their own decisions. Their first son was around seventeen years old when he decided to learn automechanics, because he was not coping with secondary school. He still lived with his parents but, said Gopaul, "He was independent." Prakas, on the other hand, has not coped well with his independence. "Das why he deh in problem now!" said his father. Laksmi, too, expressed her displeasure. "He feel embarrass when you talk to him. Well, who feel embarrass deh pon their own!" Prakas, who was present throughout the interview, hung his head, ashamed. The problem was that "He a tek wife and lef wife steady." She was referring to the fact that he has had three consensual relationships outside the home. The family is embarrassed by it and his own siblings have stopped talking to him. On top of that, his father interjected, "He gat rum! He loves rum!"

"You still drinking?" I asked. Prakas remained silent. "Oh, yu stop!" Laksmi was contemptuous. "How regular yu drink?" He was not allowed to answer. Gopaul said he drank once a week, and Laksmi confirmed that it was now only on Sundays since he has returned home. "But when you had this problem, how regular you used to drink?"
"Well . . . actually, everyday!" He spoke for the first time. Laksmi was relentless. " 'Actually', boy! 'Actually everyday'!"

"Who you used to drink with?"

"With friends. In shops."

"How you feel now, now that you not drinking?"

"I feel much better, healthier." By this time, Gopaul had had enough. He exploded: "Healthier, raas!"

At this point, Prakas's five-year-old son shouted, "Daddy! Daddy!" Laksmi quickly put him in his place: "Boy, quick! Move out a deh! Listen to me! Get out from there!" He had interrupted the conversation of adults without asking to be excused. It was now Gopaul's turn: "Le' me see yu book wha' yu write!" I had been observing him earlier struggling with his lettering, and now offered a word of praise. "Oh, he doing some good writing! The man can write!" I shouldn't have said that. I was greeted with a chorus of sarcasm from both parent and grandparents: "Write? Write? Write?" Gopaul continued: "Two months we deh pon im, and he can't write 'A' yet!" The boy had already filled six pages with the first four letters. "Never mind," I insisted, anxious to return to Prakas's problem, "He learning! He learning!" Laksmi got another opportunity to underscore her disappointment with her second son. As soon as he told me he had four children, she interjected. "Four? Ask how much yu min'! One yu min' now! Two children live on West Coast, where di mother take somebody else! One nex' one gone wid he mother!"

"Dem want it so!" Prakas explains, embarrassed. At this point Gopaul left to do his regular afternoon puja and Laksmi finished chipping bora for the afternoon meal.

Prakas is ostracized by his brothers and sisters, while his parents reserve nothing but contempt and ridicule for him. The reason lies not so much in the fact that his unions have been "common law", but in his unsteady character and its effect on the family. Common-law unions, in the sense of unions formed consensually, are not unknown to the Indian community. As Smith and Jayawardena (1959:368–69) observe, such unions are sometimes the result of elopement, sometimes of second or subsequent *"marriages"*; Prakas's unions do not seem to be either. Parties in an elopement usually legalize their union afterwards or have it sanctioned by family and priest. And not having been first-time married "under the bamboo", as the traditional Hindu wedding is called, he cannot be considered a married man but one now separated from his wife.

His children, therefore, are illegitimate. What is more, the children, whom he does not support, live, not with their father and father's kin, but with their mothers, which for a patrilocal culture is offensive. In the African community, Prakas would not necessarily lose face for his serial polygamy, and conceivably might even gain in reputation. His sexual and family life, therefore, is more reflective of stereotypically African than Indian traditions. Sexual profligacy is one of the stereotypes held by Indians of Afro-Caribbean men.

Drinking and Manhood

The great social emphasis placed on marriage means that young men continuously talk about it as an ideal, so that their failure to attain it when they enter adulthood is a source of great psychological stress. At the same time, this does not seem to pose a threat to the attainment of manhood among Overflow male youths. The reason for this is that manhood is determined by a number of other social behaviours typical of adult males. Among these is the participation in and maintenance of male bonding activities, particularly public drinking. When a young man is able to do this without sanction, he is a man, regardless of his marital status.

"He gat rum! He loves rum!" With these words Gopaul declares the diagnosis of his son's problem. Heavy drinking of alcohol is a male pastime in Overflow, particularly in its concentrated rum form. Jayawardena (1963:47) calls it an example of the hedonism he found among unskilled estate labourers in Guyana. In Overflow beer is also consumed, but rum is the preferred drink. It is central to the festivities that accompany the life cycle rituals, and to male bonding among adults, young and old. Prakas's problem, however, and that of some others, was not only that he drank heavily, with all the expenses that that implies, but also that he would lose control and get into brawls. We may thus distinguish, as the Overflow community does, "drinking" from "having a drinking problem". Drinking is an institutionalized form of recreation for men, but it is also an important adjunct to all festivities, including all but one of the life cycle rituals. A drinking problem manifests itself when it goes beyond the established boundaries of drinking, both as to frequency and occasion, as well as to proper conduct.

Recreational drinking, when it does occur, takes place in the evenings after work, rarely going beyond 9:00 p.m. Mostly, though, it is the weekends that men reserve for it, beginning Friday, peaking on Saturday and easing off on Sunday, especially the last week of the month, when the fortnightly paid workers are joined by the monthly paid.

It is about 5:00 p.m. There is only one group occupying a table at Jammy's. There were Sarge, a former trawler worker just returned from a one-year stay in the United States; Shrimpy, a university graduate who felt cheated by the former government and left his job to start his own catering business; Nanath, a self-employed electronics technician; Baker, a job-hunting accounting clerk, who operates the hire-car that has been transporting the group; Narine, a carpenter, who, though not a close friend of the rest, also lives in Overflow; and Baga, an unemployed but close friend. They are all intoxicated. They came in from midday. Two empty bottles of vodka and about thirty Bristol cigarette butts are on the table. Three of them attempt talking all at the same time, their speech slurred.

"Hear, hear, you think dem men stupid? Cedras goin' kill some o' dem white turkeys for Christmas!" Shrimpy is highly agitated, rising to his feet and gesticulating with his finger. They were talking about the American-led invasion of Haiti. "Boy, you ain't know what you saying. The American gat weapons that follow Saddam round he house! Now they got a gun if you shoot it, the bullet will not land until it find a human target!" Everyone erupted in laughter. Soon they left with two more bottles of vodka for Sarge's house, where cooking and more drinking will take place.

This sort of scene is quite common. Sarge's was the only group on this Friday afternoon, but on the following day, at a somewhat later hour, Jammy's was filled to capacity, spilling over to the adjoining shop. The din was high, with men arguing, in the manner of Sarge's group, or playing dominoes or draughts. This continued well into the night, some leaving, others coming. By 9:00 p.m., with the music set at full blast, men were dancing as well.

Jammy's is not the hottest spot in the village. This reputation belongs to Baju's, which on any Saturday is full to capacity by 4:30 p.m. Men of all ages share the same drinking spot, the bar, and share also the same drinking preference for rum. This is not to say that beer is not popular. It is, and Little T, adjacent to Baju's, sells only beer, but rum is more popular by far. They pour the rum in large pint-sized glasses, which they then fill with "chasers", that is any form of bottled soda. Chasers, they believe, help them to remain sober for longer. The bar is an important weekend institution. It functions as a meeting place, where new friends are made, work is discussed, gossip spread, news transmitted and businesses are arranged. Marriages have been known to be contracted at the bar. It is a convenient place to the ruling People's Progressive Party for inviting guests to the wedding of a party member, or supporters to a fun day. Naturally, it is the place where political attitudes are shaped and reinforced.

The other main occasions for drinking are births, weddings and Sunday projects, any event other than a funeral that brings men together. Mention has already been made of the disappointment of Shivnarine's friends at his scaling down the nine-day for his daughter, robbing them of its festive aspect. Sundays are generally reserved by the younger men for sports and "projects". Guyanese play a popular adaptation of cricket, called softball from the soft rubber ball with which it is played. Countrywide softball leagues enable many communities to promote and support their own teams. "Projects" are light jobs, often of a domestic sort, that are organized by a few friends. They thus afford friends the opportunity to come together. The host will "put on a pot", that is provide the food, while his friends bring along the rum. Drinking will continue long after the "pot" has been eaten.

Despite the heavy use of alcohol, as I have said, the Overflow community makes a distinction between drinking and having a drinking problem. Most men drink, and they do so on the weekends, and quite heavily. Thakur (1978:304, footnote) sums up the importance of drinking thus: "The social function of (rum) drinking in Guyana could hardly be overstated. It sometimes provides the avenue into new social groups. Drinking has often placed me in ideal situations where information has been volunteered." In this sense, drinking is seen as an integral part of the rhythm of social life, and not much is thought of an occasional intoxication. After Saturday night, many would have ceased drinking for the week and after Sunday very few would bother to indulge. It is this few who seem unable to help themselves that people talk about. They not only bring

shame on their families, but squander what they earn and should contribute to the household. Prakas, apparently overwhelmed by his family's low regard for him, compounded his problem by drinking everyday. Another good example of the problem drinker is that of the Singh
brothers (in the example below), who thought nothing of turning up at
a wake with their own bottles of rum. Dranath, an automechanic who
drinks while he works, has a different sort of problem. His alcoholism
does not prevent him earning a livelihood, but it gives his clients the
chance to underpay and cheat him. This is when his wife retaliates with
abuse, which is virtually daily.

Recognition of the dangers of heavy alcohol consumption led
Rampersad to kick the habit. His thirteen-year-old son once confessed
to him that he was too embarrassed to bring his friends to their impov-
erished home, accusing his father of squandering his substance on drinking. "People working less than you,", he once told his father, "are living
better than we!" Rampersad said he gave this reprimand serious thought,
then went to a dispenser, got some vitamin tablets, and every time his
friends came for him, he would excuse himself from drinking rum, because "it was time to take a tablet". In time, his friends got used to
ordering juices for him. Not even beer does he now drink. This personal rehabilitation soon began paying dividends, for he was made the
head of the temple in his community.

Heavy use of alcohol by Indo-Guyanese men is so widespread that, not
surprisingly, it figures in domestic disputes and crimes. In a study of male
adult crime in Guyana, Jones (1981:54) reports that of the 368 East Indians
criminals interviewed 17.4 percent of them exhibited firm evidence of drunkenness at the time of committal,[*] compared to 5.3 percent of the Africans
and 23.1 percent of the "Others".

The only life cycle rite that is non-festive, and therefore does not include drinking, is that which attends death. The following describes a wake,
its gender segregation and recreational character.

Golal was only thirty-seven when he died. The wake is being kept
at his mother's house, where all his ten other brothers and sisters are
staying. The wake is held every night until burial, and for ten days after,

---

[*] Jones's Table 4.11 reads "Evidence of drunkenness at time of conviction", which makes little
sense to a discussion he begins with "Being drunk at the time of the offence ought in theory
to be inversely related to planning" (See p.53).

at the end of which the mourners may resume the intake of salted food. As soon as the women enter the house, they proceed upstairs, from where they can be heard singing *bajans*, that is religious songs, and reading from the *Ramayan*. Their husbands remain downstairs, where they participate in the games of dominoes and cards, joined by other men arriving in groups of four or five.

The men keeping wake are relatives and friends of the deceased and friends of relatives. It takes only a short time for the house to become busy and noisy, players arguing and joking. Shridath, a leading troopchal (card) player, was dissatisfied with Moorthy, his partner, holding back the trump. "Ask anybody who ever play with me. Ninety-nine percent of the time I lead with trump!" Moorthy retorts, "Since we [start] playing tonight, only one game you lead with trump!" When a few games later Shridath loses with five trumps in his hand, the entire section of the house following their game erupts in fits of laughter. Meanwhile, Lucky and Jimmy, along with two others, are already gambling. But they do it on the sly, assigning Ramanan to hold the stakes secretly. They soon have no need of the secrecy, because Budhai openly started his own table. Kalli comments, "Now the real wake start! They goin' play till morning. Especially if Ali turns up!" Ali is famous for his gambling. Golal's brothers are moving around accepting sympathies and explaining how he died. Kanhai claims that he was so upset when he learned of Golal's death, that he went and drank a whole "half" at a new place near the Defence Force camp. He reports that the price there is so good ($500 will get you two halves plus a fish), that he will be going there anytime he wants a drink.

By 9:00 p.m., with the games and the gaffing in full swing, the brothers offer the guests cigarettes, coffee and salted biscuits. Soon, however, some of the wives come down, and call on their husbands to take them home. They are going through the gate when the two Singh brothers are coming in. Their reputation is not good in Overflow. Heavy drinkers and ganja smokers, they are also accused as animal thieves. They bring with them two bottles of rum. Clearly sensitive that this reflects poor taste, one blames the other, but proceeds to ask for a glass. "It look too bad! It look too bad! I tell him don't come in with the drinks. Hear, na, you could get two glass or cup for me, with water?"

By 10:30 p.m., all the guests have left for home, leaving the young men involved in gambling. The following day, Golal's body arrived from the funeral parlour. His eldest brother had already shaven his head to perform the last rites. He made five offerings of pinda to Jamraj, the God of Death, praying that he accept the departed soul of his brother. The body was then taken to the West Coast, where before cremating it the brothers performed a puja, encircling the funeral pyre. The next morning, relatives gathered up Golal's ashes and threw them into the Atlantic, signifying his return to Ganga Mata, Mother of Water.

In this wake there is a sharply expressed gender segregation, the women upstairs, the men downstairs. In the coastal regions of Guyana, where most of the land lies below sea level, houses are built on stilts long enough to create sufficient space underneath to be used for household purposes other than sleeping and receiving guests. The more well-to-do families use it as a car port. This is where men congregate when they drink at a friend's home, and this is where they congregated at Golal's wake. It could be said that they remained "outside", attending to the social and secular aspect of the wake, while the women went "inside" to attend to its religious aspect. Women are more ardent religious observers, whether Hindu or Christian. Indeed, girls are socialized to clean the family shrines and say prayers. A woman is the *Lakshmi* (Light) of the home.

The games engaged in by the men serve a dual function. Primarily they serve the function of keeping company with the bereaved, rather than being simple forms of relaxation. That is why there is no drinking, a clear rule that the Singh brothers breached. But at the same time, they are yet another extension of male bonding activities. Kalli's comment about the *"real wake"*, not to mention the laughter, joking and argument, attest to this. The only difference to the rum shop, other than the location, is the critical absence of rum.

The funeral itself reinforces the importance of maintaining gender distinctions. Burial according to Hindu traditions requires special rites by the eldest male and male siblings. They are ritually required to shave the head as a show of mourning and to perform a puja at the pyre. In the case, say of Shivnarine, who has no sons, the rites would have to be performed by a male relative, perhaps a brother or uncle. Thus, death (the end of life) reinforces the cultural demand at birth (the beginning of life) to have sons.

Conclusion

The picture presented here is of a community in which traditional cultural norms and ideal practices form the basis on which patriarchy is reproduced. To a significant degree that is so. But as I have also tried to show, two factors, education and unemployment, are countervailing factors, both of them having had and continuing to have a profound effect on the most central institution in East Indian life, marriage, and the relations between men and women. Education and other Western influences, Roopnarine et al. (1997) argue, bringing about significant changes in the way East Indians fulfil their roles as fathers. On the basis of data collected by Roopnarine over a fifteen-year period on three generations of fathers in four families living in the west bank village of Chinesefield, the authors find significant changes taking place in care-giving in the third generation. Up to the second generation the fathers were quite traditional in their relations with their children, affectively distant and strict. But a more educated third generation are showing signs of departure from these traditions, getting involved in the delivery of the children, showing personal warmth in relations with them, extending care-giving practices once expected only of women, and more egalitarian spousal relations as well. "Increasing numbers of third-generation men and women," they conclude, "are exposed to patterns of social interaction and lifestyles that are prevalent in North America and Europe, and women are challenging the tenets of patriarchy in East Indian culture. Simultaneously, there is movement away from traditional Indian values such as arranged marriages, timing of childbearing, and conservative sexual values" (p. 78). But the picture is a mixed one, however, as some members of the third generation remain very traditional (pp. 73, 77).

Here in Overflow the situation is similar, although our data point more to continuity than to change. The pattern of socialization follows the strong sense of ethnic identity shared by the Indo-Guyanese people, but with very significant changes. Indo-Guyanese culture at the level of this village reproduces very strong gender role segregation and identity. The home is the centre of the female universe, but for the male this is shared with public places, where he achieves and maintains manhood in solidarity with other males. The critical factor inducing changes in these traditions is institutionalized education. Here, girls are the winners, at least up to the secondary level. Both girls and boys are afforded the chance for upward mobility, but judging by their numbers and performance, girls have seized the advantage. The cultural expectations placed on the male for domestic and public leadership propel boys who do not show more than average intellectual ability into the labour force at an earlier age than they would have entered it had they completed secondary school. Many questions posed by these developments are left unanswered. Who do the educated females marry, and when? Is the gender role segregation any different among educated spouses? Anecdotal evidence would suggest that a woman's higher social status is a factor contributing to instability in the conjugal relationship of the traditional sort where the man is the undisputed boss over his wife. For example, in a case which came to our attention, a female accountant's bigger salary gave her greater leverage in decisions affecting her husband, while her frequent business trips abroad with her male boss aroused his suspicion of marital infidelity. Both factors combined to bring about their estrangement.

The educational advancement of women as a contributing factor to marital instability is a new development insofar as it adds a different dimension to one of the two problems Jayawardena (1960) found. In his study of the Blairmont and Port Mourant estates he cites as a major source of conflict the process of incorporating a new bride into her husband's home. But a second source "lies in the incompatibility between the cultural ideal of the supremacy of the husband in his household, and the economic realities which reduce his actual power and increase his dependence on his wife in the management of the household" (p. 100). In present-day Guyana the educated woman presumably drawing a competitive if not larger salary than her husband is likely to pose a serious dilemma for him. Unless, of course, he does not subscribe to the male supremacy ideal. Nothing we encountered in Overflow would suggest that men are being prepared to assume any other but a dominant role.

The socialization of boys to be men is clearly related to the socialization of girls to be women, since the respective role expectations are constructed in relation to the opposite gender ideal. Karran (1994:194) in depicting the background of Indo-Caribbean women in Britain identifies a fourfold oppression: as worker, as racially Indian, as an object of male, particulary African, sexual fantasy, and as persons socialized to be "wives, mothers, lowly paid workers and potential victims of sexual aggression. The internalized socialization is also a form of oppression." This may seem an extreme way to classify socialization, but it accurately pinpoints the position of most Indo-Guyanese women as willing subordinates within as well as outside the family. In Overflow, on public occasions, for example at meetings where both are present, a wife always defers to her husband and never expresses views or opinions that contradict his.

This "subordination", however, has to be viewed in context. Mohammed (1995) brings to the analysis of gender relations the concept of *negotiation* and argues convincingly that power relations within the Indian family in Trinidad were "negotiated" relations, as Indian women, due to the shortage of their numbers and other factors brought about by the indenture and new cultural and social contexts which gave them an advantage, challenged the traditional expectations of their sex. Their "bargains" resulted in the reconstitution of Indian patriarchy, which now included "the almost equal education of girls and the notion of careers outside of the home as opposed to that of primarily a domestic role" (Mohammed 1994:40). And in an earlier paper on the lives of two women, Mrs Droapatie Naipaul and Mrs Dassie Parsan, Mohammed (1993:212) shows how both their mothers defied their husbands – Mrs Naipaul's Trinidad-born mother to have all her daughters educated, Mrs Parsan's mother to have Dassie married to a lower caste man. But this "negotiation", Mohammed argues, was at the same time a collusion with Indian men for the sake of preserving the ethnic identity of the group as a whole. The complete overthrow of patriarchy within the Indian family and community would have meant at the time the end of an Indo-Trinidadian ethnic identity. The point is that both femininity and masculinity are ever being constructed and redefined, even the notion of Indian female sexual morality, as evidenced by the chutney-soca controversy in Trinidad (Niranjana 1997). Trinidad is not Guyana, to be sure, but the structural conditions are similar.

Male supremacy often generates wife-beating, the use of physical violence to subordinate wives. Although we were not exposed to any during the data-gathering phase of our study, it should be mentioned, if only in brief, since it constitutes an important aspect of the male dominance which both Indian males and females were socialized to accept. Wife-beating was quite common throughout the indenture period, and mutilations for alleged infidelity were not unknown. It continued into the postindenture period. Jayawardena (1960) mentions it in a number of the cases he cites of marital instability. In a sample survey of 120 East Indian wives Parsad (1988) found the following: five out of every six had experienced physical violence from their husbands, and of these one in eight experienced it every day; the time of highest incidence was late at nights and on weekends; lower income husbands were more likely to hit their wives than those from high educational and income levels; wives suffered more violence from dominant heads than from those with whom they shared in decisions; husbands were ten times more likely to use violence and twice as likely to abuse sexually when under the influence of alcohol than not. But what Parsad found particularly disquieting was the fact that 52.5 percent of the wives considered wife-beating acceptable under certain circumstances. He listed these: non-attention to domestic duties; answering back when partner was drunk or under stress; talking to strangers or gossiping; embarrassing partner in the presence of others; threatening to have extramarital affairs or to separate; having extramarital affairs; going out without partner's knowledge or consent; dressing up a lot; and quarrelling with him about money, children, his extramarital affairs, etc. The women blamed themselves for provoking their husbands into assaulting them. Non-justified assaults, however, were mainly alcohol-related, but even here "both spouses rationalized the use of violence on the basis that the offender was partly unaware of his actions" (p. 52). Parsad's explanation for this blaming of the victim was the East Indian wife's socialization "to be passive, dependent, barely socially discernible and dedicated to her family", a role which, he opines, has contributed to the "relative stability of the East Indian family" (p. 53).

Wife-beating also occurs among the Africans, and we saw the extensive justification of it by Grannitree men. Grannitree women also share the view that under certain circumstances the victim is to be blamed. There is a marked difference, however. African women, not surprisingly, seem less willing to accept this position, as was evident in the concession by the man most ideologically convinced of a man's right to beat a woman that some women will "*lick yu iina yu bombo klaat*", meaning that women do initiate and return physical violence; in the Grannitree barkeeper's call for equal treatment; and in the confrontationist attitude of her female domino partner. Indeed, the status position of these two Grannitree women in relation to men is quite different; it would not be possible to find two women playing dominoes in public, in a bar, with men, anywhere in Overflow. In their comparative study of conjugal violence in Guyana, Danns and Parsad (1989) found that Afro-Guyanese wives were more likely than Indo-Guyanese wives to retaliate and inflict violence as well as to initiate violence. If the right to beat one's wife at will, and without contestation, is a sign of the achievement of manhood, it is clear that in this respect at least African Caribbean males have a more difficult time asserting their manhood than their Indo-Caribbean counterparts.

5

Riverbreeze

Riverbreeze is a working class community near Roseau, the capital of Dominica, a country in which over 80 percent of the population are Catholics. Apart from the very devout who attend mass each morning or pray the rosary, most adults have to rise very early, to look about sending the children off to school and preparing themselves for work in town. Even in the early morning bustle, any observer may find evidence of the gender division of labour regulating the activities of the household. Outdoor activities, such as cleaning the yard, watering the garden, and disposing of refuse are performed by young boys; heavier outdoor tasks such as "cutlassing", are for the most part performed by older males.

Mr Fabien asked me where I was going so early. I told him I was going to see what time Riverbreeze got up. He laughed. *"They get up early. Some biddo laglise* [staunch Catholic women] *go to church 5:30 every morning, even when church is 6 o'clock – they have to say their Hail Mary before!"* But, he said, the main reason they get up early is that almost everybody is employed, and some have to cook before going to work. He himself was just going home from his night shift as a watchman. I passed the playing field. No one was there training, though a football league was on. By 6:30 a.m., the streets were busy with kids hustling to the shops, unlike in the afternoons when they take their own time. Almost everyone of them came for bread and other breakfast stuff.

I asked one of the girls if this was normal activity in the mornings. Yes, she replied, for her mummy prepared lunch before going to work. She left her brothers home, one cleaning the yard and the other washing plates. She had already cleaned her room and had her hair combed for school. She was no more than nine or ten years old.

Walking up the lane I noticed a boy between ten and twelve years old sweeping the yard. Further up, I saw another about the same age watering flowers. Greeting him good morning and leaning across, I told him he looked quite professional, the way he handled the hose. He should be by now, he replied, laughing, because this was his job; cleaning the yard was another chore. He did not have a sister. Yet a third boy the same age group went up and threw garbage in the skip. There was a middle-aged woman doing the same. Both boys and girls are involved in household chores. It appeared to me that sweeping, watering flowers and disposing of garbage were done by boys. On this morning I counted four cleaning yards and three emptying garbage. The people I saw going to and from shop were mostly girls and young women.

Activities related to indoors, such as the early morning purchasing of food for breakfast, are mostly performed by girls, and are regulated by their mothers. The exception to girls going to the shop is at night, when parents consider it safer for boys.

In our fieldwork experience itself we were before long confronted with sexual patterns of behaviour we could anticipate among the males and females participating in the research. Females always outnumbered males in the discussion groups, often by as many as five to one, and in one instance early in the fieldwork by eleven to one, despite even-handedness in our mobilizing, while males invariably came later than the females. This was true for all ages. Boys, for example, would rather leave and come back than sit and wait for a meeting to start; they preferred to find the meeting already in progress or about to start. It struck us also that in the adult mixed groups, regardless of their numbers men always volunteered to lead the prayers and they certainly dominated the discussions. Sometimes they were quite self-conscious about it.

Prior to the start of one meeting, the lone man present said to me, "It look like you sent notice to only one man and all your notices to only the women!"

"They'll come," I replied; "maybe you responded to time." We eventually started with twelve women and three men. By 7:00 p.m. there were fourteen women and nine men. Altogether, twenty-eight persons attended. After the meeting, one of the men said to me: "Why women take over is because all the men went off to war years ago and they had no choice. However, when we are present, we just have to take the lead!" Another young man joined in: "Women or mothers give OKs when fathers are absent, but when we are here or at home, we give the orders and OKs to the child."

A mixed core group of ten women and three men was asked to list the type of activities men and women would be engaged in at three- or six-hour intervals during the day, beginning at 6:00 a.m.

Men	**Women**
6:00 a.m.	
Sleeping	Sleeping
Exercise	Stretching
Praying	Praying
Making coffee	Making coffee
Sweeping	Ironing
Weeding	Washing clothes
TV/radio	Preparing children
Sex	
12:00 noon	
Working	Working
Gardening	On the phone
Gossiping/chatting	TV
Sports	Baking
Music	
6:00 p.m.	
Listening to the news	TV soaps
Eating	Washing
Chatting	Bathing
Sex	Prayer meeting
	Seasoning meat

Men	Women
9:00 p.m.	
Socializing	Reading
Sex	
Midnight	
Sleeping	Sleeping
Sex	Sex
	TV

Apart from personal hygiene and nutrition, all the domestic activities identified as men's were outdoors in the yard, and during the early morning. Women's activities were not only indoor but throughout the day. The men placed more emphasis on their ability to have sex at virtually any time of day, which, of course, does not tally with the time the women identified. Either the men fantasized or the women were evasive. Listening to music, involvement in sports and socializing were identified as activities by the men, but not the women, while attending church was identified by the women but not the men.

Children are socialized to recognize and be a part of these divisions. Both boys and girls play *Juil,* but in this game the boys chase, catch and imprison the girls, whose role is to avoid being caught and to resist. Another game usually played by girls is "I declare". The objective is to declare pieces of land in any country of the world as one's own but avoid it. The piece of land is represented by a circle. It exercises the memory as well as giving children a sense of the outside world. During the football season, when people turn out to support their favourite teams in the Riverbreeze league, boys as young as four or five may be seen organizing and playing their own football game, while the adults watch the main match. The girls present occupy themselves with skipping or running about, but usually under the supervision of their mother or an older sister.

The education system recognizes and reinforces gender divisions, even in the way children assemble. Even in the Summer Vacation Programme which engages children aged seven to twelve years in art and craft and sports, children line up according to gender.

When I arrived at the college, they were just getting ready to go out for a walk to the Bay Front. There was a mad rush out of the classroom. They were to assemble on the grounds and walk the quarter mile distance in an orderly manner. The volunteer tutors, all female, were having a difficult time imposing order. The older boys were especially difficult and seemed to take delight in teasing the girls. I held on to one of them, chatting with him about the programme and about his behaviour as we walked.

"Sir," said he, *"those girls like that! They like the boys to tease them!"* As expected, they lined up in twos according to gender. The girls held hands, but the boys had difficulty doing this. Riverbreeze children thus grow up to associate order with divisions based on gender.

We asked a group of teenaged boys and girls to play at being mothers and fathers and to write two letters, one to their "son" and one to their "daughter". The results not only confirm the indoor/outdoor division of labour, but also bring out prevailing ideas on the relations between the genders. First, a parallel-gender sample of two of the letters, mother to daughter, father to son.

Dear Karnish,

When you get out of bed, you should start off your mornings by doing these:
Clean the house, including rooms
clean bathroom
clean refrigerator
clean louvres
scrub your nike
wash your hair.
When you're through, there's money on the counter. Take it and come and meet me so we can go shopping in the Mall. I think it's time you start taking up responsibilities around the home, because you are growing up and you'll soon be on your own.

Love, Mom.

Dear Jack,

How are you doing, hope fine. I'm just writing to tell you that you must do this [sic] *chores while I'm out.*
Clean the room, the stove, the windows, throw the rubbish and the $15 on the fridge can be used. Everything in the house is under your control. Make sure that your sister is studying.

Dad

If we were to take Mom's letter to daughter and Dad's letter to son as letters to self, we see not only the sort of work girls and boys do, but also the sort of expectations for which domestic work prepares them. Girls tidy the house, but are also called upon to ensure their personal hygiene. Without the habits that come from such training, women cannot function on their own. There is thus a direct link between a girl's training in domestic chores during childhood and adolescence and being able to function in subsequent years as women. Father's letter to son involves some of the indoor chores assigned by Mother to daughter, namely cleaning room, stove and windows, but they specify throwing out the rubbish, a chore identified by adults as a boy's. Two other details are striking. He is free to use the sum of money left on the fridge any way he chooses, unlike the daughter, who is allowed to spend money but together with her mother. Second, son is put in full control of the house and enjoined to ensure that his sister studies. He becomes head in his father's absence.

The cross-gender letters provide interesting comparison.

Dear Kimbe,

From today you must take on this [sic] *daily chores such as:*
1. weed yard
2. water plants
3. sweep yard
4. throw rubbish
5. wash dishes
6. wash cars
7. scrub the concrete
8. clean room

Because you are growing up to be a young gentleman and soon you'll be having a girlfriend and believe me girls don't like guys who can't do nothing for themselves. The earlier you start the better your future, and by the way, when you're through, you can take the rest of the day off.

Love, Mom.

Dear Jackie,

I am just writing you to see if things are fine with you. I hope you got the note I left you. It has $45 wrapped in it. This money is to go to the market. I would also like you to scrub the toilet, face basin and bathroom, chlorine the yard, wash the plates, then empty out all the cupboards and spray it. Clean the dog mess, pick the cherries and make the juice, clean the fish and stew it, also clean the fridge. Take the rug out and dust it, including the furniture.
P.S. No boys allowed in the house. No phone calls on my phone.

Love you, Daddy.

The chores identified in Mother's letter to son are all the typical out-door chores, except washing dishes and cleaning rooms. Those in Daddy's letter to daughter are also typically indoors, except going to the market and the very menial cleaning up after the dog. This latter is probably revenge-inspired, since it is part of the yard chores. Of critical interest are Mother's justification for the chores and Father's postscript. In the former, the chores are not to prepare her son to manage on his own, but to be more accept-able to his spouse, and then as long as the chores are completed, he is free to spend the rest of the day as he chooses. Daughter, on the contrary has no such freedom. She can neither call out nor receive boys into the house. Assuming she can finish the work assigned by her "loving" dad, she must remain a virtual prisoner inside.

By the time children reach adolescence the gender-based chores un-dergo a shift, with girls having more to do in the house, while boys tend to have little or none at all. This change was apparent in another of our mixed adult group discussions and one with adolescents. The adult group of fifteen which met to consider the kind of tasks parents gave children was confronted with a hypothetical family with a boy of twelve and two girls, one fifteen, the other six. The gas ran out while the mother was cooking. Which child would she send to buy the gas? The immediate and universal response was *"The boy!"* Only when they reflected on the boy's age did some of them agree to send along his bigger sister to help.

They all agreed, however, that that sort of thing is more a man's duty. Explained one of the women, "Take rubbish, for example, you would more send the boy to throw the rubbish." Turning to other chores, the women felt it okay to send seven-year-old Delia to the shop, but the men disagreed strenuously, because, so they said, of the high incidence of child abuse. The mothers agreed that they would not send their girls to the shop at night. Do duties change with age? "Yes!" was the universal response. "It change at age thirteen to fourteen," explained the men. "I used to cry about that!" complained one woman, referring to her adolescent years. One of the men's complaints, however, was that at age fifteen to sixteen he was still made to wash plates and go to the river to wash clothes with his mother. "Of course, nothing wrong with that!" retorted one of the women. *"In my house washing dishes still maintain at that age. Every one following in line take up the chores of the bigger one before, boy or girl!"* Claude was insistent, however, that at thirteen to fourteen boys do nothing at all. *"I think the biggest task young men do at that age is eat."* They agreed that girls do more work at home, because they are closer to their mothers, while the boys go out with their peers and get involved in sports.

From this part of the group discussion, it is apparent that the general customs regulating what chores boys and girls are assigned may be overridden by other factors. Shopping is a girl's task, but it may become a boy's task if it involves strenuous physical output or has to be done at night, when dangers lurk. In other words, it is customary to maintain the gender basis of allocating chores, but not at the expense of the personal security of daughters. Boys may also be assigned chores normally reserved for girls if a mother insists. Oftentimes the rationale given in such instances is to ensure *"that their* [future] *wives won't 'cut style' on them."* A man should not be entirely dependent on his woman; he should be able to help himself against being exploited. A second point of note is that the shift which takes place in post-puberty gender roles takes place in relation to boys and not girls. Just at the time when girls are forced by their greater domestication to do more housework, boys come under the greater influence of their peer groups.

In the sketch of a normal Saturday by the adolescents, the general point made by Claude that adolescent boys did nothing came out strongly. Saturday was, in the words of one of the girls, "a time for free up". Yet the girls had domestic chores, while their male peers had none.

Boys	**Girls**
9:00 a.m.	
Relax	Wash face
TV	Sweep
Play music	Play music
Sleep	Clean up
Phone calls	Phone calls
	Reading
	Washing plates
	Making breakfast
	Market
12:00 noon	
Phone calls	Phone calls
Basketball	TV
	Eating
6:00 p.m.	
Sports	Playing rounders
Chatting	Coming home
9:00 p.m.	
On the road	On the road
TV	TV
Playing dominoes	Sitting on verandah
	Inside/in bed
	Talking with parents

When the above Saturday routine was shared with the whole group, one of the boys commented, rubbing his belly in satisfaction, *"We livin' sweet, y'know!"* Living sweet may reflect a temporary freedom from responsibility, for we found males at older ages doing what they said were their own Saturday routines, laundering their own clothes or cleaning.

Gender-based divisions also govern Dominican concepts of space and time. During the annual village fête in July, it is the boys who were mobilized to shuttle the drinks and other commodities between home and stall, or to help collect empty bottles, walk around selling peanuts, or even man the stalls, way into the night, long after the girls their age and older had been sent home.

In the late afternoon when people begin to return home, the streets come alive. Boys and girls are running errands, women are stopping to chat among themselves, and young men are playing football or basketball, or hanging out in groups on the corners. But by 7:00 p.m., the streets are generally cleared of the women and the children. "Riverbreeze girls are serious," a young man in his twenties told us; "You won't find them congregating on the street corners!" He and other men in the company put it down to the way "our society differentiate between what is behaviour for boys and girls. While it is on [alright] for me to be with the boys and enjoy and get on, it is not proper for girls; that would tarnish the ladylike character they have to maintain." The streets, it would appear, are quite properly a male domain.

One of the implications of this ordering of gender is a tighter control over girls than over boys. During the early period of fieldwork this was strikingly evident. A nineteen-year-old girl just finished with school and now working as a secretary, told us she welcomed the research project. *"Long time something like that needed to educate parents that children must be treated alike. I still have no liberty, but my twelve-year-old brother can go anywhere with no questions!"* Further along we met a thirty-six-year-old father of five. Two of his three daughters sat with him, while the third, a baby, was being attended to by her mother. Did he have sons? *"Yes, but they somewhere, maybe by the park playing."* He did not know for sure. This loose rein over boys was, according to Godfrey Touré, one of our informants, the reason for the negative behaviour of our youths. We leave them up to *"spoil"* other people's girls. Houmphoué and a group of older men we met echoed similar sentiments. Parents, they argued, gave too much leeway to boys. In his days, Houmphoué could not do as he pleased, coming home late at nights the way he saw young people doing today. This touched a nerve, and another member of the group began to complain that his wife had given his stepson his own key. Although the boy had begun to work, he was only eighteen years old. When he was that age he could not come home late, let alone possess his own key. Now the teenager no longer listened to him because he felt himself a big man with his own key to the house.

The changed practices were clearly upsetting to these men, but there seemed little they could do. For one thing, they themselves were very much part of the gender divisions asserting themselves in the Riverbreeze and wider Dominican community. For example, at a birthday "drink-up" in mid June, female guests began complaining of the lack of help they got from males around the house. A female who had heard that the host assisted his wife in preparing the drinks and food said to the wife, *"Thank God you have a man who can use his hand!"* After a hot debate, in which the men boasted they could cook just as well if not better than most women, the general consensus was that gender role divisions were becoming a thing of the past, for most modern families engaged both men and women in home classes. Nevertheless, the fact of the debate itself, plus the observed instances of gender role divisions in all stages of the life cycle, would tend to make the birthday consensus more a hope for the future than a reflection of reality.

During the preparation for the annual village *Fête des Reines*, the gender role divisions were very evident. One of the carpenters, who was involved in the core group set up by our research team, tried to provoke some comment with the remark that since women always wanted to be like men, now was their chance to prove it; he was willing to give up his hammer and saw. They must know their place, he declared in triumph. The women took him on, of course, pointing to the many fields in which women did just as well, but agreeing that there were some jobs more fitting for men because of the physical exertion required. As the work progressed, both genders worked well together, women passing the strips of wood and nails, men applying the hammer and saw.

The prevailing gender role differentiation in adulthood was underlined for us during a curfew imposed by the state. While most of Riverbreeze were complaining bitterly of the restrictions on their social life, a young woman told our assistant: *"For me, curfew could go on for the rest of the year, for it will cause us to see our men more often. They don't have a choice but to stay inside! Everyday is curfew for us women!"* Her friends agreed, one of them underscoring the gender bias: *"Men like to spend time with 'the boys', while we have to stay inside.* If we go out and stay two minutes, is man we have!" The looser rein over boys also means greater freedom for them to model their own behaviour after that of older males. And given the dominance of young males on the street corner and on the playing fields, it is not so easy for concerned parents and adults to pull in the reins when confronted with a wayward son.

The minister was present at the fête. The team he sponsored was play-ing. A group of young boys twelve years old and younger was playing their own game of football on the gate line. They drew attention to themselves by the foul language they used to register disapproval of a bad pass or a miskick. A woman called one of them by name. No more than six, the boy was already noted for using foul words. Where, she asked him, was your respect for the two gentlemen (the minister and me). The boy flashed her off with a gesture of the hand and turned up his nose. His peers laughed. One of them, however, quietly drew away from the group as the game resumed. After the minister drifted off to meet others, I asked the lad why he withdrew from the game. The boy in question, he claimed, was a bad example he had been told not to follow. Now he was afraid that the woman might tell his parents he was a part of the poor behaviour and put him in trouble. What trouble? *"Well, I may not get to come and see football again or I may get a beating, because I have been warned of this type of friends."* He spoke from experience for he was nearly beaten once before for finding himself in a similar situation. Some of the boys appeared quite amused by the language others were using as they played, on occasion urging them to repeat. Their behaviour mimicked that of the youths. For after the league match was over the players on the losing team were embroiled in an argu-ment about the outcome. Those criticized defended themselves with foul language, those praised were rewarded with high fives. I looked around only to see the young boys doing the same. One player remarked, "This is the usual thing in Riverbreeze football, always ready to criticize!" Even when they win, the arguments are heated and punctuated with foul expres-sions. From the games I witnessed, this appears to be the norm.

The behaviour of these boys follows the pattern set by the footballers. As males, they are free to watch the matches by themselves. Our six-year-old exercised some self-discipline and distanced himself from the behav-iour of his peers, precisely because he valued the looseness of his parents' reins. And although evidently children can be sanctioned by any adult, the lightness with which they all treated the presence of the government minister and the other adults suggests that there is not much the latter are able to do. They face two options. They could seek to change the behaviour of the older males, the youths, whose example the boys imitate, or they could quarantine their boys. Neither course of action could produce a meaningful impact, for football means a great deal to the community, which turns out to see them play. Indeed, a young woman commented that the football league gave the women the opportunity to support their boyfriends and to bring their children to see their fathers in action. A member of the national football squad, who represented Dominica, took part in the competition. Foul language, however, is not confined to the football field or its environs. As in Grannitree, any lively discussion among the youths involves the liberal flow of badwords.

The older youths and young adults are not the only role models for boys. Cable television exerts a powerful influence on the young, and on the adults as well. For example, it is through television that American basketball has become quite popular not only in Dominica but also throughout the rest of the Caribbean. One of the motives women have for hurrying home is to catch the soap operas on television. From the available evidence, children are generally left up to watch television.

I stopped to speak to a gentleman I usually see sitting on his verandah, an unusual sight since most men his age (about thirty years old) are usually on the plaza, by the bars or just leaning on the street corner. He works with the government, while his wife is a nurse. His eleven year-old son was sitting on the floor watching a movie. Two other young men, obviously friends of the family, came in. One of them asked, *"How can you have Junior watching TV alone, considering those X-rated programmes?"* and without waiting for an answer switched the channel to sports. It had, he felt, too much nudity and violence. Junior was quite vexed. His dad replied, *"Mr Clarke, he knows* what *to look at, and besides I monitor him!"* Clarke complained that foreign cultures spoil our young people, who try to imitate what they see. Dad added that he placed no restriction on Junior, once homework was done. But this did not satisfy Clarke, who expressed strong views against children being left alone to view such programmes, since they *"affected their whole outlook towards life"*. Dad conceded. *"What to do!"* he mused. *"Even without TV children nowadays will do and learn anything out there. So, it is better to just deal with it before somebody else tells them!"* The two other men disagreed. Clarke said, *"You have to teach kids these values from early, so they can grow with it!"*

Apart from revealing the freedom with which an adult friend can reprimand one's child, we see here the concern which many people feel about the influence of television. His assertions to the contrary, Junior's father was not in a position to monitor what Junior was watching, for he was outside on the verandah, while Junior was inside the living room.

Riverbreeze adolescents and young adults share a youth culture in which sports, organized recreation, music and face to face socializing play very big roles. Reference has already been made to football. During the season, street games involving six players a side are a common sight. The Riverbreeze Football Competition is taken seriously enough for a minister of government to sponsor a team. And though from one angle this could be interpreted as a political manoeuvre, from another it merely recognizes and encourages one area of social life with the potential to contribute to the national pride of Dominicans. National sports like football, cricket and athletics are sponsored and supported for the contribution they make to national identity.

It was this sense of the potential in sports that elicited regrets from a young man that his parents discouraged rather than encouraged him. The remark was triggered by a woman passing with her son who had just finished playing football. *"This woman attends every match her sons play in and supports them to the fullest. That's how I like to see parents support their children!"* He himself once had the potential, he remarked, and if his own mother had supported him like this lady supported her sons, he would have reached far. But looking on sports as an unprofitable distraction, his parents prevented him from going out to play and participate in outdoor activities, insisting instead that he bury himself in his books. The woman who was sharing in this discussion tried tempering his remarks with the comment that everyone was different and should not be judged by the same yardstick. But he stuck to his line, observing that in families like that of the woman and her sons the bonds are stronger because all of life is shared. He was clearly envious.

Sports serve to bind male youths closer. Discussing viewpoints is just as important as playing together. During our fieldwork the finals of the

National Basketball Association in the United States were being played. Some young men proceeding to a bar to watch tried to persuade one of their peers to go along with them. He told them he had no intention of swapping the comfort of his home for a bar just to watch the game on television. *"It's not a matter of comfort,"* one of them replied, *"You enjoy it more when your friends are around and you can talk of the different plays!"*

Music offers another important medium for socializing. Every Wednesday evening one of the local sound systems stages a jam session. Youths are drawn from even outside Riverbreeze. After the entry event staged by our research team, the young people stayed around for the music while the older men and women left for home. Then as soon as the tempo changed to soft, slow tunes, they too disappeared. The disc jockey explained that the change was calcu-lated—he knew how to make them go home. *"All they want is hot music to rub!"* The "hot" music refers to the heavy DJ reggae, and "rub" to the accompanying pelvic dance movement. Thus, through the music also come formed attitudes to sexuality that are gender constructed.

Sexuality

The strict control over the girl child, matched by the loose reins over the boy child, has implications for both female and male sexuality. On the one hand, a semiofficial ideology stigmatizes women for any sexual expression before or outside of marriage, even though a majority of Dominican chil-dren are born out of wedlock, and within marriage itself for any sign of being too sexually active.

A group of women who were already mothers was asked to react to the following hypothetical case.

Jane really did not want another child, as the two earlier pregnancies were very complicated. In addition, things have not been well lately between Jane and her common-law husband. He hardly helps her with the two children and most nights comes home drunk and forces her into having sex. He also beats her up frequently. Because of her difficulties during pregnancy, and having so little space between the two children, Jane had to give up her job after the second one. Things are really tough for her. Her friends tell her she now looks older than her own mother. She really wants the children to get bigger, even preschool age, so she can go to work. But three weeks ago, Jane discovered that she was pregnant for the third time.

What the women focused on was the shame brought by their own first pregnancy, not because it was unplanned, like Jane's third, but because at the time they were not married. *"I had disappointed my father." "I could not face my mother." "You are ashamed of yourself and of what people around think. I used to tie my stomach because I was a nurse and in those days you had to or lose your job."* Pregnancy before marriage was something degrading. But another source of shame was the evidence of too much sex. One of the discussants who was already married by the time she became pregnant the third time, revealed that the source of her shame was that she was still breastfeeding the second child. *"Not that I did not want the child. I was so disappointed. I would go out, but as soon as I entered the house I would cry. I was concerned about what society would say. They would think that all I was doing was having sex."* Even within marriage, which legitimizes sexual intercourse for females, a woman must not appear to be too active.

Given public attitudes towards female sexuality, but at the same time the prevailing practice of extramarital sex, it is not surprising to find a developed ethnopharmacopia of abortifacients, even though there are strong feelings that abortion is murderous and contemptible. Ingesting the following brews and substances is believed able to cause an abortion:

Marigold with salt
Castor oil early in the pregnancy
Hibiscus flower
Coke and Phensic
Coke and Andrews liver salts
The contraceptive pill

Lifting heavy loads can do the same thing, and is more acceptable because the abortion would be considered a miscarriage, even though the intention is the same.

Men, by contrast, appear to have greater sexual freedom. This notion led one of our female informants to declare that she would have preferred being male, in order *"to have plenty girls"*. She claimed that this was frequent *"woman talk"* among her friends, who all felt able to do everything males could do, including all the male sports such as football, cricket, basketball, except have plenty men. Some of them allowed their boyfriends this freedom. For her part, she valued most the sense of independence nurtured by a mother who brought her up to shun the control of men. That's why she would much prefer to be the second woman for her boyfriend than to get married, for in marriage she would have to do her husband's bidding. Now she doesn't have to yield to her boyfriend's pressure, not even to let her hair grow instead of cutting it short.

The idea of marriage as reducing the independence of women is a theme which surfaces in the literature on Afro-Caribbean conjugal relations. According to Roberts and Sinclair (1978) many women prefer visiting relationships for the independence they afford. Marriage brings improved social status to many women but it also ties them "for worse".

The sexual problem facing men is not whether to have sex before or outside marriage, or to get a woman pregnant, or whether to have more than one woman. What they face instead is the question of how open they ought to be about multiple partnerships.

This morning the barber was relating an incident with his girlfriend. She was upset with him for going out with some girls. He claims he sees nothing wrong, as the girls are his friends and there is nothing between them. Just then, she appeared from inside and gave him a hard stare. If she had a good male friend he would not react that way, since he knew what kind of girl she was. Why can't she see him in the same light? I commented that given what was happening around us, it was difficult for a woman not to believe one was having an affair if one went out with another woman. "Regardless!" he insists, "she can deal with it differently." We were joined by a young man from Riverbreeze. At once, Barber shifted to him: "How can you let your girlfriend leave you? You must leave them! Woman cannot leave man!" This brought some laughter. By then we were joined by a young man in his thirties. He continued, "When you have a back door on to the other side of the road, why not use it to let the girls come in and out? Why use Main Street to let Riverbreeze people see everything you do?" "Macho," concluded the second fellow. "He playing macho with two girlfriends. Now that one leave him I have to see him go mad!" Mr "Macho" finally defended his honour. "Which man now doesn't have two girlfriends, or more than one? Must be a *dummy!*" Barber replied, "I . . . I am sure I only have one!" loud enough so that his girlfriend inside could hear. Macho would not let up. "You could fool me, because you undercover and they don't find you out yet! But I do mine in the open!" More laughter. Whenever Barber paused to make a point he directed it inside. He and his girlfriend were not on speaking terms. Macho continued: "Once mother-in-law is involved or interfere in your relationship, it will break." Even before he had the second relationship, her mother kept pouring in her daughter's head to leave him. "One day brain must respond! That's what happened!" The conversation then turned to the difference in thinking between men and women. Women are the way they are, one of the men said, because of men. Men spoil them, so now they are upgrading themselves to compete with men for what is available. All men want is sex; yet women always into their books! When a woman will be thinking of bettering herself, the man will sit and think and plot how and where he is going to get his next grind! Shouts of "True! True!" from those present. "That's why they are doing better than men! It's men's fault that women are taking over!"

The main point being made here is that it is natural for men to keep two women. Except for Barber, who protests for the benefit of his spouse that he has only one, the debate is not over whether to have one or to have two, but whether to be discreet or open about it. Barber and his other clients believe "Macho" begged for it by being open. Macho denies that this was the cause and blames his mother-in-law instead. We have already seen the envy of at least one young woman that men are able to practise multiple partnerships while women are not, an envy which she says other female friends of hers share. But whether it is true or not that men have more than one woman but women no more than one man (and, given the roughly equal sex ratio, it cannot be true), the fact is that it is believed and this is as powerful a socializing agent as if it were true.

But age may introduce an element here, for during the fête a young man admitted that he once kept more than one woman, but that after a while he had to get serious and make a choice. "I'm not getting younger; I have to decide for one!" He had just witnessed a former girlfriend pass by with another man. Multiple partnerships may in fact be more characteristic of younger than of older men (see Chevannes 1986:41–43).

The men make a third point: it is a man who should leave a woman, not a woman leave a man. Barber expresses it like a shibboleth of the male gender. Macho's failure therefore reflects badly on all men, because in gender relationships the initiative should lie with the male, not with the female. When a woman leaves a man, the man becomes acted upon, rather than the actor, a reversal that destroys the image of man being in control.

Their final point is that there is a difference between men and women: men are preoccupied with having sex, while women are preoccupied with getting ahead. This difference they say explains why women are achieving more than men. There may be some substance to their point, for it also came out in the log of daily activities discussed above.

Where for most women first pregnancy is a source of anxiety, it is generally greeted by Dominican men with a sense of pride and, possibly, relief. *"Yes, I can breed!" "I am man now!" "I am a father!"* Consequently, among men, the feelings against abortion are just as ambivalent as those of the women. On one hand, many regard abortion with the same contempt as murder, and refer to the woman who has undergone one as *"murderer"* and *"cemetery"*. On the other hand there are those who are willing to give weight to situational factors, such as the marital statuses of the sexual partners, or the impact of the pregnancy on the woman's career goals.

Being cited as the father of the unborn child is generally a necessary but not sufficient condition to establish paternity. After the baby is born, men and their families of orientation, especially their mothers, must verify on sight that the baby is theirs. They look for family traits and points of resemblance to members of their own family. "All my children are fair," said one of our informants who was in doubt, "but that particular child born darker than the others." In another case the young man's mother forced him to have a paternity test done, although he said he had no doubt about his partner's faithfulness. Not even marriage is immune to this custom. An informant told us, *"Although I was married when I had my first child, my husband's mother came to visit the child and her first comment was 'Sa se pied nou!'* [That is our foot]." A child who it is thought does not really belong to the designated father is called a ready made. The imagery is that of a suit of clothes that could be bought from a store by anybody, instead of being measured and cut to fit.

Mother or Father

Despite the pride in becoming fathers, Dominican men find that their sons grow emotionally closer to the mothers than to themselves, just as they themselves felt closer to their own mothers than to their fathers. This became a subject of discussion first by a group of young men, and then by a group of young women, none of whom had yet fathered or mothered a child, and finally by a mixed group of fathers and mothers. The young men expressed stronger attachment to their mothers: *"I do not have a father." "I could die for my mother, but I am not bothered about my father!" "I have a strong love for my mother but I sometimes felt like murdering my father!"* Mothers, they said, were more loving and understanding, while fathers spent too much time correcting and asserting their authority, and were generally less approachable.

For the mixed group of adults, two short skits, each on a separate occasion, were used to evoke reactions. In the first the topic was parent-child communication in the transmission of values. The plot presented a young man living with both parents, who everytime he wanted to go out came to his mother, never his father, for permission. One day, his mother was fed up and sent him to his father. *"But Mammy, I asking you. What are you sending me to Daddy for?"* Reluctantly and with some fear he went to his father, but was sent back to his mother. Now quite irritated, he began to complain that everytime he needed to go out it was a problem. Mammy eventually agreed, provided he washed the dishes.

Claude's comment was sharp. "Mothers do that all the time," he said. "They do not like to discipline the children. They let the father do everything, then the child grows up not liking the father, because he is the one who is always beating!" To which the mothers present nodded in agreement or said, *"Is true!"*

However, in a subsequent discussion, two and a half weeks later, when the topic was reward and punishment, the mothers were not so quick to agree. The skit used this time depicted a situation in which a son had taken $20 from the sum of money set aside to pay the electricity bill. His mother said, *"If you wasn't taller than me, I would beat you. But I cannot hide it, I must tell your father!"* On reaching home, Father took out his strap and administered a flogging.

Reacting, one of the women in the group expressed displeasure at the mother passing on the boy to his father for punishment. Her reason was that children usually take advantage of those situations, since fathers may come home when the child is already asleep or the mother may have forgotten to complain, so that the child gets away without being punished. All the women agreed with that. Claude's reaction was the same as in the first skit, but he got embroiled in a heated exchange with Rita, who had objected strenuously to his argument that the father's flogging could have resulted in abuse. "Lucky for him," she said, "he got the strap! Stop painting fancy pictures and get down to reality!" When, therefore, he accused Mammy of passing on the dirty work to Daddy, making Daddy look like the bad one, Rita was the first to shout, "That's not true!"; she was followed by the other women in the group. She then went on: "If it were a girl, the father would not have looked for a strap, but his first reaction would be to knock the girl about. In fact, the mother would not even send her to her father. Instead of talking to her like she did with the boy, she would slap her across the face!" Other mothers in the group agreed, "Is true." Marie, the woman who played Mammy in the skit then said that if it were a girl of the same age as the son she would let the father punish her, but that if the daughter were younger she would administer the punishment herself.

The disagreement with Claude was therefore not over whether mothers pass on the task of being disciplinarian to fathers – they do – but whether their motive was to make fathers look bad. The women argue that they do not shun the need to discipline, unless the child, girl or boy, is too big for them to flog. Implicit here is the belief that men are physically stronger. The essence of Claude's point is that sons' warmer feelings towards mothers and more distant feelings towards fathers are a consequence, intended or otherwise, of the father's role as disciplinarian.

In Dominica, fathers discipline their daughters also, but from the young women's "seed group" it would appear that this does not prevent some of them from valuing relations with father better than relations with mother, but there was no discernible trend. The group of eleven identified negative qualities on both sides, but we noticed that there were more negatives about mothers than fathers. Fathers' negative qualities were: their failure to praise or encourage; poor communication; and lack of support. But the list of mothers' negative qualities was twice as long: plaintiveness; quarrelsomeness; not being ready to let go ("They stretching it!"); poor communication; lack of preparation for adulthood; domineering. There were also more positive qualities attributed to mother (open, loving, encouraging, good listener) than to father (responsible, more outspoken). The fact that mothers have more positives and negatives is not surprising, since they interact more with the children. This is the essence of R. T. Smith's concept of matrifocality (1996). In the end, some felt closer to mother – *"She's open, she has a youthful mind"*; *"My mother encourages us to do better"*; others closer to father: "I am my father's favourite child, because when I was growing up he told me everything. I was waiting for my mother to tell me; I mean is his duty too, y'know, but she should have told me. I share my secrets with him. I never informed my mother when I first menstruated; I told my father."

Fête des Reines

The village festival, which opened on the Sunday, lasted for the entire week. It was the result of a community effort. The attendance was good. There were two levels of organized activities. One comprised all the stalls with food and drink and games. These operated throughout the entire week. On the other level, the festival organisers provided for a different activity most nights: a Band night, a Calypso night, a Debating night and the Miss Riverbreeze competition.

The games section included the Lucky 7, a game of chance played with a pair of dice. Young boys, many under fifteen years old, were the main participants. They were allowed to play well into the night, unlike their female peers who by nine o'clock were either sent or taken home or in the company of adults. Many of the boys assisted their parents in the stalls, but occasionally stole the chance to drink a bottle of beer. Stall keepers, who were overwhelmingly female, had no qualms about selling to minors. There was also bingo; here on some nights most participants were women. Even when men played in greater numbers there was always a large presence of women. Moreover, this was the only game controlled by a woman.

Gender role divisions were also evident in the main activities. Both Band and Calypso nights were performed by males, confirming their dominance in the music industry. In the debate, both sides allowed the male to speak first even in the case where he was much younger and more inexperienced than his female colleague. The Miss Fête des Reines contest was, of course, a female affair, involving five contestants, two of them from outside the community. One of the Riverbreeze girls was crowned queen.

On the fourth night of the Festival two teenagers squared off for a fight, stones in hand. One had thrown Alkali, a strong smelling liquid, over the other. Two young men parted them, and as he walked away, one of the peacemakers remarked, "That's why I stopped going to the disco – too much violence among those young people!"

As both the Festival and the Football League demonstrate, Riverbreeze is a very active community, displaying a high level of organization and community spirit. This is a nice community, observed one of our informants, but for the drug problem. Her reference was to a small enclave in Riverbreeze, known as Stone End. Other Riverbreeze residents point it out as the place to avoid, because of the gambling, drugs and foul language. Indeed, the atmosphere there is unfriendly towards the stranger.

Today I decided to join the group involved in gambling. In it were an ex-policeman I once knew, two other young men and a woman named Dean. There were five other onlookers, four males and one female, including a basketball player I also knew. One of them asked if I was a policeman. I was clean-shaven. Even as he asked he was rolling a stick of ganja. "What do you think?" I asked, but before I could finish, the basketball player asked if he didn't think I would have arrested him were I a policeman. "We would have to fight for it!" was his come back. He then gave the marijuana to the basketball player, who claimed he did not smoke, but from the look he received from those present I learned otherwise. With my ex-policeman friend nodding to me, they were now sure I was not a cop, so they felt free to let off their strings of foul language and curse words. The men were all in their late twenties. As they gambled, they cheated one another. We witnessed one of the men who had lost a hand pass on cards to his partner. Dean, believing she had the winning hand, deposited $58. She lost. Their celebration of the trickery was surprising, but even more so was their own revelation of having cheated. When told, two others joined in the laughter. "Bitch!" one remarked, "good for her!" But instead of being upset, she turned the tables on them. "Is no sweat, because when I won the $75 on Sunday, is Jake [the ex-policeman] that set me up!" Jake was embarrassed "Shit!" he exclaimed. Then she explained how she did it.

Stone End's values are so different from those of the rest of Riverbreeze that one could argue that that community serves as a kind of reverse image of what Riverbreeze should never become, much the same way the image of hell functions for the Christian. The fear and aversion for the place and for its residents are quite real. Stone End itself is very real. In more than one respect it is a very small miniature of a Joetown.

Conclusion

This description of socialization in Riverbreeze focuses on a striking regularity, namely the gender divisions present at all stages of the life cycle. These divisions are structured in day to day activities. At the same time, there is ample evidence of changes taking place in the people's concepts about gender roles, in the direction of greater equality, although in reality such changes are not yet fully evident.

6

Motown

Motown is situated in the western half of the city of Kingston. It was founded around 1954 by government, and the houses sold to victims of the 1951 hurricane. Two main avenues running east–west for 300 metres are crossed by half-a-dozen streets running north–south; and on these avenues and streets live an estimated 3,000 people. It is one of those communities often called "blue-collar". Its residents are primarily weekly or fortnightly wage-earners, or self-employed artisans and traders, but not a few are trained professionals and clerical workers. On the same street one will find a middle-class family of professionals and not far away a house whose occupants are unable to afford electricity.

Motown is an open community. It boasts a very popular football club, a youth club, a citizens' association, a Golden Age Club, an all-age school serving a much wider area, but it also has features of a "garrison community" (Stone 1980), a community under the armed monolithic control of a political party. One side of Motown is an area where Jamaica Labour Party supporters are wary about entering, the other an area People's National Party supporters are wary about entering.

From one perspective, we have a stable community, whose houses are occupied by residents who either own or inherited them, though they also share them with tenants. Consequently, in Motown we found evidence of a strong sense of family. With the help of an informant, Beatrice, we sought to identify the main social features of the occupants of the thirty-six houses on Farley Drive.

The overwhelming majority of houses are occupied by vertically and horizontally extended households, headed by their elderly owners and/or their children and grandchildren. This owner-resident pattern gives Motown, or at least the Farley Avenue section of it, a strong sense of family units and provides the basis of its stability. Of all the adolescents of school age on the avenue, only six are in high schools, including one living on his own with the support of his migrant parents; the rest attend the all-age school. Because the homes are owner-occupied, out-of-school unemployed youths are provided with a sense of security. But, if Beatrice is correct, at least one-third of the residents share their space with tenants. This adds to the variation, and, coupled with the unemployment among the young people, to the volatility that draws the attention of the police.

A characteristic of stable communities is their ability to maintain social organizations. Motown's social organizations not only meet regularly, but are active. The Citizens' Association's Easter treat for the elderly, for example, pulled out 108 adults and fifteen children, while the Golden Age Club's fun night drew twenty-four adults and two girls. The Golden Age Club was founded nearly thirty years ago, in 1967. The Motown Youth Club sometimes finds it difficult to get a quorum, but it is by no means dead.

By contrast, the community is at the same time subject to antisocial activities more typical of inner-city than blue-collar areas. In February 1995, a toilet bowl was stolen from the all-age school. The president of the Citizens' Association referred to the incident as "part of the vandalism programme". Two months later, in April, Heathcliff, Dahlia's ten-year-old son, explained his absence from school as his teacher's instructions, because of the theft of the school fridge and stove over the weekend. The Anti-Crime Task Force, still called "ACID" by the people (from its original acronym), has been quite active in Motown, and, according to informants, is the main reason why the streets are not more populated at nights. Motown is alleged to have its share of drugs and gangs. Shortly before the start of our fieldwork, Dandimite, an up-and-coming DJ artist, became the victim of what was believed to be gang feuding. And during fieldwork, Motown became the end of the road for two men involved in a running gun-battle with ACID.

The Street as a Social Arena

Motown streets comprise an important arena for social intercourse, particularly on weekend evenings. Then, they come alive with the hustle and bustle of recreational activities, street-corner gossip and gazing about, drinking and playing loud sound system reggae music. Many householders do no cooking on Friday night or Saturday night, preferring instead the jerk chicken or roast fish, or sometimes roast corn, chicken-foot soup or "fish tea" (soup made from fish and vegetables) that are available from their street-side chefs and vendors. This kind of weekend "liming" is characteristic of most urban communities in the anglophone Caribbean, whether Baxter's Road in Bridgetown or Gros Islet in Castries.

On Friday, I had a walk through Motown with Horval, the Motown Youth Club president. Horval is twenty-eight years old and lives with his parents. They operate a shop on Farley Drive. He has one child, who lives with its mother but spends time with him sometimes. People were out on the streets – adults, male and female, children, teenagers, all in age groups. On Farley, near Wexford Avenue, five boys between six and ten years old were playing marbles on the unpaved sidewalk. A few boys and girls were riding bicycles up and down and some male teenagers were together listening to music and sharing jokes. The adults, mainly men, were clustered in groups, four groups of them on Wexford alone. Further up Farley a group of youths were engaged in a basketball game, the lines of a basketball court clearly drawn on the asphalt. On Farley Drive, Wexford Avenue and Burke Road we passed a number of streetside jerk chicken drums and men and women eating and drinking. Down Daisy Crescent we meet Beulah and Marvalin. Beulah is a slim-bodied woman about twenty years old, the girlfriend of Marvalin's brother, who operates a barber shop in their backyard on Farley. Marvalin is still a teenager, no longer in school, the mother of a nine-month-old baby who, when not with her, is with the child's paternal grandmother. She and her babyfather no longer have a relationship. The two of them join us as Horval introduces me to Reds. Reds is sitting on a truck wheel in front of his establishment, a bar popularly called "Reds' Bar", but officially named "Sharon's Lounge", after his daughter. The four of us enter and order soft drinks. There are four men and three women playing the gaming machines. The music is too loud to talk, so everybody else just watches, as winners collect drinks from losers.

It is now after ten o'clock when the three of them walk me to the bus stop. Marvalin introduces me to Dahlia, her mother, whom we pass. She promises an interview. The streets have undergone a noticeable change from when we began – the women and children have disappeared, leaving the males, adult and teenaged.

In Motown, the street is a recreational arena, where boys and youths play, where people meet and socialize with their friends. According to Beatrice, who lives on Farley, even late into the night the streets used to be crowded with people involved in diverse activities ranging from gambling (*"Almost every road had a gambling table, but the men also played cards and dice"*) to listening to music, to enjoying the company of peers. She used to feel quite safe walking home from the bus stop any hour of the night. Now, she no longer feels as secure. She attributes the reduction in night activities to the frequency with which ACID is known to swoop down, forcing people, youths and mature adults alike, into early retirement. Even so, the street remains quite lively. For example, minutes to 2:00 p.m. on one Sunday afternoon, we encountered five groups, comprising twenty-three men and boys and three women, in the twelve-minute walk from the intersection of Helsinki Way and Farley Drive to Marvel's home.

Group 1, five boys. One was about sixteen years old; another very young (about four or five years old); the three others about seven or eight. The big boy and two of the seven-year-olds were patching a bicycle tube, while the others watched. I hailed them. The big boy gave a cool, *"Yeah!"* The others giggled. I smiled and walked on. From behind I heard one of the seven- or eight-year-olds call, *"Hey, sah, da bwaai-ya sayin' im like yu!"* The *"bwaai-ya"* responded, *"An im se im wi . . ."* I did not catch the rest of the sentence, but got a fairly good idea of what was said, for the sixteen-year-old shouted, *"Hey, move from ya wid yu batty-bwaai argument!"* I turned in time to see him brandishing the bicycle tube at the fellow who made the obviously offensive remark.

Group 2, three male teenagers. They are standing up leaning against a fence, two on the outside, one on the inside. One of the two outside is relating an incident (a movie? real life?). I catch only a few words, *"Den di ada [other] yout' jus' duck and start let off!"* He crouches in demonstration and stretches out his hand, his fingers tensed in the shape of a gun.

Group 3, five male teenagers sitting on the kerb having an animated discussion about football.

Group 4, a roadside stall. One woman is behind the counter, selling two packets of Coolade to another woman while a third waits her turn, her scandal bag crushed in her palm.

Group 5, a group of seven youths. Six are sitting on the wall laughing, while the seventh is stooped facing them and giving a command performance.

This is early Sunday afternoon, an hour or two before the traditional mid-to late-afternoon dinner. After dinner, there are more people on the road. There is a basketball game and a football match in progress, boys standing at gates talking to girls, nicely dressed women and girls (no men) coming from or going to church.

Music plays a very big recreational role in Motown, and therefore classifies as a street activity. Early in the fieldwork we were informed that if we wanted to bring people out to our animation meetings it was not enough to use the usual pamphlet or word-of-mouth invitations. All we had to do was string up some music.

Sunday 5:00 p.m. On Wexford and Roxbury a group of boys six- to twelve-years-old were playing cricket in the open land, watched by eight adults and ten young girls. Three young men were transporting some speaker boxes, which they mounted on the corner of Farley and Wexford. Some others were erecting a makeshift food stall, while across the street six "big" (mature, adult) men sat expectantly. I was curious, so I asked what was going on. Roast fish and chicken would soon be available, so they were waiting. One added. "Yu don't see anyt'ing yet. Wait till di music start play!" I moved on. Young children, mainly boys, were riding bicycles, boys and girls walking along or standing talking, music playing from various corners.

According to our informants, roadside sessions like the one being prepared were once a common feature in Motown, while Dandimite was alive. Through him, other DJs used to frequent Motown. The sound systems would be strung up, they would provide the liquor and "man just chant" (meaning, the youths were given opportunities to DJ). Dandimite was one of those DJs known for their gun lyrics. But at the time of his murder he had begun to change to more "conscious lyrics". The murder, for which another member of the community has been held, and the subsequent crackdown by ACID have led to the general decline in street life, and in the music sessions in particular. The music activities we encountered during field-work were mere echoes of the recent past.

The large number of males socializing on the street represents but one side of the pattern of social life in Motown. The other side is the yard or home. As soon as one gets to know the people living there, one can observe a tension between exposure on the street and the influence of the yard or home, as far as the socialization of children is concerned.

Gender Preference

Within Motown, women and men are equally divided on the issue of preference of one gender over the other. Arguments for and against are strongly influenced by the difficulties in growing up the children. Boys may be preferred because they will not bring in a pregnancy; girls may be preferred because they are more controllable.

Dahlia has nine children, six of them boys. Interviewed in the presence of Marvalin, one of her daughters, she gave a number of reasons why she preferred boys to girls.

"Boy children-dem show me more love dan di girls. For instant, when they were younger, only the boys always tryin' to help me in my house-work, not the girls. It's a fac'." Marvalin overhears and objects. "Mama, don't do dat. Please, don't do dat!" She was angry. "Marvalin, it is a fac'!" "Mama, yu know se yu a tell lie, now! Mama, me no help yu?" Dahlia explains that she had problems with Arlene, Dainty and now Marvalin. Stanley used to go down on the floor more than Marvalin. The boys helped more in everything. And, if she was going out, Marvalin would never say, "Mama, yu lookin' good!", but her son would come and look and say, "Mama, don't wear dat dress! I don' wan' see yu in dat!" Or, "Mama, I don' like yu 'air style! A wan' yu comb it dis way." Marvalin, she says, "don' have any time fi mi, as a girl. My boy children have all di time fi mi. Dem sit down and wash sheet, wash everyt'ing."

Dahlia advances two reasons why she prefers boys. First, her sons were more helpful in domestic chores than her daughters. She does not say it, but their numerical preponderance and birth order over the girls must have been a factor. We once saw Stanley, her twenty-three-year-old son, cooking. She taught all her boys how to cook, she said. Her second reason, however, was the greater personal attention she received from her sons. She implied that because Marvalin was a girl she ought to have received greater gender identification from her, but this did not happen.

Not everyone would agree with her preference, based on these arguments. Sister Claudia, for example, the mother of four boys and four girls, prefers girls, because she can bring them up to become loving and be able to sit down and discuss things with her. Her last daughter from time to time invites her to Florida to spend time. She is scheduled to visit in May. "Boys," on the other hand, "are very stubborn; as dem grow to be big man, dem start put on dem clothes to go out at night. Yu see im?" she asked, pointing to her grandson. "When im come in, mi no know." He is nineteen or twenty years old. Her girls used to stay at home. The daughter she goes to in Florida is a nurse, and one of her sons is a doctor. He has three children, two daughters and a son, and his last daughter is a doctor like himself. "But im not even send one cent" for her. "Im spen pan di daughter-dem, im kids dem, yu know. Him lef' 'ere during faadn [farthing] days and mek imself what he is now. Im a doctor, one kid mix medicine, another a doctor like imself. Im grow up im kids, so A don' have anyt'ing bad to say bout im, but as a mada im should know! Yu know what A mean!"

Sister Claudia's reason is not of the same order as Dahlia's, which is the amount of domestic help a mother can count on. All her sons used to wash their own clothes, cook and share household chores with their sisters. Nor is her gender preference based on kindness, though she accuses her medical doctor son of not remembering her. One of her sons, a garage owner, does live with her and is very kind towards her. Rather, her reason is simple: she had less control over her sons. Indeed, she tells us, she had to put one of them, Timothy, out of the house. The only girl that gave her trouble was Precious, who, she said, "love man. As ar boyfrien' gone to work, she gone wid aneda man. But," she said smilingly, "she no talk to likl rif-raf, only bigshot man; an' as dem talk, dem gone a Sheraton!" Precious is either a prostitute or very loose, but her waywardness is offset by the docility of the other girls. By contrast, all Claudia's sons gave her trouble.

But, to return to Dahlia, there is a third reason for preferring boys. "To be honest, I always t'ink about pregnancy, wid di girl-dem not havin' any faada fi di kids, yu understand." But, "if [di boy child] pregnant anybody, it will lef' out a street". How did she feel about Marvalin's pregnancy? "Boy, mi no feel good bout dat. I am not feeling good bout dat. Me never want Marvalin get pregnant right now. I did want Marvalin finish up ar schoolin. Me really vex over di pregnancy. She done a'ready have di baby, so mi hav fi see it. An' is a sweet likl baby. But mi no want fi si di faada!" She was vehement. She explained that the pregnancy occurred after she had left to spend some time with her mother in England. Had she been here, Marvalin could not have gotten out of hand. But because she was not, Marvalin "mix up and get link-up wid dis black boy. He is twenty years old and Marvalin was only sixteen!" Dahlia thinks that as a man of more experience than her, for he was Marvalin's first man, he should have protected her. She took it so hard that her pressure went up. And not only she, but her sons – they were going to chop him up. God made her return from England just in time. That was last year. Marvalin is now seventeen.

Boys are preferred, thirdly, because they leave pregnancies *"out a street"*; girls get pregnancies *"out a street"* but bring them into the home, and with the babies come new economic and social responsibilities. But, as Dahlia is quick to explain, the antipathy does not last for long, for the baby *"is a sweet likl boy"*, quickly integrated into the home. She takes out her venom instead on Marvalin's babyfather. Her anger stems not from a concern that her daughter was too young to be sexually active, but from the fact that as a man, one who at age twenty she expects would have been more knowledgeable about sex than Marvalin, he should have used contraceptives.

Men also are split in their opinion. Those preferring boys give three reasons. One is that they can more easily identify with boys, with whom they can share sports and other activities, and on whom they depend to pass on their name. They can't do this with daughters, because girls are not supposed to be brought up rough. Men who once used to bathe their infant daughters as a domestic chore say they cease doing so once the child reaches *"a certain age"*. The fear of incest is of concern to mothers also, and it is almost certain that most of them would discourage their spouses from this kind of physical contact with their daughters.

Second, they perceive that society is so structured that boys have greater opportunities for success. A boy could excel like John Barnes, the Jamaican-born English football player, or like Sir Garfield Sobers, the former great West Indies cricket all-rounder, or the next prime minister. *"As a daugh-ter you take a chance, but when I look on the man side, I see more goals".* Consequently, even without a high school education boys are able to make a greater contribution to the household than their high school graduate sisters. "My mother have nine of us. Nine of us my mother have! She have five girls and four boys. And from me a ten [years old] me a min' my mother, and a no notn why me a do it. If my mother a go to her bed right now, me can give her money, and none of her daughter-dem kyaan give her anything! And she love her daughter more than how she love me."

The third reason men give for preferring boys, as with those women who share the same preference, is the threat of pregnancy which the girl child poses.

"My dream is that I want a boy, because the girls, nowadays, you can-not put yu hopes too high fi dem. I [may] have a likl girl and when she reach ten or eleven yu spend a whole heap a money pon her, send her to school. Yu try yu best wid her and she breed at twelve! It affec' me bad! It affec' mi hopes, it affec' mi pocket bad, 'cause all mi money gone to waste! She breed fi a boy at the age of thirteen, who is going to school wid her, and ting like dat! Him kyaan afford notn, so I have to take up [his] respon-sibility now, plus mi money that I spen' 'pon her fi educate her to be a doctor or a nurse, and she breed at twelve!"
"So what happen to the boy when he reaches thirteen and causes some-body else to get pregnant?"

"Well, dat strain wi' come off me, 'cause him no carry no belly give me. Him breed somebody else outside. I [would] still blame him for dat, yu' know, but dat no really trouble me much. Dats why me prefer bwaai!"

Those who prefer girls advance two reasons. One is the problems that boys give in antisocial and even criminal activities. They point to the lack of control families are able to exercise over boys nowadays, as against girls, and the fact that most crimes are committed by males. Girls are more fo-cused on the house. It is for this same reason that they do better in school, for they are not as distracted as the boys are by the activities taking place outside the yard and can better concentrate on their academic work.

"The first ting goin' on in his mentality is [that] to be a man im have fi go shoot police, go rob a bank, go do all kin' of wrong things. While the girl will say 'Bwaai! I want my body look attractive and nice, and fingernail, and ray-ray [so forth].' Di prime minister gonna see her and say, 'What an attractive girl!' Bam! She is the prime minister wife!"

Their second reason is also quite interesting, namely that girls will not abandon their parents in old age. This argument, "old age pension", used to be advanced as a rationale for having so many children, and was thought to have disappeared with the lower fertility rate that now prevails. Here it resurfaces, but in the context of men believing that daughters will more quickly take care of them when they are old than their sons will.

The contending views emerged sharply in one of the mixed core group discussions organized by our team of animators. One of the women objected to a view expressed by Patrick, one of the participants, that girls are more easily led astray than boys. David then placed the arguments in a perspective that simultaneously explained the basis of gender preferences, as well as the roles of mother and father.

"I think the question you asked [was whether] I prefer a bwaai than a girl. We still have fi look 'pon where the problem arise from. Yaso [right here] a wi yard; me call di road my yard, and di community my yard. So, I talk of what I know, and the crime rate in my community, ninety-nine and a half percent is man do it! I never hear of a girl get herself in trouble, more than getting pregnant. Patrick is saying di bwaai might say him a go a park and him gone a park, but somebody in the audience can say that is not true, because him wi' say him a go a park when him really gone rob a thing or two. We have fi set the goal straight. The difference with the man is that we can teach him fi play football; we can teach him cricket, cycling, and whatever trick him can catch on to. But if him kyaan do him book work, but him have a little basic education, him can go a technical school, because him can play a little sports. With the girls now, you have to sit her down and say, 'Look, you have to make use of the book!' If I have a girl, I would need most help from the mother fi bring her up."

Boys get into crime, girls get pregnant – these are the kinds of trouble each gender gives. But in bringing up boys, fathers have more options. There are more avenues to success than through academic excellence, so that if the boy fails in school, a father can encourage his progress through sports, or "whatever trick him can catch on to", provided he has some basic education. A girl's options are limited to education, but for them to make the best use of it, fathers need the help of the mothers. Regardless, therefore, of their gender preferences, a father plays a greater role in bringing up sons, a mother plays a greater role in bringing up daughters. It follows that fathers are more to blame for the trouble boys give, while mothers are more to blame for the trouble girls give. This in part explains why most fathers flog sons but not daughters, why most mothers react the worse to a daughter's pregnancy.

As an arena beyond their control, it is easy to see why parents would fear the street for the danger it poses for their daughters, once they pass puberty. Interest in sex and courtship does not take place inside the home, at least not within the gaze and earshot of the family. In the following fieldnote entry, knowledge of the Jamaican body language allowed us to make the following observations of a pass being made by a young man at a young girl.

As I walked along Wexford, heading west, on nearing Farley I saw a girl coming in my direction. I was not the only one who saw her. This young man not only watched her every step, but made it obvious to her through his body language that he was watching. I was too far away to hear what he said as she passed, but I saw her "cut-eye", that gesture of contempt. He was now walking up behind her. She obviously knew him. He attempted to hold her hand, but she flashed him off. Then his gesture softened. I found this quite funny, for before she had passed his body language was very macho-like, but as soon as she flashed him off his gestures softened, as if begging her to talk to him. I passed them and looked back, only to see that she had stopped and was listening to him. He never gave up trying to touch and hug her, and she was ever pulling away. But each time he touched, she would reach out and put his hand away, this time more gently, not like when she first flashed him off. It was as if she did not wish to offend him, but she also did not want him to get too close.

In the expression of sexuality, it is the male who is expected to initiate the encounter. On the street, that is outside the yard, is where encounters first take place. In the observed encounter above, a girl is approached by a young man. He signals through the use of his body, that he wishes to *"put argument to her"*, to court her. Having ample time to prepare herself, she treats him first with hostility and contempt, and then, as he persists, with hopeful distance. It is neither difficult nor unreasonable to imagine, if they continue to meet, whether by chance or plan, especially by plan, that they could become lovers, and that the misfortune that overtook Marvalin could also overtake this young girl. Should that happen, we may further imagine, her mother would blame not her own failure to prepare her daughter in handling her sexuality, but her daughter's surrender to, even connivance with, bad influences outside the home. Encounters like this are common everyday in every rural and urban community. Girls and even mature, attractive women are the subject of sexual comments and advances from young men. A young man signals his intention when he breaks from his pack and begins to *"lyrics"* a girl. Allowing him to hold her hand signals in turn her willingness to listen.

The street is a threat to girls, but from the point of view of their sexuality. In the fieldwork experience, as strangers, we found the Motown women far more approachable than the men, once we clearly establish a non-sexual intent. The concern which awareness of this threat generates shapes the gender preferences of parents, as well as the way women are socialized to regard and deal with men. The "street" is the arena where that danger is to be found most.

Motown mothers also protect their boy children from the streets, but with them the issue is mainly crime and other antisocial activities, rather than sexuality. According to a street-side vendor, who was himself smoking a ganja spliff, one can purchase anything on the street – drugs, food, car, "even a gyal". Reacting to the recent find of an arms cache in middle-class Meadowbrook, Dahlia affirmed that guns were present also in Motown, but "dem kyaan fin' it", meaning that they were better concealed. Her only concern was "to know dat none a *fimi* [my] pikni iina it". Her children dared not get involved, she said, because they already knew that she would call in the police. Once some young men came around to sell Stanley a gold chain, but, knowing it was stolen, she spoke out strongly against it and aborted the transaction. She said she put her life on the line by telling them she did not want them around her house again. Nobody should feel sorry for her and give or try to sell her stolen goods. Dahlia then expressed her concern for Alex, her fourteen-year-old son. As soon as she missed him from the house, or if he was late from school, which was often, she would comb the streets looking for him. "Everybody know dat A walk and look for Alex. Outa mi nine children, im a mi target. Beatin' kyaan help im; talking kyaan help im. An if im continue, mi carry im a approve school mek govament look after im and mek im learn trade and come out when im nineteen. No pikni," she said, "naa kill mi or bring down disgrace on mi!" If most parents were like her, children would be better. For when they start bringing home things that are not their own, "yu sen' dem back wid it! Dat is 'ow thiefin' start! I don' want anyt'ing free!"

Knowingly receiving stolen goods is a crime. Dahlia brings up her children, particularly her sons, to avoid stolen goods. The incident with the gold chain would not be uncommon, for gold chains are popular but expensive pieces of jewelry for both men and women, and there is a thriving illegal trade in them. Dahlia's problem with Alex is not that he is mixed up in stolen goods, but that he spends more time than she would like outside her control. She counsels Alex, but it doesn't work; she beats him, but that too does not work. Her last resort, she threatens, will be the approved school, a government institution for delinquent boys. But it is an empty threat, for Alex is not a criminal. He is a regular church-goer, in fact, as she later tells us, though he elects to go not to the church she sends him to but to one that is lively, where they shout and clap, " *'cause im turnin' big man"*, she accuses. Dahlia doesn't deny him this choice, but she resents the implied assertion of independence. During one of our interviews, she broke off twice to shout instructions to Alex to stay in the yard. His second attempt also involved his ten-year-old brother, Orville. Stay inside, she shouted to the two of them, where she could keep an eye on them, and suggested that they go read the Bible for Granny, or take a book.

Keeping one's child inside the yard is a common strategy employed by the parents interviewed, young and old. For the girls, parents' main preoccupation is preventing pregnancy; for the boys, keeping them from antisocial values and behaviour. Beatrice did not have much of a problem keeping Marlon off the street, and perhaps this explains why she believes that *"girls kinda little harder to raise. You have to give them more attention and protection from disgrace, susu, you know how society stay!"* The disgrace she refers to is pregnancy. *"Susu"* is Jamaican for gossip, and in this context refers to the fear of a girl child becoming the object of other people's gossip.

Marlon is sixteen years old. Beatrice raised him as a single mother, giving him a brother only four years ago. An asthmatic child, she protected him from overexertion, and took him to the hospital for emergency treatment when he needed it. As an activist, Beatrice often took Marlon, when only three or four years old, to her meetings. As a result, both mother and son are very close and communicate well with each other.

"We maybe would be closer, if he was a girl. The closeness more necessary when yu have girl children. It [is] very important to know where yu girl child is and who she is with. The idea of a girl on the street is not as acceptable, so people make greater effort to keep in their daughters. Boys are expected to be tougher and slightly safer."

But Marlon is a boy. From what he told us, she went to great lengths to focus his mind on studying. Now totally preoccupied with sixth form in high school, he explains that the reason why he is not on the corner like other young males in the community like himself is because he is different.

"I don't see myself as the typical youth. [The typical youth] . . . is like the stereotype we hear about every day. Dem involve in some negative or violent or unhealthy activity. They rebellin' against society, against the rule, the laws, yu know. But [the] main reason I am not on the corner, too, is because I personally just not interested. I mean, I play basketball on the road wit' dem-guys every now and again, yes. But I really don't have time to waste. Once yu hang out on the corner, dat mean se yu doomed to be a failure, yu know. Is jus' dat most yout' on the corner want easy money, and want plenty material things to profile. They are very easy to get influenced the wrong way. Most of them are school age and out of school, and they see plenty example of people who not schooled and who are dons, or rich, or whatever. Most of them feel that work, any kind of work, is too hard."

Marlon's characterization of youths on the street is of people who are easily influenced into breaking the laws of society, which they will do in order to get the clothes and other material things they need, in order to "profile". As for himself, he knows the youths on the corner may not respect or admire him now, "but when Marlon make it and have a good job and car and house and successful life, they will think, 'Bwaai, Marlon is a yout' who me respec', blaa-blaa, etc. But my mother respect me – she may not say it to *my* face in so many words, but she is proud of her big son, and that is good enough!" Thus, Beatrice has no problems keeping Marlon off the street. "My mother done win that struggle already. I am home most of the time. I come from school late sometimes, but I really don't hang out on the streets."

According to Marlon, the main difference between himself and the youths he describes as *"typical"* lies in the use he makes of education, as against the use they make of unlawful activities, to achieve the respect of others. He then goes on to offer what he considers responsible for bringing about that difference.

"I definitely think there is a link between closeness with your parents or family and your outcome as a young man. Especially if you are fully into your school work. If and when I get a *family,* that will be a very important thing to *me* – the closeness, the spending time together, the sharing, the discussion. I think the children and your type of friends also make a difference. Even if you don't go to church yourself, you find that church people are often nice to associate with. I don't think [however] that school plays such a very important part. School has negative and positive. Some of the boys on the corner are in school and are still into badness."

He identifies closeness with parents and the *"type of friends"*, including *"church people"*, as two very important factors. School, as such, he does not credit in this regard.

The Father's Role

One of the most important roles of a father is establishing the kind of control over his children that prevents them from falling into "badness". This is what Motowners refer to as *discipline*. And the main instrument fathers are expected to use is flogging. A father does not have to flog often; indeed, it is the threat of flogging that he exercises, for example by a stern look. But when he does flog, it is severe, *"wicked"*. For this reason, fathers rarely flog girls – it is the mothers who do. If they have to flog girls, they are not as hard on them as they are on boys. Mothers use flogging as one of many forms of discipline (other forms being scolding, denial, confinement to the yard), but it is not considered as severe as when fathers flog. In families where the father is absent, mother's brother or mother's "big" (eldest) son substitutes.

The older people in Motown blame the current decline in moral standards and lack of control over the young to a decline in flogging. The kind of flogging that was used to keep them in check is today called "child abuse", but it was effective. "When dem out of order, I scold them. Yeah, man! Slap dem wicked, too! If I didn't do that, is pure criminal I would have." Flogging as a corrective measure is a commonly held idea among the older people. Too many parents nowadays, they argue, resort to telling their children badword, and when they do flog, it is much more abusive, "beating the children for half an hour or more. One cannot half-murder children. You must have some feeling. These young parents like to talk about 'modern times', but sometimes it's useful to listen to the older heads. *Old story bring up new answer.*"

Generally speaking, fathers avoid expressing similarly warm affectivity mothers show towards their children, for example hugging. Not only is it not in keeping with the ideal of toughness that should be a part of the character of the male, but as I have said about fathers bathing daughters, warm father-daughter touching is suggestive of incest. In father-son relations hugging is suggestive of homosexuality. One of our seed group discussants, revealed that she instructed her son to report to her anyone who *touched his bottom*. "If him father wipe him bottom, as me come in him tell me, because me tell him se 'Anybody touch yu bottom yu must tell me!' Me serious 'bout it, y'know!' "

Of even greater importance than disciplinarian is the role of a father as provider. In fact, the latter provides the legitimacy of the former. In an interview we asked Marlon about his father.

"Me and *my* father now, we have what I would call a financial relationship. When I need to discuss new school fees or money to do some special thing are the times when I see him. If I had a problem? Hah! He would be the last person I would go to, to talk about any serious or personal thing. *We* don't have a friendship like I have with my mother." Does he love his father and wish he had this friendship? "Love him? No, I don't know him that kind of way. Well, yes, I wish we could have been more close, you know, to have *him* teach me certain things, but I don't really miss it. Well . . . Some things I learned from my mother I couldn't learn from *my* father or any other male . . . You see, the things like father teaching son to fly kite or ride bicycle and so on, is good, but most males neglect the concept of sharing, or dem just can't do it. Just the other day my mother was teaching my little brother to ride the bicycle. Most men think that 'gentle' is not macho, and that loving yu children is strictly for female."

Marlon did not grow up with his father, but he not only knows him, he has a relationship with him – a financial rather than an affective one. He wishes they could have been closer, but does not think the lack of affectivity has affected or will affect him, for men do not show love anyway. Yet, Marlon believes, closeness to a parent, more particularly a mother, since men are unable to be close, is crucial if a boy is not to succumb to the streets.

The case of Alex, Dahlia's son, provides another angle from which to view the problem of father as provider. Failure here has serious consequences for the affective relationship between a father and his child. Dahlia told us that Alex was troubled about something and she was going to take him to Webster Memorial United Church, which operated a counselling service. The boy was not behaving right, was keeping bad company, and was uncommunicative with her. The context was her telling of the difficulty she had getting child support from the fathers of her children.

"[Donald] have it on im brain. Im faada is in Canada and im say im wan' to go to Canada. Im see some of im friend wid t'ings and im would like to have it too. It is a red eye dat, still, yu know. Im see im frien'-dem getting money and t'ings from dem parents-dem a foreign, an' im faada deh a foreign for so many years an' im not achievin' – im might go put it on im brain." Dahlia said she once telephoned Donald's father's mother, his grandmother, but his father was not there. Marvalin also called and he told her he would send some money for her and Donald. When she told her brother, he said, "It come a'ready!", meaning that he knew they would not get it. He had low expectations of his father. "Yu can't tell im anyt'ing [good] 'bout im faada!" But Alex, Donald's younger brother, had expectations too. While Dahlia was away in England, Alex searched Marvalin's diary, got their father's telephone number and phoned to tell him he, Alex, "a go kill im, because im not helpin' im!" Their father came out to Jamaica, and when he called Alex, Alex did not look at him, but went inside the house and locked himself in. The father cried. Dahlia called to him to open the door and show his father respect, but he did not budge. She had "to decide mi mind and get bad" before he would open the door. His father started to talk to him. Alex told him, "Yu naa do notn fi mi. Everyday yu get up an' tell mi yu a go do dis an' dat fi mi. Yu naa sen' clothes fi mi, yu naa sen' shoes fi mi! Den, Daddy, wha' yu wan' mi fi do?" His father offered him a chain. "Mi no wan' no chain!" His father pleaded. "Alex, yu know me naa work. A mi mother a look after mi!" Alex retorted, "Wha yu go 'way fa, den? When yu deh ya [were here], yu never a min' mi, jus' mi mada alone! An' den yu gaan 'way again an' yu t'ink se me a go better, me worse. Me never even have a good pair of shoes on mi foot fi go a school. All mi frien'-dem a look an' say dat me have faada a Canada!" That was last year, 1993. Dahlia said their father had other children he supported, so "dis is what carrying di feelings". Alex often hears when the other children come over and talk about money their father sends. Marvalin is able to live with it, but Alex would get up and go through the door, head down the road and sit on a wall. Sometimes she would watch him sitting under the ackee tree alone, just talking to himself. A week following this interview, Alex had a good talk with the counsellor. He told the counsellor that he was bothered by his father's lack of support, leaving the burden on his mother alone, while supporting his other children. His behaviour, she said, had changed now that he had got it off his chest. She used to wonder what he could be talking to himself about so. "Now mi know," she said, "now mi know."

Nowhere in this story was there a suggestion that Alex, Donald and Marvalin devalued their father other than for his lack of financial support. A father's main role is to provide. When he fails in this he fails in every way, but when he succeeds he lays the basis for the kind of affective relationship Marlon regretted he did not have – which implies that Marlon's indifference would become the contempt and disrespect of Alex.

The problem bothering Alex was his father's lack of support. It also bothered his other siblings. But Alex had two reasons for his anger. One was the unfair burden this irresponsible behaviour forced on his mother. Even at fourteen years old, he is conscious of the hardships she undergoes singlehandedly. He is stung by the attention he sees his father give to his other set of siblings, and recalls that it was precisely to be able to support them that his father migrated, but instead of being better his own condition has got worse. The migration, then, was useless.

In one of our mixed core group discussions, a male discussant expressed the view that a man's duty was to mind the child he fathered. Then he explained why he felt so strongly about it. "My father have seventeen pikni, and him no min' none! If him never dead, me woulda kill him! If him never dead, bwaai! Because no him go out go get woman and breed woman? So why when dem get pregnant him run leave them? He was more than in a position to maintain them, but him run leave all. So if him never dead, me woulda kill him myself, and me tell my mother everyday se if him never dead me kill him!"

Anger and resentment of son towards father derives not from his role as a disciplinarian, but from dereliction of his role as provider. In the discussion both men and women expressed gratitude to their own fathers for the severe flogging, while, according to both male and female golden-agers, their children say they are thankful for the strict upbringing. Thus, the flogging a child receives does not in later life become a source of resentment. But a provider's wilful neglect does.

Alex's other source of anger was his consequent inability to uphold his standing in the eyes of his peers. As Dahlia recalls it, Alex told his father that he lacked a good pair of shoes to wear to school, yet all his friends referred to the fact that his father was in Canada. Alex's school attendance was threatened not because his shoes were worn out or his clothes tattered. Rather, his embarrassment derived from the failure of his father to support him with the name-brand shoes and, presumably, clothing, befitting his status as a boy whose father now lives in a wealthy country. Pressure from the peer group and wider community is an important factor shaping the role-expectation of good fathering. The kind of lifestyle demanded by many young males cannot be supported other than through connections with relatives abroad. According to some of our informants, the fact that many youths do have such connections explains why they, although unemployed, are able to function without any evidence of distress. But some are prepared as well to support themselves through what Marlon called "easy money".

A Peer Group

The barrel connection, according to Everton, is what allows a group of youths to engage in round-the-clock domino-playing. Everton is a thirty-year-old body-man at a garage on Spanish Town Road. He lives in Motown's west end.

Saturday night. As I walked towards Farm Row, I could see and hear the place coming alive: shops open for business; music; youths playing, adults standing at gates; bicycle riding; domino games. Bay Road was alive with music, domino, gambling, youths getting their hair cut at a gateway; three youths dressing themselves inside another gate. On Distant Avenue, Sharon's Lounge was open for business, but the area was dead – no music; three men were sitting inside. Turning on to Darliston Crescent, music was blasting from three locations – one was Ludlow's Mobile Shop, where about fifteen youths were playing or watching a game of dominoes, well-dressed and profiling in dance-hall style clothes. I stopped here. I tried engaging the youths in conversation, but the game was too exciting for them to miss a play. However, Everton was willing to talk, so we sat on the wall near Ludlow's shop, while Ludlow's music box pumped away dance-hall music and the matey rhythm. Those youths playing domino, he told me, were playing from about 9:00 this morning. "They tek turn, and tek a walk, but return soon after. Sometime they play for money, like mos' of today." The time was about 10:30 p.m., so that they would have been playing for over twelve hours. When we started talking, I counted fifteen youths, ranging between fifteen and twenty-five years old. An hour later I counted twenty. For the three or so hours we chatted, over thirty different youths stopped by the game. Everton said that it was like this most Friday and Saturday nights. "Most of these boys don't want to work. They are lazy and they don't have a trade." Most of them, he said, went to high school. Everton said that many families in Motown have some relatives abroad. The family members here depend on their relatives abroad to send out clothes and money for them, especially name-brand fashion shoes and clothes. Mainly on the weekends, they dress in these and profile in the community. These shoes and clothes are very expensive and if they were to work, they could not maintain themselves and their gifts from abroad would stop. "So they don't risk that. They don't trouble anyone, as far as I know, but if they stop get things from abroad they may start t'ief and rob people."

The males described here are, clearly, friends. They constitute a peer group, whose members span an estimated age range of ten years, from mid-teens to mid-twenties. This is most important from the socialization point of view. At fifteen, most would have had their first sex already and become sexually active, and at twenty-five would have already borne a child or two. A peer group like this also serves as a socializing medium for its younger members, who by running errands legitimize their presence within the group. While purchasing a drink in a shop we observed the following:

One lady came in and bought seasoning and some Chinese sauce. She was followed by another woman who bought half-a-chicken. It was afternoon and they were clearly looking after the evening meal. Then a young boy about twelve years old came in and bought two rizlas (ganja splif wrappers) and some Craven A cigarettes. You could tell by how he wrapped them back up in the paper and held them that they were for someone he respected. Next came a girl of about sixteen years old and she bought a pack of sweet biscuits. She probably was just passing – I cannot imagine a big girl like her leaving her yard just to buy a pack of biscuits; she'd send some smaller child. Another young boy the same age as the first came in and he bought two bottles of Dragon stout. After they were opened, he took one and knocked back the top of the other, so that whoever was to get it, would get it with the top firmly on.

The services provided by these two boys give them the privilege of hanging around the older youths, who, it is reasonable to assume, sent them, and from whom they learn the habits and manners of adult males. Rizlas are used to build splifs of ganja spiced with some tobacco. It is not too much to conjecture that before long they will themselves be rolling and smoking splifs, and, if they have parents in foreign countries, profiling in name-brand clothes. In research carried out some years ago among students at a secondary school in Kingston, we found that older members of the peer group who were Rastafari acted as socializing agents in determining the positive attitudes of the students towards the Rastafari religion. Those students who had no Rastafari members in their peer groups generally reflected the views held by the wider society about the Rastas (Chevannes 1981). A similar pattern of older members of peer groups transmitting knowledge and attitudes was also found in a later study of sexual behaviour among Jamaican men (Chevannes 1986). The older, seemingly "more experienced" members become role models and sources of authoritative knowledge for the younger members in the warm face-to-face circle of the peer group.

Friday and Saturday nights are the profiling nights, when the youths described above by Everton dress up and occupy the streets. Many of them are unemployed, according to Everton, and are not interested in working. Beatrice confirms that a large number of the youths hanging out on the streets do not work, but where Everton considers them as having gone to high school, she describes most of them as primary school drop outs. Being unemployed they are unable to support their lifestyle other than through the remittances in cash and kind sent by their relatives abroad. Given common practice in other communities, remittances in kind are occasional, perhaps at Christmas time, while remittances in cash are more frequent, giving rise since the 1980s to a number of companies that offer wire transfer services (see Chevannes and Ricketts 1996). Before that money came through the mail.

One effect brought about by the dependence on remittances is the idolization of "foreign": Canada or America. The following excerpts from our fieldnotes bring this out. They also bring out two important vital principles nourishing the male bonding of the peer group, namely Motowners' aversion to homosexuality, and the importance of commensality.

Cedarwood Corner. As I approached Cedarwood, I could see a group of youths on the corner. Some walked away as I stopped and sat with them, as usual. David got up and said he was hearing a vibe, "but me naa say anyt'ing". What kind of vibe? He looked away, saying, "Bwaai, me naa say!" The rest looked at me, then at each other. Then Norbert said, "Bwaai, me a hear dat unu [you] a batty-bwaai from university. A yout' from round Cayman Crescent say im know unu, an unu an' Mr McDonald and Fatman a frien'. Im see unu wid dem a move iina di community, an' dem a university man-dem, too." David asked if Mr McDonald, Fatman and I were not friends. I first met McDonald in the community, I told him. He asked if I didn't know him from university, and when I told him no, he asked, "Den a who know im from university?" He then questioned me about Fatman. When I insisted I did not know who Fatman was, he promised to show me one of these days. James then said, "Bwaai, look 'ow me a move wi' di man [you], an' now me a hear dat im a one a dem!"

What was all this about? The Cedarwood corner youths knew of the research project and had already given views on man-woman relation-ships and children. Now, on this visit, they claimed they had evidence that we were seen associating with two Motown homosexuals, Mr McDonald and Fatman.

If I stayed long enough, David and Norbert said, I would be shown the youth who said so. "But, if a mistake di man a mek, den a so! If a no so, bwaai, yu life coulda iina danger, because we no like dem-ting deh roun' ya! [If the man is mistaken, so be it! If he isn't, your life could be in danger, because around here we do not approve of such things!]" David said I defended myself well, and furthermore did not look like one. "If yu a one, we will know! If yu no one, we will know! So, everyt'ing cool, seen? But cool off from di corner for a while. Anyhow, gi' me a money fi buy a Dragon!" Another youth asked for a "drinks money". I gave them $70 to share. "A money dis?" they asked. David then said, "If man no have money like 400 to a t'ouzn dollar, im mus'n come on di corner, cause im mus' know se man-an'-man [we all] a go expec' a ting. Look 'ow much a we out ya! All we a do out ya is look we a look it, yu know. So, when yu a come, yu hafi come fi leggo some good t'ing."

Our life could be in danger, they told us, implying that they killed homosexuals, though they had evidently done nothing to either McDonald or Fatman, both of whom they claimed to know were. But it was the association with homosexuals they would have none of, lest they too be branded homosexuals. And so, the minute we moved to sit with them, some got up and left. Hostility towards homosexuality and the fear of being contaminated by homosexuals were themes encountered during the research. In early April, seven male teenagers were overheard teasing one of their peers about behaving like a batty man. In May, a young man who had just reproved his friend, saying that *"man mus'n go on so over man!"* went on to explain that while viewing a televised DJ performance his peer had *"jump up an' scream an' rub up imself wid im han'-dem"*, like a girl. Also in the same month, a candidate's effort to garner support for the appointment of a Justice of the Peace was aborted because one of the candidates was, according to one of our informants, known as a batty man. These were chance observations arising out of casual contacts in Motown.

The group was not afraid of revealing a parasitic side, for after urging us to *"cool off from the corner"*, they quite suddenly and unexpectedly turned to begging, complaining that the money was too small, that they were expecting anywhere from between $400 to $1,000. The rationale they gave was that we already knew that they were on the corner because they were *"looking it"*, meaning looking out how to make a living. Seventy dollars was not good enough from someone coming from outside to learn from them. It is possible, however, that the sudden demand was a ploy to discourage us from moving in their circle.

The youth who had asked for the "drinks money" suddenly jumped up saying, "Bwaai, A coulda rob a man now!" He was on the look out to see where the barrels were going. "Once a man come dung" [from America], "especially if a barrel come too, im mus' have valuable t'ings under dem bed, under dem mattress. Some a dem carry VCR –whole 'eap a money yu can get fi dat. Dem all 'ave US dollar!"

This kind of talk continued for over twenty minutes. Thus did the question of the barrel and America arise, but in the context of the expression of a desire to commit robbery. It is questionable that by saying all this for us to hear they intended to be taken seriously, but we later found out that they had a reputation for *"badness"*; they had, according to our informants, the power to prevent anything they did not approve of from taking place inside that section of the community. The fieldnotes continued:

They also expressed their interest in going to America, because things were better there, while *"notn a gwaan ya"*. They cited youths whom they *"use to give a money to"* years ago, who got the opportunity ahead of them to go to America. One came out the other day, and "di yout' rent a car. If yu see di yout' clothes an' di tings him have on! Di yout' look good! An' over thousand dollar him leggo! A so we wan' fi stay!" "If only I coulda get there," one of them said. I turned to him, "What the youth does in the States?" They looked at one another. One of them said, "It no matter! Di yout' a mek it! But yu see when I get there? Me a do everyt'ing fi no mek dem deport *mi!*" Another butted in, "Yu see as a man leave out, im start mek it! Me? Me naa come out!" "Why wouldn't you come out?" I asked him. "How me fi come out? Me have fi have somet'ing fi come out! Like a job, or good money! Yu no see that people iin ya deh ya because dem kyaan do better?" [Don't you see that people remain here because they can't do better?]"

It does not matter what one does when one reaches America. As long as one gets there, one can make it, even if one has to sell drugs. This was the meaning behind the looks they gave one another when asked what this successful youth did for a living. In fact, so boundless are the opportunities for success that as soon as a man leaves out he begins to make it, and his success will be measured by his ability to rent a car and to make a fashion statement on his occasional visit home. This was the thinking behind Alex's unsympathetic feelings towards his father's unemployed circumstance. The possibility of unemployment and poverty are excluded from this world view; included in it is the certainty that people remain in Motown only because they can do no better; that given the chance, they would leave.

Unemployment and the search for resources figure prominently in shaping the activities and hopes of the youths. One group, for example, utilized the skit worked out and presented by our animation team at the entry event to *"raise some breads"*. The play depicted a young schoolgirl, who names three boys as responsible for her pregnancy. According to Max, one of the group members, they presented it several times and are hoping to improve on it for a bigger promotion. Bringle, his friend, explained their motivation as *"job is a hard t'ing to get"*.

While their common unemployed circumstance seems uppermost in the minds of these corner youths, the corner provides them with space for male bonding. The events on Monday, 4 July brought this out. On the corner were Jack, Mullings (Buju), Dale, Nellie, Singer and one or two others. Other members moved through, but at no time were there more than nine persons, one or two of them females.

Buju introduced me to Nellie. She is his babymother, he jokingly said, but he can set me up if I like her. "Wha' yu say, Nellie?" Nellie looked at me and smiled, but "cut" her eyes at Buju. She has two children whom she left at home cleaning the floor. Her babyfather does not help, she tells me, and she alone has to use her head to hustle to mind them. She was a student at St Andrew Technical High school when she got pregnant. All of a sudden, the streets were crowded with males pouring out of their yards, shouting, "Goal! Goal! Send di bitches out!" They were referring to the United States, who were playing Brazil in the World Cup. Within twenty seconds the streets were clear again. Three more joined the corner, saying it made no more sense to watch the match, because with Brazil scoring, "it done". One of them asked, "How di food? Unu naa run boat? [How's the food? Aren't you all cooking?]" They asked me to support the effort. I contributed $100. An argument over "dry food" versus "cook food" was settled in favour of cooked food. Next, the question of who would do the cooking was raised. Someone suggested Nellie; she took the money and left.

"Run boat" is an urban expression among young males for group cooking and eating. Members of the peer group contribute what they have, purchase the food and go cook and eat. "Dry food" refers to food that requires no cooking, for example buns, biscuits, crackers, bread, even if there is also included some form of precooked tinned meat or fish. In the folk culture dry food is considered light, insubstantial and not as nutritious. Here Nellie was chosen to buy the stuff, foods like yam, green banana, callaloo and flour to make dumplings. Nellie was the only female around at the time the decision was taken to "run boat", and so chances were the task would have fallen to her. She had barely disappeared when Dale raised an objection he had suppressed while she was present.

"Unu a go eat from her?" A youth asked why. Dale replied, "Unu never go a her yard an' see how she live? Unu can eat it, but me naa eat it!" Dale explained that he went by her yard one day only to see them defecating under the ackee tree, and the children playing nearby. "Ackee all [could have] drop iina di shit and dem wash it off an' cook it! Dem nasty! Unu never know?" Buju expressed surprise. James reminded them that he had proposed buying dry food. Amos laughed and walked away, saying, "Me no wan' none!" Why didn't he stop us, we asked Dale. He was trying, he explained, by insisting we should buy dry food, because he did not want to embarrass her in front of the group. "We good fi get di food wid shit a float iina it an' yu t'ink a gravy!" Everyone laughed. "What are we going to do about it now?" I asked. Buju suggested taking it from her and cooking it ourselves. I pointed out that she had money in it, so it was decided to give her some and take the rest. Nellie returned from shop and placed the food – yam, green banana, fresh fish, seasoning – between my legs. I was sitting on the ground with my legs stretched apart. The youths looked at me and laughed. She also laughed. Then they told her they were going to split the food and cook their portion themselves. She asked me why, and I looked towards the youths. One of them said, "Dat alright! Cool!" Nellie looked at us, smiled and said OK. She then left to do her own cooking. Buju, who agreed to cook at his house, took ours and left.

The notes describe arrangements made by the Cedarwood corner group for cooking. But in it we also glimpse certain male attitudes and values. First, along with the commensality of the "boat" comes the idea of purity. Nellie, the only female, is the contaminating source, not because of her sex but because of her alleged unhygienic domestic situation. *"Dem nasty"* was the phrase Dale used, labelling Nellie's entire domestic grouping. But at the same time, Dale did not raise the matter in her presence, not wanting to embarrass her. There is no reason to believe he could not have, but it is not clear whether her gender or her poverty accounted for his silence. Evidently, he did not think the matter sufficient to force a dissociation. Nellie remains a part of the group, but somewhat marginal. The overall effect was the strengthening of the bonds between the male members of the corner.

Conclusion

Motown, a blue-collar community, exhibits strong features of social stability combined with tendencies towards social instability. Within this context, the successful socialization of children and adolescents is a major concern of parents, particularly mothers, and this is expressed in a preoccupation with keeping children in the confines of the yard and away from the harmful influences of the street. Progress in education makes the task easier. The street, however, is an arena for male socializing and bonding, and socialization through the peer group. This pattern is noticeably similar to the male bonding activities in the Indian community of Overflow, except, of course for the tabooed presence of females on the streets, not to mention in the bars and other male socializing spaces. Although Motown girls may be seen recreating in the streets, it is the males who dominate, both by their numbers and the types of activities. For the female girl child, the principal danger posed by the streets is sexual conquest by males and pregnancy.

Motown construction of masculinity is built partly upon a strong anti-homosexual foundation, notwithstanding the strong practice of male peer group bonding. We did not encounter any similar homophobic concern in Overflow, despite the strength of patriarchy and male dominance in Indian culture, both in the domestic and the public spheres. There, the path to achieving masculine identity is clearly delineated, its main outlines being patrilineality, marriage, virilocal and patrilocal residence, headship, birth preference and so on. Overflow youths' main concern is how to accumulate enough wealth to have a "bamboo wedding", for a man is not fully a man until he marries. If we are correct about this, homophobia is not a function of strong male dominance per se. Could it be a function of weak male identity? As it surfaces strongly in the next chapter, it will be necessary to return to this point.

7

Joetown

We begin the journey into Joetown with an excerpt from notes entered nearing the very end of our fieldwork.

I stopped by the college to gather my thoughts on the areas I needed more information on. Two boys who were playing on the football field came over. They said they knew me, and I too recognized them from the community. One of them begged me my box of orange juice. I tried engaging them.

    "Suppose someone told you you were raised like a gyal pikni, how would you feel?"

    "You mad, sa?" the little black one asked. He was eleven years old. The thirteen-year-old, fair-skinned one, a student at Camperdown High, apparently found my question beneath his dignity. His retort was simple. *"Who, me?"*

    "But girls and boys are raised quite similar – only few differences," I played for an angle.

    "Sir, you really did need the orange juice! Gas must be in your head!" I laughed and asked them to tell me the differences in how boys and girls were raised, for I needed the information for the university. I took out my notebook. We sat on the wall for some two hours as they gave me difference after difference, but I managed very little note-taking because I was too amazed that such young kids could have such knowledge. Such interesting information, however, is not easily forgotten. The following is a fairly accurate summary of their most important points.

1.   "A bwaai don't wear frock, so im kyaan raise like girl!", said G-G, the thirteen-year-old. I was very rude, or my statement was. The fact that a girl wears a frock makes her different, he repeated. But how?

"Why yu think girls wear pants? Is because dem want fi look wicked like man. Is not only because dem want show dem shape!" The little dark one, Besbes, agreed and pointed out that anytime a girl wears vest, cap, pants and dem tings like bwaai, she rough!".

2.   Girls stay home, while boys "naa do dat!' said Besbes. Why? "'Cause girls can help mother more than bwaai – cook, wash and dem tings." Thirteen-year-old G-G added, "They must learn housework, 'cause dem going have to have dem own house later."

I butted in here. "So you not goin' have your own house later?"

"Yeh! But me going get a lady. You know, too, y'know!" I asked him to explain what he meant by "You know". It was obvious, he explained, that if his wife had the baby she would take care of the house. I was honestly shocked to find a thirteen-year-old associate having the baby and caring for it with actively running the house, a viewpoint I had found among men as well as women in the community. Since the woman has the child, she must have more to do with raising it, which means housework.

"So a boy shouldn't learn to do housework?"

"Yeh! But him no have to! If him learn, that good still. But if im don't, a no notn!"

"But if a girl don't learn housework . . . ?" I asked.

"Matey tek 'way her man!" It was Besbes who spoke and laughed. Immediately they started singing the DJ hit, "Matey a no Good Sinting"

"So you never hear about women who can't wash or cook?"

"Yeh!" said G-G, "but that a girl who grow up with gold spoon in her mout'. *Me* no want a girl like dat! Me wi' tek her for her money, but me want a girl who can cook and wash and clean."

3.   "A girl will trace a girl, y'know," said G-G, "just run off her mout' like she see her mother and aunt and other women do. A boy, now, im fight fi the slightest little thing. But if me and my brethren fight, now, two-two's we a brethren again. A so we grow!"

4.   At this point Besbes said he did not know any more differences, but G-G insisted, "Plenty more deh, man!" They thought for a while, and G-G jumped up. "A girl mature quicker than a bwaai, but the bwaai do it quicker!" Besbes was embarrassed. He got off the wall and walked away. I called him back and reassured him that he could tell me anything. They told me that a boy was sexually active by the age of ten, while the girl could not do that, "'cause her parents wi' shame! Nobody no want a man say im daughter a whore, and worse, go breed early!" Besbes told me. A boy gets the chance to do this, however, G-G added, because he has more "free time on di road, and nuff time a bigger man set im up 'pon a beef!"

Now I had to be very direct. "Yeh! Three times," said G-G. He and two other boys did it to a sixteen-year-old girl for money, when he was eleven years old. He had gone without lunch for several days saving up his money. Besbes said he did it only once, and gave the details: in the old house on Harker's Road with the twelve-year-old girl who lived in the old broken-down house on his street.

"Who teach you guys about sex?"

"Nobody don't have to teach a man how to do that!" G-G said. He had heard that a woman had to learn, but it was natural for a man to have sex. I asked him where he had learned that and was told in his uncle's bar. He even learned that women sometimes say "No", when they mean "Yes", " 'cause they want to test your manness".

"You mean that if a girl said no to you, you would hold her and take it?" I asked.

"It depends. If she always a behave like she want it and then say no, you hol' her and kinda force her!"

"Suppose she was only teasing you and just did not want to do it?"

"A man can know, man!" Then he turned on me. "Don't you know when a woman want you?"

"Yes," I said, "but I am old enough to know." He disagreed. "Even from this age me can know!"

"What about you, Besbes? Who teach you 'bout dem tings?" Besbes said he learned from his big brothers, and from his friends at school and on the street. 5.   One more difference, I begged. Besbes told me that girls learn from early to "tek' way a yout' money". He related how a girl conned him of his $20. She told him she would give him a kiss and maybe more, but he got nothing. When he told his brother, his brother said, "A so uman tan [women are like that]! Jus' money dem interested in!" He advised him not to retaliate, as he could still get her one day.

"But man like money, too!" I pointed out.

Yes, G-G conceded, but there is a difference. He was quite certain about this as he said it. "Most man want money fi give dem uman and mek dem feel nice!"

"But, G-G, man make money and invest it and so forth," I corrected him.

But he was adamant. "Dat is rich man. Down here so," pointing to the community", "di man-dem work fi dem uman and family!"

I told him I respected what he said and he smiled. They were anxious to go now. Some of their friends were kicking ball or retrieving balls for the young men playing. I thanked them. I remained fixed in my position for at least three minutes, just watching them. *How could two boys, one thirteen years old, the other eleven, already know so much?*

Joetown is situated in the densely populated heart of what is now called downtown Kingston. The city of Kingston now comprises the parish of Kingston, the capital of Jamaica, and the urbanized section of the parish of St Andrew surrounding it. Only two square miles in area, the parish of Kingston was once the main centre of commerce, banking and political activity, besides being the site of several residential communities (Clarke 1975). The focus of these operations has shifted northwards into neighbouring St Andrew, where New Kingston is now the banking district, and Half Way Tree the leading commercial centre, and westward to Newport, the main port.

For several decades now, St Andrew has replaced Kingston as the parish of urban population growth; now the adjacent parish of St Catherine is replacing St Andrew. Thus, the Kingston Metropolitan Area comprises all of Kingston, all of the flat parts of St Andrew and the Portmore part of St Catherine. What is left of the parish of Kingston are the markets, informal and formal retail trading targeted at low-income earners, and dilapidated buildings abandoned by their owners but now housing the poor and the destitute. This is *"downtown"*. Roughly speaking, downtown today is the parish of Kingston, while *"uptown"* is anywhere above Cross Roads and Half Way Tree in St Andrew. Uptowners regard downtown as a place to be avoided, because of political and gang-related violence; many young uptown dwellers born since the 1970s have never been there. Downtowners have mixed feelings about uptown. On one hand, uptown is where the snobs and the scornful, who stereotype downtowners, live; on the other hand, it is the symbol of achievement, the place downtowners aspire to live one day. Even Motown, though not part of the mental space called "uptown", is better than "downtown".

If you live downtown, you live among people who know "right from wrong" but practise the art and science of survival more. Chances are, particularly if you are a young man, you will never get a job uptown by giving your correct address, unless as a security guard. You stand a better chance of riding the underground railroad to the Bronx or Brooklyn and to a fantasized future than riding the bus uptown to Graham Heights. Yet downtown has its peculiar attractions for some uptowners, particularly men. Downtown is where one finds the cutting edge in Jamaica's music culture, where dance-hall fashion statements originate, the Jamaican patois acquires new words and expressions, where men come to have a *"good slam* [sex] *from a ghetto gyal"*. On any evening after work in Joetown, one may see the BMWs and Camrys parked beside the bars and prostitution houses. Many absent Joetown fathers are actually from uptown.

The community we call Joetown comprises seven streets and lanes running north–south for four large city blocks, and five streets running east–west. In the city blocks on the eastern side is concentrated more than half of Joetown's population, while the buildings in the western half and on the southern boundary house small-scale commercial establishments and government departments. There are over thirty rum bars, thirty small grocery shops, fifteen workshops, six race-horse betting shops and six beauty salons, scattered throughout the community, but with a concentration in the eastern half.

Though old, the buildings tend to be solid concrete structures, showing a coat of paint no more recent than four years old. Some, recently renovated, look quite good. The dwelling houses, on the other hand, are quite dilapidated, some showing the ravages of time and natural disasters. From one of our key informants we learn that only six buildings have been constructed since 1951, the year Hurricane Charlie struck.

Roughly 80 percent of dwelling houses are tenement yards, mostly owned by people living somewhere uptown and visiting to collect rent every month. A small tenement yard will comprise one large house or two small ones, home to between ten or fifteen people. A very large one will have either one extremely large house or several medium to fairly large ones. We gathered that two of these each had over forty-five persons living there. In between the small and large tenement yards are those comprising two or three small houses and housing fifteen to twenty-five people. A few family houses may still be found, some above a grocery store or bar and housing its family members.

To see where Joetown people dwell from the outside is one thing; to see them from the inside is quite another: well-kept, if run-down rooms, well-furnished with chests of drawers, buffets, stereos, televisions, videos and other appliances, floors immaculately shined or carpeted, walls decorated with religious pictures and plaques – the dwellings of struggling but proud people.

The People

According to the 1982 census, 3,000 people lived here. Making a rough calculation, with the assistance of four key informants over a period of three days, we estimated approximately 2,500 people, a decline consistent with demographic trends. Informants support our estimate by pointing to the number of people who emigrated, moved out, have been imprisoned or died, without much in-migration taking place.

One convenient way of classifying the people who comprise Joetown is to do so by age. We found that age correlated in some respects with function. Beginning with the elderly, we found that the most important role played by the old women was looking after infants, walking them to and from the basic school or church inside the community. Some set up small food stalls outside their gates, where they sit and wait for the occasional buyer. For recreation they take up seat by the gate on a stool, a small bench, or the upturned bottom of a bucket, just looking out or holding an occasional conversation. The old men, by contrast, may be found either at home or at the bar. At home they help with the younger children or read the newspaper; at the bar they partake in a drink and socialize with friends. A few are known gamblers.

The main breadwinners are the middle-aged women and men, no longer youthful but definitely not old. A number of the women are food vendors at their own gates, on the street or at the school gates, but most seem to be domestic helpers, janitors, store clerks, higglers in the market and owners of small businesses, all of whom have gainful occupations that take them outside Joetown. Those who are not employed may be found at home washing and performing various domestic chores. Their male counterparts are artisans, construction and public sector workers, who also make the daily trek outside the community.

The youth, adolescent and young adult, make up the largest section of the unemployed. This is the population of Joetown that is most into the informal sector, which, for the women, spans a range from hairdressing and informal commercial importing to gambling, prostitution and, we were informed, trafficking in ganja and hard drugs. We were propositioned many times. Three of those we met from this age group bore the disfiguring traces of acid burns, the retribution for "stealing" another woman's man or the wounds from a "tracing match", that is the publicly conducted quarrel between two women.

A large percentage of the men in this age group may be seen in the mornings going to, and in the evenings coming from, work, but an equally large portion are unemployed. These are at the core of the gambling, which seems to be a major form of activity in Joetown, and other illegal activities. When not gambling, some sit idly by their gates, walk aimlessly, play football or basketball in the street, listen to music from a cassette player or make their own. Only when hands are needed to unload the occasional ship do they work. This is the group from which the drug dealers, pimps, pickpockets or *teka* [takers], thieves and a handful of male prostitutes may be found. Once one gets to know Joetown, one can distinguish between the genuinely idle and drug pushers. The *teka-dem* usually travel in threes, for foiling and defence, targeting buses and other crowded gatherings like cricket at Sabina Park or football at the National Stadium. We actually witnessed a young man showing a fourteen-year-old boy how to *tek* from a pocket. A few are deportees, feared for their notoriety. Said one to a teenager, *"Yu a notn fi me kill yu, an' yu know dat, 'cause me kill nuf idiot like yu a 'ready!* [It takes nothing for me to kill you, and you know it! I have killed many other 'idiots' like you, already!]" Some deportees are believed to have brought back the tabooed practice of homosexuality.

The deportees are not the only signs of American presence in Joetown. Basketball is immensely popular among the young people, and many of the names are replicas of famous American teams and players. For fashionable clothes, there are the expensive LA Light™ footwear, sweat suits, Patrick Ewing™ T-shirts and gold chains. Only through remittance, theft or hard drugs can a man *"dress like Mr America"*, as one of our informants put it, and deck out his girlfriend the same way. "They live in a fantasy world – USA means little sweat, plenty money and easy life. USA is like name brand. Every yout' have fi identify himself with New York, or im naa say notn!" If they do reach the United States, they find easy work – "drugs and thief". When they return home, "dem don't want to work, dem run the place hot!"

In Joetown sex is discussed openly by men and women, but by young men in language reflecting the more violent aspects of ghetto life. To have casual sex with a woman is to *stab it, to murder her wid love, to kill it, to kill her wid agony*. Early initiation is normative. One mother was upset with her fourteen-year-old daughter, calling her *"stupid"*, not for getting pregnant but for bad timing that was going to cost her a whole year out of school; waiting for a few months, she would have missed only half the school year and been able to return the following September. Prostitution, generally female, but on a small scale also male, is regarded as a form of hustling, tolerated but despised.

Gambling is a round-the-clock, week-long activity. A mainly male activity, it takes place non-stop, on the street corners, in the yards. A serious activity, it receives the undivided attention of its players. Men are at their inhospitable worst when gambling. They must never be interrupted. Ludo is a popular gambling game, and several Ludo clubs may be found in the community.

The area is also known for its gangs, though it is not what could be called a garrison community, like two other adjacent areas. As mentioned in chapter six the term *garrison* was applied by the late Carl Stone (1980), a political scientist of the University of the West Indies, to those politically monolithic communities and constituencies controlled by armed paramilitary gangs belonging to either of the two major political parties. Young males, on reaching adolescence, run the grave risk of being drawn into the underworld of hard drugs, gun-toting, robbery and other crimes. Guns, easily available, as elsewhere in the inner city communities, bark from time to time.

Because of the poor quality of housing in the area, its crime-ridden nature and high unemployment, we found no resident with anything resembling pride in their community. Quite the opposite: shame of living there, and the desire to escape was the prevailing emotion. A few are nevertheless proud that the ghetto produces outstanding people, athletes, professionals, leaders, who, despite the odds, or perhaps because of it, rise and achieve national fame.

The log of visits to the community by one of our animators over a three-month period reads as follows:

June 18   Visit aborted due to gunshots
June 22   Information that "war" will soon break out
June 26   Community very tense

June 29   Community still tense
June 30   Fire in a large tenement yard; some of our informants homeless
July 4   Tension very high; residents give views on violence
July 6   Shootout; had to seek refuge in a yard
July 8   Another shootout
July 17   Visit hairdresser to get insight into the happenings
July 31   Peace dance; peace dance shot up
Aug 3   Community very tense
Aug 9   Planned meeting aborted due to stone throwing
Aug 14   Shootout; my hairdresser shop informant shot on the corner; one
          dead, four injured; community very tense
Aug 20   Tension still high
Aug 24   Phone call to community: still no-go
Sept 9   Drive-through shooting
Sept 10   People afraid to come to animation meeting
Sept 17   Hairdressing parlour broken into, second time in one week
Sept 21   Tension high; vendor shot at gate last night

Shootouts are not daily occurrences, and over the research period those were the worst three months. They were occasioned by the revival of a four-year-old feud, when a major don was killed at point blank range by a *press button*, a child-assassin. Nonetheless, as citizens of the ghetto, Joetown people know the volatility of their community, the factions, the warning signs and temperatures, the causes, and the precautionary measures to take, such as sending the children to the safety of the countryside to escape being shot or being drawn into the war by stashing or carrying guns, or by becoming gang members outright.

This is the setting in which children are socialized into ideas and values which determine how they view themselves or which govern their day to day interpersonal and social relationships. Infant boys at play in basic school express anger by verbally or in gesture threatening to shoot one another, or tease infant girls with an erect penis; they practise rolling imaginary ganja splifs; a thirteen-year-old describes himself as "a rude yout'", because he fears no one; a group of boys between eleven and thirteen years old use an abandoned house for gambling at half-past-eight in the morning – school, one of them says, is "borin' stuff", and for girls.

Most children of school age do attend school, but a large number, mainly the boys, do not. We were surprised to find so many girls over twelve years old attending high school. They may be seen bustling out early in the morning, in larger numbers than their male counterparts. A few are drop-outs, due mainly to careless or intended pregnancy. We found them sexually active but aware of contraceptives. Girls of primary and high school age are generally watched carefully by community and family members. The few we observed playing basketball up to dusk and after always had a brother or their mother close by. Those who have been unfortunate enough to fall victim to the gang rape known as *battery* – we were told of two, aged fourteen and fifteen years – carry the humiliating nickname of *Mattress*. On the whole, the girls in Joetown are noticeably clean, well-dressed and presentable when appearing in public, even when wearing their "batty riders", as some do.

A noticeably large number of Joetown boys who should be in school may be observed gambling, playing marbles or basketball, or just walking the streets. When not accepted into adult gambling circles, they create their own in abandoned houses, at the back of yards, in tracks between houses, even in the churchyards, and there gamble for marbles, elastic bands and money. Stealing is another major activity: empty bottles, school children's lunch money, people's pockets. Some are couriers and messengers for drug dealers.

The number of boys attending school is larger than the number of those who are not. Nevertheless, the two groups are indistinguishable in terms of their peer group relations. They not only mix socially, but the ranks of the drop-outs swell from time to time, as parents when faced with too little money for school send their daughters but keep back their sons. Girls thus have a greater association with schools than do boys; have less pressure to prove anything; and usually manage to graduate unless they get pregnant. Boys, on the other hand, are subject to the pressure of having to contribute to the household and to their girlfriends; of proving their manhood and heterosexual orientation; of knowing how to withstand hunger and deprivation; of learning from very early how to be tough; of being able to win and survive at all costs. Those who finish high school are generally very bright, but find getting a decent job very difficult. Many end up working as manual labourers, finding it extremely difficult if not impossible to remain untouched by the myriad illegal activities that are the trademark of the hustler and survivor.

But school is not exactly a haven. At the March PTA meeting of the all-age school, parents heard of a pencil stabbing, of a boy pushed down and getting his hand broken, of the most unpleasant badwords being used among the students, of a threat by a student to borrow *"Longman* [a known gunman] *gun"* and shoot a teacher *"through her hole"*, or of a teacher told by another student that it is because *"her man naa give her no money"*, why she is taking it out on him. Parents were visibly embarrassed.

Finally, the preschool children: there are more girls than boys attending basic school, a pattern we already observed in Grannitree. According to one basic school principal in Joetown, the girls receive better care from parents, more lunch money and attend more regularly, than the boys. Those preschool girls seen alone on the street were usually on errands, as a way of socializing them, for which parents will praise them. It was a rarity to see an infant girl unsupervised on the street. The only case observed, that of a four- or five-year-old, merited the contemptuous remark of an elderly lady that the child's parents were *"low dong"* [contemptible] for allowing her on the street alone. No such care is extended to the boys. They too run errands, but they are allowed the freedom to pull their toy trucks, wheels and skates along. Boys are noticeably more poorly clad than girls. On one of our field trips early in February, of the six little boys we passed on the streets, four had on only briefs and shirts; the other two were fully clad but barefooted. Informants confirm that from the age of four boys are expected to tidy and dress themselves, but girls are tidied and dressed by their mothers up to seven or eight years old. This is not only due to the greater care and concern expected by the community, but also because girls learn to plait their own hair much later.

At a basic school meeting early in March the male principal and two teachers complained of children using their exercise book leaves to roll splifs and stuff it with their pencils; of little boys peeping on the girls in the bathrooms and holding up their crotches; of boys wincing with pain when touched because of the welts inflicted on their bodies by their mothers; of the re-enactment by the students of the latest quarrel or fight in the lane.

Midday. Nearing the end of the street, I see six boys in an abandoned house and peep to see what they were doing. One ran, scattering the money and cards they were using to gamble with. "I am not a police! Here is my ID." "Show mi di police ID now," the leader took me on. "If me did a police yout', me 'oulda drape unu long time an' gone wid unu! [Were I a young policeman, I would have long since arrested and taken you away!]"

Three of them said they were living with only their mothers, two with grandmothers. Only one had both mother and father. What about fathers? One in prison, a second in the Bronx, a third "*mi mada don' see im since she pregnant*", and two living uptown, Cherry Gardens and Liguanea, two upper-middle-class suburbs.

Why were they not in school? Four gave the standard explanation – "*no lunch money*", "*no clothes*", one found school boring, another lied about being on holiday. Not surprisingly, of the six of them, four attend school sometimes, while the remaining two had not been in school since Grade 2 or Grade 3.

What about the sisters? One of the two with an uptown father smiled. He is about thirteen. "My sister look like she like di book. Yeh, man. She pass fi Wolmers [High School] an' mi uncle tek har. She bright. Me no bright." The Bronx-father one put in: "Yeh, man. Girls love borin' stuff." The one with both father and mother explains that when things get rough and they cannot afford to send both his sister and himself, they send her, for which he is glad. "Sometimes me tell dem fi sen har 'cause she young. Me can read." He is eleven years old.

For survival two of the boys beg on their way from school, one claiming that according to his mother it is his lunch money for the next day. Three hustle by running small errands for uptown buyers in the market, or pushing "sky-juice cart" with Juicy.

I asked them what their mothers did for a living. Two sold in shops, one vends food in the market during the day and works in a bar in the night, and two were domestic helpers. The one whose father was in prison said he didn't know what his mother did for a living. But from the giggling of the others I guessed she was probably a prostitute. He was clearly embarrassed, so I did not push the issue. Taking leave of them, I encouraged them not to give up, pointing out that many persons have made it from worse situations, but was taxed $10 by the leader of the group, with the Bronx father.

Back in the street, I paused long enough to absorb what these boys had just told me over a box of orange juice and to make some notes, before setting off again past a video shop. The owner was filing away cassettes while screening a blue movie. There seated before the video were my six little friends, all seeing blue. And the owner never even looked at me standing in the doorway with my mouth half-opened. It was nearing one o'clock.

These fieldnotes capture a number of major and recurrent themes: first, the training in risk taking provided by certain games, and, connected to these, the role of gambling and other forms of illegal activity as a way of life; second, the role of the yard, the school and the street in the construction and reproduction of ideas about gender; third, the parenting crisis facing the citizens of this inner city community; fourth, the meaning, place and management of sexuality among the people.

Risk Taking

Every form of illegal activity involves a risk. Gambling involves a double risk, that of losing and that of being caught. In Joetown, the games are primarily Ludo, dominoes, bingo, crown-an'-anchor, drop pan, horse racing and cards. Ludo is played by four persons. In it a player's fate is determined primarily by the throw of one die, sometimes two. Throwing sixes entitles the birth of one's four "men" to be born out of "Hell", one by one. Once one or more men are born, a player manoeuvres his way to "Heaven", step by step with every count thrown by the die or dice. On the way, however, one may become the object of "a kill", bumped off and unceremoniously flung back to Hell, there to languish until another throw of six procures a rebirth.

Ludo involves some element of strategy, which enables a player to dodge a kill by distancing his men from his opponents or by spacing their progress to heaven. Most often, however, whether one succeeds or not in dodging depends on sheer chance, the throw of a die. The element of strategy also allows friends to cooperate with one another. For example, one may exercise the option not to kill one of Player X's "men" as against one of Player Y's. Indeed, it is so generally expected that there will be some form of give and take, that a group of youths sometimes play a game of Ludo they aptly call *"corruption"*, in which it is every player for himself, "without mercy". The game clearly also reinforces social values.

Ludo boards often encode ideological messages, as in one depicting Jamaica as hell, "Zion" as heaven (a clear Rastafari influence; see Besson 1995), or social relationships, as in another depicting rival groups of youths. The posture and gesture with which the dice are thrown, the verbal expressions accompanying every throw, are ways of trying to influence fate.

Unlike Ludo which is only part chance, *Bingo* is entirely a game of chance, as one's fate is determined by the number picked out of a bag. But it allows for many players at one time, as many as there are cards to distribute. *Domino* is also played with four persons, but, unlike Ludo, in partnered pairs. Players, however, are not completely at the mercy of fate; it does involve personal skill. The chance element in domino is the "hand" of seven pieces that one draws blindly from out of a randomly shuffled pack. Thereafter, the outcome of the game depends on the combined skills of "reading", that is the ability to infer the pieces being held by one's opponents and one's partner, on the basis of remembering what pieces they have played up to that stage of the game, and coordination with one's partner to outplay the opponents. Domino, therefore, involves both strategy and chance. It is played with a great deal of loud, verbal expressions, including a liberal flow of badwords and physical gestures, which make the game characteristically male, and is usually watched by a coterie of friends. Domino is intensely popular throughout the Caribbean.

Crown-an'-anchor is a guessing game. The idea is to guess which face of the die (crown, anchor, diamond, spade, heart, or club) is facing up when the crown-an'-anchor man lifts the cup. Participants simply stand around and lay their bets on the symbol depicted on the crown-an'-anchor table.

Drop pan is a lottery, a game of thirty-six numbers, each number a symbol for one or more related concepts or things. Introduced by the Chinese in the early decades of the twentieth century, the game is played by a banker, or owner, who, by dropping a number in a pan, "plays" a number (see Chevannes 1989). His agents through the community sell numbers, turn in their sale to the banker and pay out to the lucky winners. Of all the gambling games we found in Joetown, this is the only one in which people's dreams and omens are interpreted to determine the numbers to buy.

Horse racing is also a daily affair, but rises in participation on Wednesdays and Saturdays, the only two days of the week for local racing at the Caymanas Park track outside the city. On the other weekdays, many betting shops receive bets on foreign horses and post results.

Finally, there are card games, simply called *Card*. Here the most popular form, the one being played by our six little boys, is *pitapat*. The chance element lies not only in the hand one gets, but also in the replenishing from the randomly shuffled pack.

In Joetown, gambling is intense and popular. When men are gambling, they do so with a concentration that brooks no interruption, as we once discovered. It does not matter that the amount of money at stake is small; it is still money. A man was stabbed to death the year previously in a fight over a few dollars. The popularity of gambling has given rise to a number of clubs whose only rationale is the playing of the game. Domino clubs are not peculiar to this community – indeed there are regionally and nationally organized competitions between clubs and teams. But the idea of a Ludo club, however, is a local one, as far as I have been able to ascertain. Club members are primarily male young adults and adolescents. The few female members are usually the girl-friends of the males. In one of our early field trips on a Sunday afternoon, we counted no fewer than twenty-five persons at one intersection in Joetown gambling *pitapat* and bingo. They were brought outdoors, according to our informant, by the Sunday closure of bars and other establishments, where the many forms of gambling take place during the week. On another Sunday afternoon we counted fourteen people at the same intersection, nine of them young men, three older men and two young women.

Except for horse racing, all these forms of gambling are illegal, all a part of the vast informal sector. Because of their petty nature (bets ranging from two- to twenty-dollar bills), they attract little or no sustained attention from the police, but remain a potential source of being picked up, especially if the police are unable to pin the bigger charges.

Our six little gamblers already know how to play pitapat; they also know it is illegal, think that they could be locked up, and know how to be on the look-out for and to escape the police. But they obviously feel quite safe gambling inside their community. Even at this young age, we are told, they learn to become couriers for the real gamblers, namely drug dealers and gunmen, savouring not so much the risk of losing but rather the possibility for gain. The following rather long excerpt from our Joetown fieldnotes describes a man of only fourteen years old, who was the same age as our six when he was drawn into the big time.

I needed to know the name and possibly have contact with one of the boys who, I kept hearing, were so bad that their mothers had to run off and leave them. I checked with Cat. I was quite surprised to find that the boy lived just around the corner. Cat warned me of how dangerous this boy could be, and especially the "big man who im spar [in close friendship] wid". I took my chances and knocked on the gate. He came out to me, after peeping through his gate. He is tall and well-built. His pants front was open, revealing a pair of underpants or shorts.

"Yes sa? A yu always a walk up an' dong dis community? Yu a police?" I explained that I was from the university and the aim of the project. He laughed and asked for my ID. Satisfied, he began speaking about school, that one day his son would go there. I asked if he had a son. He laughed.

"I'm only fourteen plus, so me no have no time fi pikni. A later business me talkin' 'bout!"

Then he wanted to know if I was checking on any and every person, or if I had come specifically to him. I pointed out that my interest for the week was to relate to the youths, not to their parents. He accepted my answer and we moved on.

"Tell me about yourself and how you were raised." Here he laughed and said that I had respect, because, although he was only fourteen, he was a man and I did not ask him how his mother raised him, " 'cause yu can see me done raise!" I was happy. I had scored.

Dali told me he was born in West Kingston and had moved to the community in 1984 at the age of four, after his father was shot and killed, even though *"di ol' man never do notn"*. He and his little brother, twelve years old, lived with his mother. She left them and went to the country sometime ago, returning only last week. But although he and his mother now lived in the same yard he now had his own room and paid his own rent. The little brother had been sent to Manchester. Dali told me of hearing that his mother was going to New York.

It became clear to me that they were not on speaking terms. Why? His mother, so he said, had thrown away some of his stuff, and "dat is nuff money, about $50,000 wo'th". He got mad and "kinda t'reaten har".

"What is the stuff?" That was his business, he retorted and went back to asking me if I was "a police". I then opened my pouch and took out my tape recorder. This frightened him terribly.

"This is a tape. If I was an informer, I would have turned it on." I showed him that he did not even know I had it. Emptying the recorder of its cassette, I invited him to feel that it was cold, telling him to keep it until the interview was over. "Now talk to me!"

Dali spoke freely about trafficking in cocaine for a man in the community, and the fact that he could be killed if the man knew he was even telling this.

He explained how he got started. Two years ago (he would have been only twelve years old), a man tried selling him some cocaine. He told the man he did not have the money to support the habit and in any case was afraid of it. The man suggested that he sell a few grams for him to get money, and this he did. Since that time, the man has been like a father to him. He even brought him women.

"A screw di firs' big uman at age thirteen! Nice, me a tell yu!"

To my query about using it he laughed. "A seller does not take the stuff! Only idiot uptown I sell to!" Sometimes he would use "a likl whorin' gyal dong di road" to make deliveries if he himself could not, since "di police woulda easier look pussy from har dan check har panty!"

He got money for school, wears the latest fashions, rides a bike, goes to Negril, the famous beach resort at the other end of the island, occasionally, and, in essence, lives big. As he spoke, I realized he was actually wearing a pair of LA Lights™. These cost close to $5,000! He had furnished his mother's house, opened a bank account and left school. The money is banked in his mother's name, so he cannot *"dis"* her. This is part of the reason he "only" roughed her up, because she can *"soak"* him up [make it bad for him]. Dali now had, he said, at least $50,000 in the account. His cut was $10,000 off every $100,000 that he and his boss sold. Clearly then, his mother was aware of his activities.

Was she afraid of him? *"Like puss!"* He told me that once he had hit her, but later gave her $10,000 in a letter to say he was sorry.

How did Dali protect himself in such a dangerous activity? He let down his trousers further to expose the *"metal"* bulging in the waist of his underpants. He told me it was a .22, assuring me that it did not even clap louder than the firecrackers the kids played with on the street. Only once he has had to use it: after his boss and he had broken into a store to get cash to buy some stock, he had to fire at the store owner. He swore he never killed the man.

"A not a murderer! An' a wan' leave dis t'ing before A have fi kill someone!" His plan was that after he patched things up with his mother, she would take him over to foreign as soon as she settled down. She was only waiting her plane fare to leave.

Dali had dropped out of St George's College in first form, not being able to take any more of school life, he rationalized. A fight with an uptown student earned him a two-weeks' suspension. He never returned. One day after that he knifed the boy in Cross Roads. His intention was to kill him, but the fear of prison restrained him:

"A love mi freedom, yu see, sar!" He thought of himself as bright and might return to school once he gets the chance to go the United States.

We suddenly turned to the subject of girls. "What about them?" I asked.

Clutching his genitals, he said: "A gyal fi get 'hood [penis] in har 'ole, man!" He had his first sex at age eleven, and by age thirteen joined in his first battery with five other boys in the Pentecostal Church on the lane. After that experience, he tricked a prostitute and the eight of them almost killed her *"wid hood!"* She could barely walk when they were through. When it came to *"cunt"*, he boasted, he had no mercy, *"pure agony!"*

Just then, Dali's mother appeared out of another house and asked if I was pushing her son into drug business. I explained my purpose in the community. She asked me for my ID and took some time to be convinced. Then Dali chimed in: "T'ink yu did say yu no business wid mi!" She offered no response. She turned and was about to leave, when I asked her for a possible interview. She had two jobs, she said, and therefore was rarely home. She gave in, nevertheless, and we agreed on Sunday, the twenty-sixth, at 6:00 p.m.

While I was negotiating with his mother, Dali had disappeared. Now he returned with two cold soft drinks. He offered me one, boasting that he owned his own fridge, TV, video, stereo, *"everyt'ing!"*

Resuming where he had left off, he went on to tell me that his job restricts him from having a girlfriend, so he had to *"buy a piece"* whenever he got horny.

Drinks over, he told me he had a girl to check. As I got up off the steps where we had sat speaking, he mused that I was *"cool"*, and offered the following advice, for my own protection. After coming to see his mother on Sunday, I was not to return to speak to anyone else in the yard. Otherwise, people would think I was on drugs, for they knew he sold it, or his boss might think I was up to something.

I respected his advice, I told him, and left. I walked through the western half of the community but could not do any more work for the day. I headed home. It was 7:30 p.m.

At age twelve, the same as our six pitapat gamblers, Dali is absorbed into a game which yields higher stakes. But he knows that the risks are also high, the loss of his freedom or his own life, whether from the police or from his boss. But the sense of power he derives outweighs the dangers.

Although the objective of the interview was to construct a profile on a tough and wayward youth, so tough that his mother had to pack up and run, as he was described by Cat, our main point here is to suggest that there is a coherence between the risk-taking games the boy children in Joetown occupy their time with and the crime and illegal activities the community has a wider reputation for, and further that communities and their informal structures, informal institutions and social life should be counted as agents of the socialization process.

It would be absurd to say that socialization in risk taking necessarily leads to crime. Bof's case below is one of several examples of youths who have little taste for crime, big or petty. They desire and struggle to make it out of this ghetto. Where Dali had gone only as far as first form in school, Bof went all the way to fifth form at Kingston College, or "KC", as everyone knows it, with seven Ordinary Level passes in the CXC. Notwithstanding this achievement, he failed to graduate, having, so he told us, committed two *"unpardonable"* offences, as he said the principal put it: pushing another student off the stairs, in an explosion of anger built up over two years of being *"messed with"*, causing the poor victim two broken arms and a leg; and accusing the administration of stealing the large benefactions to the school, instead of building auditoriums and upgrading playfields, as arch rival and neighbour, St George's College, had done. In addition, he still owed the school $600. This he could pay, but had opted instead to improve his two CXC Grade 2 passes in Physics and Biology, with the hope of doing medicine at the university. How he will manage this, Bof does not know yet. His father had broken his farm work contract and run off somewhere in the United States. He has neither written nor returned since.

Now with seven Ordinary Level passes, Bof has been unable to get a job. He said he regretted his stupidity in turning down an offer which paid $2,500 per fortnight, confident at the time of doing better with seven passes. Now he is desperate, searching hard and earnestly, for he does not really want to turn to the gun.

Then he explained that he had been asked four times to hide guns for older men. His quiet disposition and reputation as a KC student made him the last person to come under suspicion. With much of the *"blood money"* he received for his services he was able to put himself through school. One night, though, he was nearly caught. As he said this, he shivered. He had just been given a gun to deliver to Johnson Street. On reaching the bridge across the drain, there in his way stood three policemen, three of the most famous and deadly. He almost froze. With the .38 in his waist in back, he tried walking as normally as he could, hailing one of them as if he knew him. But just as one of the lawmen was about to call him for a search, another he had not even seen called out, *"Mr KC!"* That marked the turning point for him. He then and there thanked God, resolved to stop the nonsense, and concentrated on his CXC exams.

But Bof is not out of the woods yet. He confided to us that he had a second motive in resitting his examinations, and it was that the more he studied, the less likely he would be drawn to the gun. Socialized in risk taking, *"Mr KC"* desperately wants to shun illegality and crime. And he signals his want by dissociating himself from the street activities engaged in by his friends and the members of the Lucky Crew. While they engage in their ludofest he sits beneath the street light studying.

If socialization in risk taking does not necessarily lead to crime, it is also evident that a life of crime implies a predisposition to take risks, which is what Dali has, and what Chris has. It was clear from listening to the members of a Ludo club jeer and tease one another while playing that most of them engaged in some form of stealing. Once when Chris dodged a *"kill"*, David teased him by remarking that his dodging was similar to the time he dodged the police in Cross Roads. On their way through Cross Roads Chris had asked them to stop, and going up to a man and introducing himself as a security guard, he picked the man's pocket. Only his artful dodging prevented the police from nabbing him. When Chris protested that he was a security guard, Cat corrected him: "Security guard when you are employed, sir, an' pickpocket when yu see a careless man or when di money run out and yu not employ!" Picking a man's pocket need not arise from desperate need, as is clear from this example. The opportunity having arisen of a man carrying himself carelessly, a security guard seizes it, helps himself to the man's money and dodges a kill. Dodging a kill on the Ludo board thus becomes a metaphor for dodging the police in real life, not only in the past but in the future. If done once, it can be done again.

Where picking pockets and other forms of theft are generally male activities, women engage in their own versions. A particularly creative one is *crutchin*, a form of shoplifting. During a diversion created by accomplices, usually two male *teka*, the article is snatched and quickly placed in the crotches of the thighs, where it remains gripped "like how yu hol' yu man wid yu big foot [legs]!" The *crutcha,** who should be big and fat – the bigger and fatter the better – and who must wear a long skirt, must be able to walk in a normal fashion and for a fairly long distance, the article held firmly by the inner muscles of the thighs. *Crutchin* therefore requires training, and one is not allowed to graduate until she has mastered the skill of *crutchin* fairly large objects like a water bucket and walking up and down the yard. Articles of clothing, and appliances such as blenders, fans, and even small television sets are targeted.

The Street, the Yard and the School

We turn to consider three different arenas of influence on the young, which, in this community of Joetown, also function like two poles of the gender axis, in one direction manhood, in the other womanhood. Street, yard and school are not only socializing agents, as such; they also serve as embodiments of social identity.

By "yard" people refer to the space behind a fence and a gate, hidden and protected from public view, where people are domiciled; where they cook, eat, sleep, relieve themselves, wash, bathe, and so on. Most yards in Joetown are what the people know as "tenement yards", private space shared by as many families as there are rooms to rent. They share the bathrooms, toilets, kitchens and standpipes, as well as the actual courtyard, sometimes paved, often not. In the rooms are personal possessions and valuables, like the furniture and appliances Dali proudly boasted about, chests of drawers, dressers, television sets, stereos, videos, blenders. Almost all the homes we entered were well kept, floors shiny or carpeted from wall to wall.

The yard is the only place where mothers are able to control the socialization of their children, not only because they have them within sight or earshot, but also because of the sense of responsibility which other adults in the yard exercise towards younger children. As Erna Brodber (1975) noted, it is an important social space for settling interpersonal and other problems among women. People who are unable to get along with others in the same circumstances and surroundings are considered selfish. Protracted disagreement between, or quar-

---

* Though obviously derived from "crotches", in the Jamaican dialect the pronunciation is identical to that of "crutch". It is the sound I wish to convey.

relling among, neighbours who have to share the same resources ultimately necessitate the departure of one or other.

Betty's yard classifies as a small one. There are seven rooms in the house, each with a female tenant. Three of the tenants, including Betty, have spouses. Between them all, they have nineteen children, ranging from infancy to teenage. Lacking space for the children to play, the yard accommodates two kitchens and three bathrooms. Two have toilets; the third is a simple outdoor enclosure behind which the men bathe. Sharing the common circumstance of this yard, the tenants know well and care for one another. We once observed a young man eating from the plate of three different mothers. Betty's children get along very well with the other families, adults and children alike. The children go to school together and return home together. We even observed them sharing food with one another.

The yard is the place children first begin learning their gender roles and certain social values. Betty is thirty-nine years old and the mother of seven children, ranging in age from her firstborn daughter of twenty-three years to the baby not yet two years old. Only three of them live with her: the baby, of course, her five-year-old son Kane, and twelve-year-old daughter Nadia, all children of her present spouse. The twins are with her aunt in Westmoreland, where she migrated from. These she has not seen since they left over five years ago. Two others are in Rockfort, the eastern outskirts of the city, with her own mother: her son who left for his grandmother when he was twelve, and her firstborn.

Twelve-year-old Nadia is taught to tidy the house, a one-room apartment divided by a thick curtain and made to look very neat and welcoming, furnished with the television set, stereo, crib and three-quarter bed on one side, and her parents' bedroom, hidden from view, on the other. She makes the small bed, washes up dinner plates and runs errands sometimes. She is also taught to bathe and care for the baby. Five-year-old Kane learns only to wash the cup he uses and to run to the shop occasionally. She gives him little to do, *"t'rough im likl"*. But he sometimes helps her dust the furniture, if Nadia is not around. Before Betty sent Ralston to live with her mother in Rockfort, she used to require him to wash his own clothes and to learn how to cook, from he was about ten years old. One thing that she never made him do was *"tek out di chimi* [chamber pot]*"*. Nowadays she expects Nadia to do it, a task Nadia told us she refuses because she is not the only one using it and it sometimes splashes out on her.

Nadia's work around the house will increase as she gets older, "because is not everyday she gwain 'ave mi aroun' di house". Betty's spouse, however, objects that Betty is pressuring Nadia too much, complaining that Betty is lazy. Betty defends herself: "She is a girlchil' an' she mus' learn, 'cause as dem reach thirteen, fourteen, a go up, dem fin' bwaai-frien' an' 'ave children an' go live wid im, so dem mus' learn from now!" Being home more than he, it is her position that carries final authority.

Nadia attends school nearby, and is required to be home immediately after. Except for private lessons, she must find herself home within ten minutes of dismissal. Betty does not allow her to play basketball, Ludo or any other game on the street. Kane, though only five, is allowed the freedom of the abandoned factory nearby to play. At Nadia's age, Ralston was allowed much more freedom. He was different, Betty says. He used to stay out late, sometimes going to spend the evening with his grandmother without informing her. It never bothered her, however, and she was never worried for him.

One of the most valued qualities Betty tries to instil in her children is the willingness to share. She herself gives away things easily, because, so she says, she was born in February. Nadia, who was born in December, is mean. Her little son also is mean. He will give to strangers but not to her, unless she first gives him. In addition, she fears for him because he is soft. *"As yu touch im, im cry!"* She wishes he were as tough as some of his schoolmates.

Other qualities she drums into them are *"manners"*, meaning good manners, especially towards adults. For lack of this she says she punishes them. She rarely has to, so much so that her fellow tenants accuse her of growing the children bad. The last time she flogged Nadia was because she was playing in the house, endangering the valuables. Kane she beat two months ago for playing with matches in the house.

Andrea is another woman who looks to the yard to keep her children from the dangers of the street. She is the thirty-four-year-old owner of a bar. Two of her three children live with her, a seventeen-year-old son and fifteen-year-old daughter. Her last child, a boy of ten, was taken by his father when the two of them broke up. She let him because he was a man of substance. The child is in prep school and doing well. Her daughter, Keesha, just had a baby, so at thirty-four years old, Andrea is a grandmother.

The tenement yard is a small one. Many of the tenants are her relatives – nephew, cousin, sister, an apparent strategy, Andrea admits, to protect one another. Her own quarters are well kept. She takes personal pride in her shiny red steps, on which she has slipped no fewer than three times.

Keesha is her favourite child, and always was, even though she loves her son because he is her firstborn; and even though Keesha disappointed her with the pregnancy. From the beginning, she confesses, she wanted a boy, since girls tend to get pregnant and rude towards their mothers. But she and Keesha have shared life together *"as only women can"*, she says, suffering the absence of her spouse, Keesha's father, in a way that drew them closer. She is certain she could never have been as close with her son. In addition Keesha is bright. The worst she ever placed in school was twelfth out of a class of thirty-eight, the best fourth out of forty-two. All the more reason, then, for her disappointment at the pregnancy. But now that the baby has come, she has quickly adjusted to the idea of being a grandmother and taking care of her grandchild while its mother returns to school. Andrea remains proud of Keesha's brightness, and, as it turns out, her athletic talent as well, for she has won many medals. It was the streets that spoiled Keesha. By her own account she used to beat her by punching her up so hard that when she was through, she *"sorry fi har"*. Keesha loved the street, in stark contrast to her big son, who confined himself mostly to the yard, and who, if he went on the street, it was to a movie with one of his cousins, then home and to bed. Keesha was different. "A dem tings deh me an she use' to 'ave problem fa; plus she 'ave a nex' frien' who like fi trouble people, an' [when people] come complain to mi, mi beat har! [A] girl mus' stay in di yaad and fin' someting to do, 'cause when I was grow up I did not 'ave any free time."

She did not know Keesha was sexually active. Had she known, she said, she would have encouraged her to protect herself, since she knew she could not have stopped her. But she would not have let it go without saying something, as she did when she surprised her son at age fourteen putting a condom in his pocket. She said nothing. With the pregnancy, however, Keesha changed. She dropped her bad friends. Now, according to Keesha herself, there is nobody in Joetown she could "pattern", that is use as a role model. "Sir, dem call nuff a di girl-dem here 'Marky Belly' an' 'Bu'n-up Face', an' 'Cemetery', an' 'Whore'." That's why, Keesha admits, she has no friends now.

Being on the street does not look good, even for a "big woman". Were it not for the bar, Andrea says, she would be found nowhere else but her yard. "Girls mus' stay a dem yard and fin' someting fi do!" Out on the street anything can happen, "worse t'ings dan di bwaai; dem can rape har!"

Despite all her problems with Keesha, Andrea confirms unhesitatingly that it is easier to raise girls. Girls rarely get mixed up in gangs, drugs, guns and such badness, and the reason is the role that the yards play. That is why she was particularly pleased with her son. He stuck close to his own relatives living in the yard and avoided the influence of the street. Even so, she would monitor the time he would leave for the movies and calculate the time he should return. Youngsters who get into trouble, in her opinion, do so because "dem mada kyaan talk to dem". For Betty, Andrea and scores of other Joetown women, the yard represents a protective circle around their children, especially daughters. They are less concerned for their sons, even though they admit that the dangers of the street pose greater problems for boys than for the girls.

What, then, does the street represent? By *street* is meant all that space outside the confines of the yard. It is a somewhat residual category. For Joetown, it refers to the three lanes and nine streets which form the grid within which our study was confined, but from the point of view of the yard it refers also to the bars, video shops, street corners, even the abandoned house where our six little gamblers were ensconced. So that a man who it is known may be found at Shirley's Bar will be said to be *"out a street"*. Compared to the tidiness and pride in the yard, the street strikes a stark contrast: potholes everywhere, uncollected garbage, and sometimes a broken sewage main overflowing through a manhole. At the start of our fieldwork in February we counted no fewer than six such broken mains, but three were quickly repaired. The actual streets are busy all day and into the night with people. During fieldwork they became desolate only twice, as a result of the shootouts between rival gangs.

The street holds one key to the socialization of the children in the community, especially the boys. One little boy grasping the contrast between yard and street told us, *"Di good tings wha' mi learn mi learn dem a mi yaad"*, not on the street. The bad things, he implied, he learned on the street. As mentioned before, it is the young men (teenagers and adults) who control the street, regulate its flow of life, make it safe for some, unsafe for others, engulf the prepubescent male, only to release him a pubescent boy fully socialized into values, predispositions and behaviour that leave many parents, the mothers especially, at loss as to what to do to counteract them.

Noon. Today I check to see if Mrs Morgan will have time to complete the interview we had started about a month ago. I find her, but she is busy stacking up crates all by herself, in between keeping an eye on the stove at the back of the bar. She can't see me now, but I can come back Friday. As I am leaving she says: "One of my nephews is here with me. He is sleeping. I'm going to wake di lazy cruff. Yu can talk to him. Maybe you can find out why him won't work." She disappears upstairs. While waiting, I walk to the front. Out in the street five boys, aged somewhere between twelve and fifteen years, are playing football, three against two, pausing now and then to let through a car or motorbike. The game is intense, full of expletives at every hard tackle or near-goal. One of them wore a pair of boxer shorts that kept sliding down to expose his bare bottom, much to the excitement of four girls watching from the sidewalk. It's quite a long wait. Mrs Morgan's nephew obviously likes to sleep. I look back inside at Mrs Morgan; she shrugs her shoulders, as if to say "Di lazy boy having trouble finding the stairs to come down." I look back out onto the street. Football had stopped. Two of the boys are now fighting. Excitement. The girls are jumping and going wild with amusement. One of the fighters produces a knife. A man whom I had passed seated on his stool on the sidewalk jumps up and snatches the weapon. "Fight, like old days!" he says. "Fist to fist! No weapon!" Then he sits back. The boys are now rolling in the dirty street, punching, tearing, slapping each other. One blurts out: "A yu did start it, yu know! Mi done, sa!" With that, the fight stops. Then strangely, they simply resume the game, as if the fight never took place. The fighter from the side with two now declares he is tired. His opponent taunts that he did not tell him to fight, meaning he should not have wasted his energy doing something he cannot do, namely fight. After conceding three goals, they decide to drop him in favour of a bystander. In vain he pleads. "Res', man! yu tired!" they tell him. He protests: "But di bwaai clap mi t'ree time, an' mi tell im fi stop!" That, obviously, was what started the fight. The others simply remind him that his opponent is not only not complaining but had scored one of the goals.

Fighting is quite normal among boys. By fighting boys are toughened and given skills of survival. Thus, even between friends, one should not lose a fight. Pleading tiredness was, to the boy's friends, only an excuse for losing. This meant he was soft. Softness and feelings in a man earn no respect on the street. Boys are trained to be tough, to defend and give good account of themselves, to win. Losers are punished, as the following demonstrates.

I am in the community quite early this morning. As I enter the lane I notice a crowd, in ring formation. A fight was in progress. Two boys, one about thirteen years old, the other about fifteen, were locked in struggle. I was there some five minutes watching, when the older one struggled free and dashed for a rock. But before he could use it, his opponent wrested it from him and smashed his knees, first the left and then the right. Weakened, the bigger boy collapses under the punches of the younger, and the fight ends.

   Then came a most telling sequence. Out of the cheering crowd stepped a man, who then proceeded to rain down lashes on the loser with the buckled end of his belt. *"Damn wotlis* [worthless]*!"* were his words. A woman also swooped down and fired a slap across the poor boy's face. They were, I was shocked to find out later, his parents. Only as the boy cried for his knees did his mother realize he was hurt, seeing the blood soaking through his trousers, and realizing, grasped his hand outstretched for help. But even as she gave him help, she could not help but curse him a string of badwords, *"Fuckin' wotlis!"* Her only encouraging words, as she helped him away, were: *"One day, yu gwain murder im!"* His father, meanwhile, would have nothing to do with him. He left before I could see where he was headed.

Like the other fight, this one also drew spectators, none of whom offered to intervene to part the two boys. There is no explanation why in one fight they were encouraged to fight without weapon, while in the other no attempt was made to disarm them, except, perhaps, the lethal character of the knife. But what stands out as constant is the expectation that a boy should know how to fight. He should be able to handle himself. And this, in the second fight, required what some would consider the unfair advantage of a rock, but which was obviously not seen as such by the spectators. In neither incident was any move made towards arbitration. Indeed, sanctions were applied against the losers, and in the second of the two, the winner was given accolades by the spectators. *"Yu rough!"*, *"Big up!"* were some of the praises heaped upon the thirteen-year-old, with one man adding that the boy was as good as he had been when he was his age. Sympathy for the losers, even if felt, was never expressed, at least not then and there, on the street. Instead, bearing in mind that these were teenagers and not young adults, what seemed to matter most was the display of the ability to win a fight. That's what boys should be trained for.

We cannot say what would have been the attitude had the contenders been fully grown men. It's not unlikely that knives, bottles, ice-picks or guns would have been brought into play. The single largest category of murders, according to reports of the Jamaica Constabulary Force, is domestic, that is arising from disputes between people related by bonds of blood, friendship, or acquaintance, people who know each other. If one is socialized not to lose, why shouldn't one try to win at all cost?

It is the male who is the target of socialization by the street. The owner of a grocery, which is also furnished with gaming machines, confirms that "girls hardly come here to play, but di boys flood di shop".

I spend almost an hour there, while she tells me how easy it is for boys to be led astray. "I see boy come here from country, and in less than two weeks im into drugs," she says. Girls, too, are easily influenced, she agrees, but into keeping men early. "Although dem a screw hard, dem a use all sort of protection." Look, she points out, how many little cliques of boys there are in the community, "but only few girl groups you will see. Boys gamble, thief, hide gun, sell drugs, even rape in groups. An' when you see a small group, it soon turn big."

That there is a kind of opposition between yard and street, paralleling to some degree the gender differences, may become clearer from the attitudes adopted by Joetown residents. One has been mentioned already, namely the exercise of protective custody over children, particularly the girls. It is six o'clock. A girl playing basketball is approached by her younger brother and told it is time to go inside the yard. We approach and interview briefly another young girl on the street. As we leave we look back to find her being debriefed by a woman we had not noticed before, most likely her mother. A mother will time her daughter's arrival home after school. If she is late, she has to give an explanation. As Durant-Gonzalez (1976:35) observes concerning girls away from the yard in the rural St Mary district, most girls on the Joetown streets are moving about purposively, going or coming from somewhere. Boys have a freer rein.

A second attitude is resignation. Eight boys between eleven and sixteen years old are playing marbles in an empty yard. Noticing our interest in them, a friendly middle-aged sidewalk vendor describes them for us: four lived with their mothers alone, three with both mother and father, and one with neither mother nor father. The last was dirty in his appearance and quite vulgar, his every sentence coloured by choice expletives. She tells us that his father is in prison serving life and that his mother had run away leaving him. He sleeps in an abandoned house, and depends on the sympathy and kindness of many mothers round and about. He is, she says, the leader of the group. And don't believe, she adds, that they are following him for marbles alone. Somehow, he gets "a likl dirty girl like himself an' all a dem battery har in one a di ol' car in di back, night an' day!" He is rotten, she says. Only thirteen years old, he has shown her own fifteen-year-old how to "screw a girl". She too gives him food, because she feels sorry for him, but "im bad-bad, like sore! Yu know dem ketch im wid gun, an' mi 'ave fi hide im an' beg fi man no kill im – t'ief a bad bwaai gun!" So why allow her boy to mix with him? Her answer was a surprise: she could do no better. In any case her son, also, was already spoilt, from when they used to live in the West, though "im not so bad!"

We confirmed her opinions about the boy by engaging him and the group, but the main point here was her resignation to this corrupting influence. There was nothing she could or wished to do about the situation in general, or her son in particular. Only thirteen years old, and calling himself "a rude yout' who no fear no bwaai", the young leader gave us a sound lecture: School was a waste of time. Shabba Ranks, Roun' Head and a host of other DJs were not as educated as we, yet did not have to walk up and down the streets of the ghetto claiming to be researching about boys an girls, but in danger of getting hurt even with our "University cerfitikit". "Di school business," he declared, "is a fraud. A man 'ave fi learn to live, from people who go t'rough di rough and tough. Dat no teach iina school!".

Not all mothers, however, are so resigned. As a third attitude, many try to fight fire with fire.

I first stopped at Albert's mom to remind her of our appointment – "any Sunday at 4:00 p.m." – and then headed toward Ramgoat Lane, just from gut feeling. I was driven towards a thwacking sound coming from a tenement yard, every thwack accompanied by a wail. Five persons crowded the gate looking in, one of them one of my informants. From her I learned that a mother was *"murderin' di bwaai because he use im mada money go buy drug!"* The boy, she said, was fourteen-years-old, not attending school, and now taking cocaine. Something hit me hard, like being shot, though I have never been. Pressing against the gate, I listened to the *"murderin"* like the others, only I felt sick, where they were being entertained. *"A true! Lick out im klaat! Lick out di drugs"*, one man commented, while the four women laughed. I stood there for what seemed like at least ten minutes, when I felt compelled to intervene. She had dashed into the house for hot water to carry out her threat to burn him up, to which came shouts of *"Don't do it!"*, *"Laad, Gad!"* from the women, and from the lone man, *"Bu'n im mek im stop!"* I opened the gate and went inside, my informant following apprehensively, *"Min' she bu'n yu up instead!"*

"Lady, fi Gad sake, no do it!" She was coming out of the kitchen with a battered-in kettle. "Who di hell yu be? Yu business wid me an' mi pikni?" The people at the gate laughed, with this new twist in the drama. As I told her I came from the university to study how boys were raised in this community, she started to cry "A mi parents decide how dem-ya jangkro-ya turn out!" She was now weeping. "Mi do mi best. No faada from im a six!" The boy's father was raped and killed in prison by other inmates, so another convict told her, and she had done her best since. But because the boy had to go hustle for them to survive, he had got mixed up with bad company and now started on drugs. She was about to whack him again when I noticed the motorcar fan belt in her hand, and noticed too that the boy's hands had been tied. I pleaded with her not to. Wiping her eyes on the already soaked collar of her blouse (she seemed to have been crying while she flogged him), she untied his hands. He was bleeding around the neck and shoulders, and through the mesh vest he wore could be seen marks all over his back. The drama over, the small gathering left.

The boy confessed to using cocaine only once, but the little bit was enough to knock him out. For ten minutes I pleaded with her not to employ beating as the method to get him to desist, but to seek help instead. She knew no one she could turn to, so I suggested one of the ministers of religion in the area. By now, other tenants were beginning to arrive home from work. She seemed ashamed as she noticed one lady coming through the gate shaking her head in pity. Leading me inside her apartment, she showed me pictures of herself when she was happy and living uptown, and took at least five minutes to tell me how her parents had disowned her when she got pregnant with the boy's sister at age sixteen, and how, when after four years they had forgiven her, she got pregnant again "wid dis wotlis wretch! A coulda kill im!"

She was totally frustrated and it was obvious. She told me she would have killed herself and him, had it not been for her upbringing as a Christian Seventh Day Adventist. The boy had been caught smoking ganja six times, and now this cocaine. Although she knew flogging would not help him in his position, she could do nothing else but *"lick im and lick im!"* He had taken her week's wage, leaving them penniless, bought the cocaine and then came home *"like se im a go dead!"* When she realized that he was only knocked out and not going to die, that was when she began to *murder* him. Realizing she actually had no money, I gave her $200. This made her cry again. The boy too, who had been sobbing quietly, now began to sob loudly. Pointing out to him that he was killing his mother, I got him to pledge that he would go to see the pastor, who could direct him where to get help.

I started to feel the pain inside me ease. At least I was allowed to help, and the fear that she would burn me with the hot water was gone. The kettle was already cooling on the floor. I felt I had to ask her about her daughter. Her story was the same as I have been hearing since the start of the research: the girl was alright. She had graduated, living with her aunt, working as a secretary and doing more CXCs. The boy, too, is bright, even brighter than the girl. "But see wha' im do wid fi-im brightnis – tek out mi money go buy drugs, 'bout dem tell him se it no strong!" Encouraging her not to give up, and reminding her to take up the problem the following day with the pastor, I left a hurt and frustrated mother and a bruised boy.

Kaila's method of dealing with the dangers of the street was to flog her son, Troy, in the merciless and brutal way referred to as *murderin'*. This was the way it was described by the basic school principal at the PTA meeting in March, when he raised as his final point of concern the way the children, especially boys, were punished. *"Half-murdered"* was his term. That he found cause to raise it was an indication that this type of punishment started from an early age. His plea that parents beat their boys less only elicited the quiet comment from a mother, *"Ongl* [only] *lick can help some a dem-ya bwaai-ya, an' yu have fi start from early! So Mr Jakes can stay deh!"*

Usually, this type of beating is carried out by fathers, the strongly held belief being that a woman's licks are light and therefore not useful. One man in a bar conversation explained that fathers had to attend to how boys were being raised, "cause di yout'-dem iina di ghetto-ya is like leggo-beas' ", and that he himself "bus' di bwaai backside if im mix up wid di nasty bad bwaai-dem iina di community". This was essentially the same reason given by Cat and Denver, who both shared the opinion that "di mada kyaan control da part deh!". Cat was explaining in the presence of some members of the Lucky Crew that when he gets home from work, he receives a list of all wrongs, and "all who fi get beatn get it". When Chris objected, arguing that the responsibility for beating lay with whoever saw the problem, Denver agreed, yes, the mother also flogged, but the "sturdy" beating was father's responsibility. Obviously, where fathers are absent, mothers have no choice but to punish in this male way. This could explain why Andrea felt that a simple flogging with a strap would not have been effective against Keesha's street-oriented ways, and that she had to punch and box him up.

Along with this gender division in the type of punishment meted out to children, especially the boys, is an implicit belief that the more wayward and intractable the behaviour, the more severe the punishment required to correct it. Not that mothers do not have the responsibility to punish, but heavy duty behaviour requires heavy duty punishment.

Believing in this method, parents pay little attention to assessing its effectiveness. Kaila, it turned out, had "murdered" the boy many times before. She later told us that he regularly used to fight with other boys, steal money from the tenants, and have sex with girls all over. Her method then was to talk to him, much to the frustration of her spouse, who, of course, could not beat him since he was not the natural father, but who had warned that the boy would drive her to her death one day or "bite off her ears". She was always defending him when he complained. When they broke up over Troy, she came to her senses, she told us, and "stop lettin' im ruin my life". That was when she began to "murder" him. She burned him once with hot water; tied him in the house for an entire day without food; tied him in an ants' nest until he had sores all over; chopped him with a plate; cut him on his fingers with a knife; and still Troy had not changed. She would probably have killed him, she believed, had God not intervened. The very day she was "murdering" him with the fanbelt, her brother arrived from the country and took him back with him to St Ann, to tend his cows and fashion walking-sticks for tourists. He was a very stern man, a "slave driver" who used to overwork her as a younger sibling and keep her from talking to boys when she was growing up, "like he was my father", but who was also kind, generous and, unlike her, still a Christian. Thus, Kaila still believed that what Troy needed was the firm hand of a man. This was what God in his mercy had provided in the person of her brother, and in the opportunity of a remote parish.

Given such difficulties in bringing up boys, one would have thought that most Joetown citizens, certainly most mothers, would state a preference for girls. It is not as straightforward as that. Although everyone acknowledges that the only problem a girl may give is "di belly", some women still prefer boys. In the words of one of our core group discussants, "Although dem stubborn, you can see the boys giving trouble. But you don't see the girls until it's too late, because dem sneakin'!" A boy does not turn to badness all of a sudden, but a girl will become pregnant overnight.

In a discussion group of five fathers, with nineteen children between them, seven boys and twelve girls, three had a daughter as their favourite child, and two a son. Their reasons were based on either the outstanding achievement of the particular child, or the failure of one from the opposite sex ("him turn worthless"; "she start breed"). In the end, the preference was not gender based. "Believe me, it no matter whether is boy or girl. The truth is I envy Daryl here with him good son, but I feel is the pikni who make you proud you have fi love most – boy or girl."

Thus far, we have been presenting the street in the community of Joetown as a kind of personification of certain values and behaviour shunned by all parents, male and female, who are concerned for their children. The street they have little or no control over, the yard they do. But we have to avoid leaving the reader with the impression that the people's conceptualization of the street is all negative. This is not so. True, the street harbours grave dangers, from which they strive to shield their children, particularly the girl children, but it also provides opportunities, to which they expose them, particularly the boy children. And they do so from early. It is part of the process of toughening them to survive.

Survival is an important objective of the male socialization process. It requires first of all an ability to defend oneself against being taken advantage of, an ability to fight. Asked the most important social skills she values in her two sons, Ursi replies, "being able to survive. Dong ya yu 'ave fi firs' know 'ow to survive, an' 'ave manners an' everyt'ing else combine." Odene, her fifteen-year-old son, is a very soft and gentle boy, so soft that if she talks to him in too hard a tone he cries. After passing the Grade 9 Achievement Test he began attending high school, where the boys used to prey on him, stealing his books and school equipment. One day Ursi discovered that this soft and gentle boy had begun carrying a knife to school. She said nothing, did nothing.

Members of the Lucky Crew accused Cat of treating his daughter, his firstborn, rough. "You a turn di young lady iina a bwaai," Dave added. Cat responded: "A likl girl over deh-so always a beat up my likl girl. Yu know wha mi do? Mi beat har. Mi say, 'Listen. Yu mek sure di nex' time she touch yu, t'ump har iina har eye. 'Cause any 'ow yu come 'ome to mi, mi gwain beat yu, 'cause I'm not goin' to be dere all di time! Learn to fight!" The others, including Junie, protested that Cat was trying to make a boy out of his daughter, one of them whispering to another, so that Cat could not hear, that Cat was behaving that way because he had no son. All agreed that it was more necessary for a boy to learn to defend himself. He must learn to survive.

A second concept encoded in the word "survive" is the ability to hustle, to create a living out of nothing, to beg, even steal. Our six little gamblers learn to survive, pushing Juicy's cart. For them to have been so employed, they would have had to show initiative, to suggest to Juicy, perhaps, that they could help. One informant reminisced with pride that he started working at twelve years old.

Third, to "survive" also entails being able to surmount the odds. Members of the Lucky Crew confounded us with example after example of men who made it out of the ghetto, in support of an argument that notwithstanding the edge that the girls received in educational opportunities, very few achieved beyond the level of secretary. Where job opportunities are concerned, girls are able to get jobs more easily, sometimes with fewer qualifications than their male counterparts, often because of good-looks, but also because they do not appear to be threatening. The boys, however, learn that they will never get jobs by applying for them, that their only hope lies in "contacts", friends, acquaintances, relatives, who already have a place in the world of work, or in giving uptown addresses. In chapter 3 we pointed out that this perception of gender-based opportunities finds some validation in the tracer study conducted by Dennis Brown (1994). It would seem therefore that being able to surmount odds also entails being able to make the correct choice of vocation.

These are some of the things implied in the concept of survival. In essence it means being able to meet the necessities of life in the face of great odds. Surviving makes sense only if there is struggle. And so, valued at high premium, it evokes a sense of historical tradition, in the struggle to survive the infamous "Middle Passage" across the Atlantic ocean, and the centuries of enslavement. Survival makes sense also, only if there is victory. The main folkloric figure of the survivor is Anansi, the spider-hero of Ashanti background (see Bascom 1982), who not only survives but uses brain to triumph over brawn. With a socialization pattern like this, and with such historical and cultural traditions, Joetown dwellers face life with some optimism.

In a final comment concerning the representation of street and yard, I would urge strong caution against absolutizing this dichotomy, and draw attention to a fact that may already be clear, namely that in some respects the two reinforce each other. Parents look to the street to toughen boys and hone their survival skills, and they reinforce this in the yard. The issue of male sexuality also represents a point of convergence between these two arenas of Joetown socialization. But before discussing it, it seems more appropriate to focus on the role of the father, one of whose roles is to provide safe passage for his children, particularly his boys, through the dangerous street. He does it by a firm hand.

Pa versus Faada

Based on the problems highlighted thus far, it would be fair to infer that there is a serious parenting crisis in Joetown. The absence of fathers in significant proportion and the inability of single mothers to cope with the children, especially the boys, are two dimensions of the crisis. Where fathers are present, they do make a difference in keeping a tight rein, but under the strain of the social character of the community.

Early in our fieldwork, we were drawn into a bar by a loud and heated discussion between twelve men, most nearing middle age or older. The subject was women. One of them was making a point that "Yu have fi screw a woman good, 'cause money alone kyaan do!" This met with strong objection from another man, who asked if that was what they were teaching their boys. At this point the discussion shifted to the raising of children.

"Men don't have so much fi do with raisin' children," one man said.

"Yu right! 'Cause a man kyaan stay a im yaad! If im stay, di uman tek set 'pon im. She call im lazy, if im tek a day off from work!" The speaker was around forty years old or so.

"A man who stay a im yaad mus' tu'n wotlis!" interjected a third. "Bare [nothing but] quarrel and uman business! Kyaan tek it!"

So, the mother raises the children while the men work and spend most of their spare time at the bar or with friends, playing dominoes, or, in the case of a young man in the corner, a little gambling.

This led me to enquire whether any of them had a spouse who also worked. Six of them had. Said one, "My girlfrien' work, but she no have fi do dat and mi a work so hard! So she do her work and tek care a di yout'-dem!"

A young man, about twenty-five years old, offered his opinion that fathers should help care for their children, especially their boys, for they needed a strong father figure. "A pure [only] uman raise pikni iina Kingston. That's why so much crime! 'Cause uman no really understand boys. Nuff [people] love di girls-dem more, because dem put dem head to book early!"

Two others commented that boys *"hard ears"*. One of them described how he had to box down his son, concluding that that was why he preferred to let the mother deal with him, for "Boss, mi ignorant [quick to anger] bad, and mi wi kill im!" The young man who brought up the argument explained that he took his boy to the clinic. Four others said they did the same, but when it came to caring for the children, it was a woman's job. One even had his wife's mother and sister at home to help his wife bring up their children, while *"mi look di money!"*

Here the bartender joined in the conversation. "On a serious note," he said, "we have to stay home and see to how wi yout'-dem a grow, cause di yout'-dem iina di ghetto ya is like leggo beas'!" He explained that he did the flogging himself and "bus' di bwaai backside if im mix up wid di nasty, bad bwaai-dem in di community!" His son was soon to leave to join his uncle in the States and he was glad to be getting rid of that problem. Only his two girls will be left, and "is only breed you have fi watch dem 'bout. Not so for the boy! You have to watch his company, drug, theft, everything!"

An old man, at least sixty-five, spoke for the first time. "If di uman-dem lef' wid di bwaai-dem, and we agree se dem no fully understand di bwaai-dem, then no wonder so much crime! For di bwaai-dem no fully brought up! Not like when my faada check mi homework every night when im come home! That's how it was when I was a boy. And I had to answer to him, not my mother! The fault is the fathers'," he concluded, why "di little bwaai-dem roam di street like goat!"

Another man explained that the mothers cannot manage the boys, for the boys are stronger. They need the men's strength. "So," concluded the young man who said he helped his babymother by taking the boy to the clinic, "a dem yout'-ya shoot up the lane later! Dem have pa, but no Faada!"

These fieldnotes highlight the earlier discussion pointing to the need felt by parents for firm discipline and harsh sanctions in male upbringing. It is this felt need that in part justifies the division of labour between mothers and fathers. Mothers are responsible for the day to day upbringing, while fathers ensure that the boy turns out right, by applying the kind of discipline which only males, by their physical strength, are able to. Thus, the portrait of the Joetown father has a hard texture.

That there is a serious problem of deviance among the boy children is recognized and taken as self-evident by the bar patrons, who seem unanimous in locating the cause of it in the failure of fathers to establish control. We should note that the group spans young and old. Once on a visit to a woodwork shop we found the owner-craftsman with his ten-year-old son. The lad was there, so our informant said, not to assist or to learn the craft, but because *"im mada kyaan manage im"*. As a matter of fact, he explains, the boy makes a mess of things and slows him down, but he has little choice, for the boy responds to his authority, not to his mother's. Two other men, on hearing the conversation, verify that they have the same problem. One of them says that his woman cannot manage their eleven-year-old *"stallion"*, so he packed him off to the country for the summer.

The discussion in the bar also brings out a dilemma facing fathers. In order to be effective fathers, they realize the need to be present much more in the yard, but to hang around the yard is either to be subjected to nagging and gossiping, which they associate with females, or to be accused by their spouses of not fulfilling their role as providers. However, from the final contribution of the twenty-five-year-old member of the group, it could be deduced that the dilemma is only an apparent one, that it is possible to supervise boys without having to identify with the yard, to be a *faada* instead of just a *pa*.

According to the definition, being a *pa* simply means siring a child, whereas being a *faada* means assuming responsibility for its upbringing.

We came across ample evidence of both in Joetown, enough to conclude that in this very volatile inner city community, bringing up children, especially the boy child, is a very complex and challenging task.

The road was drawn up to represent the two NBA Finals teams, the Rockets and the Knicks. I needed to speak to these boys, so I asked out loud who was "Patrick Ewing". The smallest boy, about nine, said he was.

"*Yu* too winji [small], man! Patrick is seven foot tall!" The tallest said he was Patrick also, so I asked, "Who is Hakeem Olajuwon?"

"You know the game, man!" remarked the little Patrick Ewing. With that I felt I could beg them for five minutes of their time.

"Which of you is your parents' favourite child?" Only one boy thought he was. Little Ewing felt only girls were favourites. In fact, he said, *"favourite"* is a girl thing. He explained that "the way a boy flex in the area" means that a mother does not too-too [much] enjoy his actions, so he can't be a good or favourite boy.

"What kind of actions?".

"Smoke ganja, touch girl, play 'pon the street, curse badword, hustle, tease people, have sex wid a girl, or wid a woman if she lay her legs open, fight."

"You have done all these things?"

All said yes, except the oldest, who was about sixteen. He had never smoked ganja or hustled downtown. Why? *"Mi mada woulda kill me!"*

This led me to ask my six friends about their parents. Only two had a father who visited occasionally. None lived with a father alone or on a regular basis. They all lived with their mother alone. One said his father was in prison; another that his father was dead; two had fathers uptown (presumably the two who visit occasionally), one did not know his father, and one had *"a man who say him a mi pa iina States"*. I must confess I was a little shaken. I had met this sort of thing before. The boys who are the freest on the streets are the ones most likely not to have *faada.*

This description of their fathers by these six basketball players reads like a repetition of the earlier description given by our six little gamblers: one father in prison, one in the Bronx, two uptown in Cherry Gardens and Liguanea, and one *"mi mada don't see im since she pregnant"*. Of that six, only one lived with his mother and father.

"Dead" and *"in prison"* are two frequently given explanations for the absent father. Dali's father was killed – innocently, according to Dali, but

not so innocently, according to Marva, his mother; so was Troy's father, killed by a fellow inmate in the prison. Serving a life sentence was the father of the *"rude yout'"*, who lectured us on the fraudulence of *"di school business"*.

Multiple relationships are a third source of paternal absenteeism, including the dual marriage practice discussed extensively by R.T. Smith (1996). Many fathers are residents uptown where they already have stable, sometimes marital, unions. The father of Ursi's big son came from a middle-class family and even now lives in a middle-class suburb in Spanish Town, a circumstance that Ursi is proud of, despite the fact that he never owned up to being the father of the child until the boy was big and had started looking like him; despite also his lack of financial support since – *"im no min' im pikni, but im have class!"* In Merline's case, her babyfather lived right inside Joetown, but she did not know he already had another woman. In a quarrel, the latter threw acid in her face. She and her son now depend on her mother, *" 'cause, you know, no man no want me again!"* so disfigured is her face.

The fourth and most pervasive factor for absenteeism is money, either the lack of it because of unemployment or not enough of it because of the demands, or the search for more of it through migration. There is no question that *providing* is considered a father's number one duty, even though Caribbean mothers are in every sense of the word "breadwinners" too (Safa 1995), and at no time in our fieldwork did we encounter men for whom this was ever in doubt. We interviewed informants whose fathers and babyfathers had migrated to Canada or the United States. Some forgot their children the minute they settled, even getting there; but there were others who not only remained in touch but used their financial support to exercise leverage over the children. Twice a month Keesha's father sent money for Keesha and her mother, Andrea. As punishment for Keesha's pregnancy at fourteen years old he stopped the remittances, so upset was he. Up to the time of our last interview with Andrea, a few months after the baby was born, he still had not resumed. In some cases, the hope of one day joining a father abroad acts as an incentive for a child to keep out of trouble.

We also encountered one case in which a father's absence was due to his inability to meet all the expenses of his family. Gutu's mother, Miss Sadie, has six children for four different men, the last of them being her present spouse, Eric's and Sandy's father. But he is seldom present. He sometimes leaves for long periods of time, sometimes up to six months, his return depending on whether or not he is earning money. Gutu says his mother tends to be quite *"miserable"* if there is no money and a man is in the yard. *"A man fi work. Im no serve no more purpose!"* Gutu said she once told her common-law husband. He therefore spends a great deal of the time in the country, but they are still *"together"*, that is, *"married"*.

Here, Gutu's stepfather is pressured out of the house. He is not a man if he is not bringing in the money. Joetown men know that good sex is not enough to keep a woman. Even thirteen-year-old G-G and his eleven-year-old comrade, Besbes, know that what a woman wants most from a man is money, and that is why "Down here-so most man-dem work fi dem uman an' family!" Men require money, the two little, already-socialized boys said, "fi give dem uman and mek dem feel nice!" Two things make a man, one of our older informants told us, "im private and him ability to give money to the family!" "Serious thing!" added a woman, "what else a man good fa!" Gutu's own failure to bring in the money, because he was unemployed, was what he believed caused his girlfriend to take their baby and leave him for another man. Now after the man "screw her and tell her she done", that is of no more use, she has come back begging for them to be friends again. He said he threatened that if she ever did anything to hurt him again she would get "what di duck get!". Being unable to provide for children forces some fathers to rely on the extended family and send the children to live with their own mothers in other communities or in the country. This strategy is used also by young mothers.

Unions gone sour are a fifth factor. This was what happened to Stacey, who claimed her spouse was a bisexual, and what nearly happened to Bev and Jonathan. These two had an argument over their twelve-year-old daughter. He did not feel he should be coming home at 3:00 p.m. to find the child on the street, and said so. She argued that he should try find a cheap but better place elsewhere for them to get the girl away from *"di little bulldog-dem in the area"*. Whereupon, he angrily told her to *"tek her fat ass out di house and go look house"*, for he cannot work all day in the sun, then leave to go look house. She slapped him. He beat her up badly, telling her that if she could not be satisfied with the little he could provide she could leave. She departed with the children. She did return, though, after several days.

One who never returned to her union was Dahlia. She and Jimmy entered a relationship, because, so she said he told her, he wanted a "fresh womb to have im yout', no done-out uman". But after four years, with "nuff beatn and all now no children", she left. Now a lesbian, she "rejec' and ejec' and dash 'way all man!"

The above experiences of paternal absenteism show the quite complex nature of the social relations between sexually active men and women. The female single-headed household, as a phenomenon with a high incidence in Joetown, is the result of many factors, cultural, social, as well as economic. At the same time, however, it is clear that many men function only as *pa*, including some of those who leave their children in search of money. Out of sight, out of mind. Anger towards the careless father who *"didn't min' mi"* was expressed by several men. Gutu's own father, *"a village ram, live and roaming"* from community to community, sired sixteen children all over the place, knowing well that as a barber he could not maintain them all. The old man is now over sixty years old, and his last child, a boy, is two months younger than Gutu's own child. Ray, another informant, is still bitter about his father, even though he has been dead five years. His father, an uptown businessman, was a client of Beulah, Ray's grandmother, who at the time was a prostitute operating out of her house. That was where he started molesting Beulah's daughter. "Di dog did a fuck mi mada and granmada same time." His mother was thirteen years old when she became pregnant with Ray. Neither mother nor grandmother saw him again until his business crashed, his wife died, and their two children had migrated. "Di madafucker come to see mi granmada 'cause him have no money and nobody!" His big son was almost forty years old before he knew about his outside brother, Ray, at the time half his own age. Up to his death, Ray said the most he ever got from his father at any one time was $150, and that was to pay for an inner tube Ray had stolen from a gas station to sell and buy food.

At this stage it may be useful to highlight a few examples of *faada* taken directly from our fieldnotes.

March 28. A man was heading straight towards Ursi. She excused herself from my interview, and for at least ten minutes he poured out his heart to her about a daughter he had whom he could not take home with him, because his wife would not accept the child, although he had her before they got married. He now ended up getting the girl's mother pregnant again, due to problems at home with his wife, and now has two children outside, instead of one. He told Ursi he had come into the community to give the babymother some money, only to realize that she now had another man and was moving away. Even at this point he was still willing to continue supporting his kids. "No one can tek yu pikni dem! Yu mad?" Ursi consoled him. She even suggested that he take the young two-year-old boy and give to his own mother to care for. He replied that his mother was now living in the United States. Ursi would not let up. "Draw a card," she advised him, to make the woman stay; in other words, consult an obeahman.

Friday, May 27. I am in the community at 8:30 a.m. I enter from Johnson Street and stop to speak to four of my friends, just to keep our friendship going. I then met Tambo, an old "brethren" (as he calls me), and could not suppress my smile as I point to his own head and his little son's. Both wore the same haircut: sides shaved clean, top high, *"No. 1"* etched on the right side. What was this all about? He explained: this was his only child. Tambo's mother had taken the child from him, because of some incident on his corner. The child's mother, however, went to Tambo's mother, lied that Tambo had sent her for the child and proceeded straight away to one of the notorious garrison communities in the west end. Tambo marched boldly into that community when he found out, and carried on "bad" before he could get the child. He did not *"care one damn if di whole* [community] *did come fi fight him"*. So, since the day before was the boy's fourth birthday, he gave both of them a special haircut and bought the boy $6,000 worth of clothes, which was half of all he had left of his ganja money, after paying off his debts.

Monday, June 13. When I left the workshop it was some minutes past four o'clock. I proceeded on Sainsbury Street, stopping to help a sick old man cross the street. A man on his bicycle with three kids on it looked back and shouted "Respect!" for the deed I had done, but almost lost control. It forced him to stop and I helped him settle the little girl on the carrier in back. "You alone have dem t'ree here, man?" I asked. He laughed. The three-year-old girl in his arms was his sister's, while the five-year-old girl on the carrier and the three-year-old boy on the handle were his. He used to leave his two with his sister, go to work and return "like now" for them. But since last Monday his sister got a job, so he has to keep her daughter until she comes home, at which time he will ride the child back home. He actually lived over the west but has no problem over in Joetown, because he used to live here. His real headache was caring for the children, especially his five-year-old daughter, plaiting hair, bathing them. His sister used to help. And where was the children's mother? Two years ago she brought and left them with him. She is now somewhere in the United States. She was "not much good from out here anyway!" His hope was to show everybody that they were going to come out to something. I helped him put the children back on the bicycle and watched him ride west.

Thursday, July 14. I was delighted to find Princess at home, having already spoken to her son Saasi. Princess is thirty-nine years old. She has three boys and one girl. Saasi, aged fifteen, attends Calabar High School; Rallo, aged thirteen, attends Holy Trinity Secondary and Roshi, twelve, Independence City All-Age. All three boys live with her. Kaye-Ann, her only girl child and the favourite, attends St Catherine High. She lives with her father in Spanish Town. She is different from the boys, gives no trouble, is helpful, obedient, calm and very bright. Her father, a construction worker, and father also of Saasi and Rallo, took her at age three or four years. It happened this way. One day after the two of them quarrelled, Princess took Kaye-Ann and Saasi (she was pregnant with Rallo) to her sister. When she returned, she found that he had come and taken Kaye-Ann. She believes he would have taken Saasi also, but reckoned that he was too young for his father to care for him. Besides, both of them loved Kaye-Ann more. Princess considers herself fortunate that Kaye-Ann lives with her father, for their one room is not adequate. Kaye-Ann herself prefers living with her father. Princess sees Kaye-Ann every summer. Her father supports Kaye-Ann, but not very well, since he does not always pay her school fees, but Princess is happy for the way he grows her. He is extremely strict and she is well-behaved. After the children's father left to live in Spanish Town, Princess found a man, who lived with, and cared for them. Joshua would treat all the kids as if they were his own, and even after Roshi was born he treated them the same way: he took them to the doctor, attended their PTA, disciplined them, took them to school, to the cinema, the beach, etc. He was a good father, extremely good. Tears welled up in her eyes again. In 1988, a neighbour and friend persuaded Joshua to become a Christian. He had one reservation, however. He could not understand how this neighbour could be Christian yet steal electricity from the Jamaica Public Service Company, sharing it with other neighbours. Joshua confronted him and he repented. He decided to take the electricity legally. However, when he told one of the neighbours who depended on the theft for their electricity, a quarrel developed and Joshua was stabbed to death. Joshua's death turned Rallo into a monster. For over three months the boy suppressed mention of his stepfather's murder. Then one day he broke down in school. He declared he would not allow himself to be killed like a fool. By age nine, he was carrying a knife in his schoolbag. Not long after that he took up with a group of guys who were known to be gunslingers.

Five snapshots of Joetown *faada*. One man thwarted by his wife from taking possession of his outside child, and under threat of losing access to the child altogether; a young man marching into a dreaded garrison community to get back his son; another young man struggling with the plaiting of his daughter's hair, and determined that she and her brother succeed, despite abandonment by their mother; a father seizing custody of his daughter; a stepfather who was a true father, whose untimely murder changed the personality of his stepson. These snapshots are not the only evidence we have of inner city *faada*. There is Andrea's third babyfather who took their child when their union broke up; Mr Morgan, whose one look is all his children need to fall in line, who accompanies them to the clinic, the dentist, the fair, and attends the PTA meetings, monitors their homework assignments, and rents children's movies for them to watch; a woodworker who keeps his ten-year-old son at the workshop with him because only he can command the boy's obedience; a father embarrassed by being called irresponsible and taken to court for a child he is not even sure is his. *Faada* in Joetown, as also in other Kingston ghettos, is an honorific term reserved for any mature adult male deserving of respect. It derives metaphorical significance from a man's exercise of his social responsibility as a man, providing for his family and ensuring that his children grow up to become a source of pride.

Sexuality

In Joetown, sexual awareness begins quite early in life. Basic school boys play out roles they obviously learn outside the school setting, but according to the basic school principal, the girls also invite and encourage boys to watch them use the bathroom. Where, and from whom, do they learn this at these tender ages? The common stereotypical answer is that they learn from watching their parents making love in the close quarters of the one or two rooms common in tenement yards. What evidence there is to support this is too little to explain such widespread belief. And there is no evidence that parents teach them. We therefore have to assume that they learn from the wider community of informal social relations, primarily from those somewhat older than they are. As Greg put it, *"nobody no really have fi teach yu dem tings. Yu know!"* He was about eight years old when he asked his mother what he was to do if his *" 'buddy'* [penis] *stay up long and naa go dong"*, to which he said she only laughed and said he was becoming a man fast. Nothing more. He began learning about sex from his *"bredrin"*, that is the peer group, and from the older men in the bars. The *"decent part"* he learned from school.

By the time small children reach the age of seven or eight, and are in primary school, their sexual socialization would have begun in earnest, though it is probably in the immediate prepubescent period that they begin to exhibit personal, emotional interest in sex. It is around this age that Ursi's younger son, whom she describes as a *"hog"*, would be caught peeping on other tenants and their lovers. But by then he would already have, like Greg, learned from his *"bredrin"*. Approaching the group of boys whom we already met being led by a street-boy who called himself "Rude", we brought up the topic of sex.

"Boss," Mr Rudeboy spoke up, "mi a tell yu di trut', mi do it regular, an' mi let off a girl pon dem yout'-ya sometimes. A shame dem shame [to talk]. But *mi* no shame, as long as *mi* no do a man batty! A dat a shame." And he uses the condom, also, " 'cause, yu see, some a dem likl girl big man a hood too, yu know!" He said he was only thirteen years old.

What is particularly striking about sexual socialization at this age in Joetown is its normality. The video storekeeper thought nothing amiss when our six little gamblers sat watching the blue movie he was screening, probably assuming that there was nothing in it that they would not already have known.

I was in the community very early. On the street there were many girls and fewer boys going to school. Women, young and middle aged, and slightly fewer men, were heading out to work. The betting shop was open, but this time two school boys stopped by the door. I walked close by to investigate, especially since there was laughter coming from the men in the shop. One woman appeared less than amused by what was going on. There was a man I judged to be about forty years old giving the two eleven- and twelve-year-olds their *"first lesson of the morning"*, as he put it: how to use the condom. He stretched it onto his middle finger and asked them whether it was to be used on finger or on *"ting-ting"*. After the two convinced him they were already aware how it was used, he allowed them to run to catch up with their friends disappearing around the block.

But this normality applies to the boy child, not the girl child, and it governs both the nature of sexual intercourse as well as the start of it. According to seventeen-year-old Barry, it is like a rule in the community that boys must begin sex at around puberty. Greg, his friend, had his first sex at age twelve years *"iina one ol' car dong deh-so"*; Denzil at age eleven, on his mother's panel bed; Ivor, on his fourteenth birthday, at the home of and with a nineteen-year-old girl.

And, as "Mr Rude" makes it clear, it is heterosexual activity that is understood, not "batty man business". Homosexuality is taboo. Denzil said his father was quite emphatic: Denzil had to screw a girl, for he, the father, wanted no batty man in the house. Ursi said she sat her big son down, let him know that it is a girl he must screw, "no batty business", and gave him condoms when he first brought a girl home. "Tek dem," she told him, "put dem in yu pocket, yu may need dem. AIDS a go roun!" Trojan declares that he plans to ensure that his boy screw a girl from early, so that the boy can know "se God mek pussy sweet, because batty is fi shit from". And Stacey, a sidewalk vendor, the mother of three children at only nineteen years old, explains how she and the father of her two daughters broke up: "Because im iina some batty business and mi fin' out." Did the community know about it? "Jesus! If dem fin' out, mi dead to raas! Dem woulda call mi batty man gyal, an' maybe aaks mi if im a dig out my batty too!" So objectionable is homosexuality that, according to one young adult informant, batty man rape is worse than the rape suffered by a woman.

Within these parameters, sex is considered quite normal among males of all ages. Among females, however, the picture is more complex.

I had just reached the No. 1 basketball spot when I saw a girl dash out on to the street with a ball. She was followed by another from next door. These two called to three others, all in their high school uniforms, and arranged for a game. Very soon the five were involved in a game of basketball. All except one, who later told me she was a netball "pro", were poor shooters. She was fifteen years old; the others ranged from ten to fourteen. This gave me my entree. "Lend me the ball," I asked, and scored three times out of five.

"This is man's game, not as simple as netball," I tried provoking a conversation.

"Anyting a man can do, a woman can!" the pro almost shouted.

"Except a few things," I taunted. Very soon we got into a heated conversation about males, with remarks like:

"Boys are just wasting time in school!"

"They play too much!"

"They have no respect!"

"Some are hogs!"

"Dem mash up di tings in the house an turn it upside down!" "Dem lazy!"

Stopping them to introduce myself I found out that they already knew I was from UWI, and that was why they were entertaining a conversation at all. Men from the community, they affirmed were dangerous and could not be trusted. That was why their parents did not allow them to play until late. They had "ambition", and did not enjoy mixing with local men, due to their reputation as "users of women". They did not even mix much with girls who "ketch man". So being from the university I was not dangerous. One other said they spoke freely because I looked harmless and must be a Christian. They claimed that they have been repeatedly threatened by Joetown men to "mek dem brok out"; but, said one of them, she would prefer to "brok out later wid a man outside than even di bes' from inside di dump!" Responding to a tap on my shoulder, I looked around to find a mother staring up at me. The girls quickly explained that I was from UWI and "harmless". Whereupon she went on for five minutes about her two daughters, both in high school, both wanting to become accountants, and how they did not "blend with dutty niega!"

After she had left, I asked them about the type of men they would be looking for in life later. "Honest, handsome, tall black man, hardworking, brilliant, talented and good family background" summarize their answers. Not one said rich. "Anybody can make money," the fifteen-year-old explained. "Plenty t'ief live in the community, and man wha' even drive Benz come here, so a girl who love money [will] get knock!"

A number of themes already discussed are clearly evident in this fieldnote entry, among them the danger of the street versus the security of the yard, and the protectiveness towards girls but not towards males. Here, with sexuality as our present focus, an important point is the pressure exerted by males to sexually initiate females. This is what is meant by men threatening to make the girls "brok [break] out". But why *break?* Out of what? The concept implies freedom from the restrictive hold of parents. This is exactly what a girl does when she gets pregnant. She, in effect, defies her mother and relinquishes her designs for her. Andrea's disappointment, it would seem, was triggered by Keesha's assertion of independence, even if temporary.

Yet, like their male counterparts, many girls become sexually active at early ages, too, but unlike them, without pressure to prove their heterosexual nature or their womanhood. Indeed, promiscuity is negatively sanctioned, even where it is imposed, as it is in battery. A girl's good reputation may be lost equally for being a battery victim as well as for being promiscuous. The term *mattress* applies to both. Girls have therefore to be protected from battery, rape and other forms of male sexual abuse. But for their part they have to protect themselves by dissociation from girls *"who ketch man"*, that is promiscuous girls. To *ketch man* conveys the imagery of trapping, usually to win monetary gain for sexual favours. It also implies selectivity. It is not every passing man that a woman would want to ketch. It must be one who can "maintain his kak [penis]", that is be prepared to maintain a woman in her lifestyle, or, as an old song put it, "No romance without finance."

This is where the uptown, middle-class men come in. Downtown women, it is a popular belief, provide great sex, a good *slam*. The bars function as contact points. The uptown men provide money, of course, but they also provide contacts and status. The term *uptown man bait* is used for a woman who hooks an uptown man into a relationship. This is what Ursi did with the accountant father of her first boy. In a tracing match, she told Pam her only mistake was to get involved with *"one low-class man"* (father of her second son), but all her other men were from uptown. The one she has pikni for *"no mind him pikni; but im have class!"* And even though her present man screws her more than he gives her anything, she can identify with him and not have to fear police coming for her, as they do for Pam and her *"t'iefin' man"*. And that thief is the only man Pam has to give her anything – all Pam's other men are from Joetown and *"a so-so kak* [they are all penis and nothing more] ". Yes, Pam shouted back, it's some of the same thiefin' money she has had to lend Ursi sometimes, though. Ursi's retort was, "Yeh! But mi still gat mi pride! No matey dong ya-so [down here] kyaan come cuss at my gate fi dem man. Mi dear, mek mi stay [leave me alone] wid mi mean uptown man-dem!" A mean uptown man, from whom little money is forthcoming, is better than a downtown low class thief, who has to dodge the police. That's the essence of Ursi's sharp but revealing words. She uses herself as an *uptown man bait*. She caught her first babyfather and now her present lover. Her gain is not the money, but the status of having an uptown man.

Man ketchin is clearly not the kind of sexual activity Joetown girls aspire to and only a thin line separates it from the more contemptible prostitution. Prostitution is regarded as the very lowest form of activity possible for a woman, not only because of its cold, commoditized nature, but also, perhaps mainly, because, as one member of the Lucky Crew put it, *"dem suck hood!"* that is, prostitutes have to perform the kind of sexual services they are being paid for, for example fellatio, which is taboo. According to Dahlia, a known prostitute, her son threatened to kill her when he found out how she earned her money. The boy is only thirteen years old and she has had to raise him alone, his father killed by the police just months after he had given up selling drugs and begun to invest the money in a gambling house and bar. "Das why," she defends her life style, *"mi have fi use what God bless me wid."*

Not quite so contemptible as prostitution is go-go dancing. There are, however, no go-go clubs in Joetown, and if there were the girls would be recruited from outside. In this way women can go to work outside and return with nobody the wiser. This was how Dainty met her uptown babyfather. As soon as he started the relationship, he asked her to leave the go-go dancing and got her a another job.

To some women, money is not just critical in a sexual relationship, it is more important than faithfulness. This was the view of an old lady who sold biscuits by the sidewalk. A man can be faithful, "but him have to be two things, a Christian and cold". That's why, she continued, a woman only wants to know that the man gives her the money, and does not bother to "plague him 'bout faithfulness. Most women I know, is di money important." And to back up her view she called over three young women, all of whom agreed with her. One of them, the owner of a nearby hairdressing establishment, said that since men will have outside relations anyway, "might as well mek sure se yu get di money!" "Faithfulness," one of her companions added, "cannot pay bills!" The third was blunt: a man's money is more important than a man, so if a man has no money, he has nothing. The old lady ended the discussion by pointing out that it did not mean that women are selling their bodies – only prostitutes did that, but a woman has little value to a man "if she don't have a front!"

Because the club members had told me how expensive braided hairstyles were and how it was the men who provided the money for them, I stopped by a hairdresser. I was lucky. She was having lunch, while her assistant braided. Those braids, she said, pointing with her chin, cost $1,000; the most she ever put in one for was $2,000. "Where the ladies get that kind of money?" I asked.

"From dem man! Or men!" She went on to explain that anybody who did not depend on a man was a thief or into drugs.

Feeling that she seemed to like me, I knew I could ask the next question. "How did you start this business?"

"A man start me," she whispered. "Dis legal!" She slept with a man about four times, but before entering the relationship she had laid down a condition: "It couldn' go jus' so!" She asked for some money to start a business and he gave her $20,000. That was five years ago.

I asked out loud, "So, a woman's life is easier than a man's in the community?"

Her bluntness shocked me. "If she is not a Christian, yes! Uman get dem pussy fi survive!" She laughed, then looked at me as if in pity. "If a man only have a kak, him no have fi work hard fi maintain it?"

"So, yu sayin' that a man's kak pressure him to steal and get into drugs and dem t'ings?"

"Yu getting' smart!" She then got up and posed as if for the camera, pushing her breasts forward and exposing a part of her leg. "Tell me, if yu didn't have money and yu see dis everyday and only money can buy it, you wouldn' t'ief?"

The other ladies laughed. I had not realized that they were observing what was happening behind the curtain cutting off the lunch room from the parlour. They told me, as I pushed my head around, that their men were paying dearly, too – hairstyle, clothes, and so forth. Only one man lived in Joetown, the others came from uptown. It never occured to me before that women would speak about these things so freely. It was almost as if they were boasting, or calling men fools. When I left we were all smiling.

The ideology governing the gender relations prevailing in Joetown seems very transactional. Men need sex, which women have; women need money, which men must find to satisfy their demand. No money, no sex. In this view women need three things: good money, good treatment and good sex, in that order, with sex coming last. For the man, not so. Sex comes first. He needs it to establish his manhood early in postpubescent life, and to be able to maintain it afterwards. He cannot live without it. This gives woman the edge, because she can always maintain control over the supply side. In Taata's words – he is the owner of an auto repair workshop in the community – women are lucky creatures, made so by God himself. "Dem got wha' man want, so dem use it fi rule wi!"

To adopt a transactional portrayal of sexual relations in Joetown, however, leaves little room for love, particularly in its initial boyfriend-girlfriend stage. Often times it is the joy of mutual attraction and sexual love that brings the young couple together in the first place, out of which develop the later gender-based commitments and relationships. Princess's son, Saasi, has had a girlfriend with whom he has been sexually active over the past two years; she is a seventeen-year-old graduating student of Holy Childhood High School, he is a fifteen-year-old fourth form student of Calabar High, both of them doing well. Saasi is very poor, most days without lunch or bus fare, and for breakfast a cup of tea. Yet he never misses school seven miles away. Knowing all this, his girlfriend sometimes travels over to Calabar to give him some of her savings, though he hates it. These two young people are lovers, whose relationship has not yet taken on a transactional character.

A better way then to portray the complex sexual relations between genders in this inner city community is to think of it as a seamless continuum, rather like a spectrum. On one end is the state of being-in-love, on the other prostitution. And in between are the various stages of conjugal bonding and ideologically determined domestic divisions and responsibilities, as well as the various types of negotiated sexuality having elements of the transactional, but not quite as cold as prostitution. The difference between one type and the next is neither sharp nor sudden, not exactly yellow, but not green either.

And yet the effort to try to put Joetown sexuality into some kind of schema runs the risk of trying to find patterns in a state of revolution, when the old order is changing but before the new is discernible, let alone clear. In some senses the sexual dynamism we found in Joetown is part of the global sexual revolution underway. I refer not so much to the presence of transactional sex, which clearly is not new, nor confined to the inner city communities in Jamaica (see Chambers and Chevannes 1994), but to the "lived and changing relationship" (Snitow et al. 1983:67) between men and women. Certainly as far as Jamaican mores go, the sexual relations in Joetown represent change. Taata's observation above, *"Dem got wha' man want, so dem use it fi rule wi"*, captures only one aspect of what seems to be taking place in Joetown, namely the sense of negotiable power some women are claiming with respect to the use of their body. But there are other aspects.

A seed group discussion late in June had seven female participants: Sharon, a young teenager; Windy, an eighteen-year-old; two women in their twenties, Pauline and Tanisha; Carole, in her thirties; Miss Joy, in her forties; and Miss Townsend, a very religious elderly woman. Except for one of the women in their twenties and the young teenager, all were known to us as mothers. Miss Townsend was also a grandmother. The discussion, which started out on the question of who determined what was right and what was wrong, got around to focusing on parents.

Miss Townsend:	I suppose that is why it's important to live with both mother and father. In my days, even if yu parents don't marry, dem live together for years wid dem pikni.
Carole:	Nowadays-pikni as dem t'ink dem a man and uman, dem gwaan go live a street wid frien'! A want to know why these children nowadays can't hear!
Miss Townsend:	Yu want to know why? Because mother and father have no patience. We have to deal wid dat problem first, or all hell pop loose!
Pauline: (vulgar laugh)	It start pop loose a'ready!
Miss Joy:	You young people take every strikin' t'ing fi joke!
Pauline:	What yu want me do? Cry? Yu no see uman get tough now! We naa cry again! We a go jail or dead!
Animator:	So what you saying is that time change, because woman has now gotten rough?
Tanisha:	Yes, miss. Is survival time now. Not what is right or what is wrong. Whether for woman or for man.

Miss Joy:	The other day my fifteen-year-old daughter tell me to leave her alone, let her prosper! "Prosper" to her is going around with a Junior Don, going half-naked, putting on a million colour in her hair and makin' it stiff like buckram. An' on top of dat, di little nastiness say me grudge her for her body!
Tanisha:	Den you never know dat is competition? Mada an daughter a compete 'gainst dem one another, who-fa [whose] body ready and who more popular.
Animator:	Is this the same for you and your mother?
Tanisha:	Me? My mada is a big uman! She jus' hol' her corner! [does not interfere]. Me and har don't go to dance together. I know what to wear go where. But some a dem [girls], because dem get plenty attention when dem wear dance-hall clothes go everywhere, even funeral, dem continue wearing it! I will wear X-rated clothes go a dance, but me naa go shop or walk up and down di street iina it, because me no want no little class bwaai come touch-touch me up!
Pauline:	A true! Iina Africa dem walk naked and nobody no say notn, not even touch dem! A waso [what's wrong] wid dem?
Miss Townsend:	A no so we live in Jamaica! Fiwi [our] man-dem blood too hot!.

From these women we learn that women today are taking on a more aggressive stance, in three directions. They can be the equal of any man in toughness and in being coarse. Prison holds no fear for them, or as a *crutcha* once told us, referring to her colleagues in the art of *crutchin, "If yu no go a jail yu no have no degree."* Second, they are aggressive towards the earlier generation, and therefore less open to their guidance. And finally, they are more competitive and aggressive in their sexual attraction to Jamaican men, who are peculiar in how hot their blood runs. This last has been known for some time, for the X-rated dance-hall clothes have become quite popular, first throughout the ghettos as an adjunct of the Jamaican entertainment industry, much to the amazement of uptown society. As Tanisha alludes, it has changed even the atmosphere of funerals. But there is no mistaking the appeal. That's why she confines dance-hall clothes to the dance-hall.

Another aspect of the ongoing change is that women are in a position to pick and choose the kind of man they want to have sexual relations with, based on the independence that a woman is able to acquire by establishing her own economic niche. One group of such women is the subset of higglers known as informal commercial importers, who reportedly prefer young men and teenagers. This arrangement reverses the role of the man bringing in the money, usually to a spouse of lower age, and taking control over his partner's sexuality. One of our informants, a schoolboy, said his sister tried to set him up with a higgler, but when he saw her picture he realized that "she too heavy. Mi would have to give her three more years when me stronger. Mi too maaga [slight in body]!"

Whereas higglers can pick and choose their man, another group, lesbians, *"rejec', ejec' and dash 'way all man,"* as Dahlia declared. We had an enlightening discussion with four self-declared lesbians: Mona, thirty-four years old, mother of three children; Dimples, thirty-three years old, mother of four; Sidonie, thirty-two years old, married, two girls; Dahlia, twenty-eight years old and no children. All four came out of long, uniformly bitter, relations with men – "nuff beatn"– a scar from a wound requiring twenty stitches, and other signs of abuse; they consider men uniformly hateful, even if they cannot entirely do without them.

Mona: Most times show me a man wha' treat him uman good, I can show you fifty or more who don't. Dat's why me have a serious hatred fi man! Any man, from him have penis!

Sidonie: Man fi dead! Mek uman run t'ings! My life change from mi stop worship man, believe me!

Dimples: Personally, a five years now a man no cross my foot, 'cause no profit no iina dat. Dem use yu an' yu no benefit!

Turning from abusive men these women turn to other women, and thus have been able to achieve independence from all men: Sidonie has a visa and three stalls; Dimples owns one stall and drives a Corolla, though she cannot read; Dahlia has six stalls, four downtown, two uptown; Mona, herself a ghetto girl, has four stalls downtown, two uptown, a van, a house in Meadowbrook, ownership of the Joetown yard where the discussion was taking place, and two bank accounts. *"No man no have no talk iina dat!"* All four of them are doing well, the result of their own creativity and lesbian relations. Mona tells of her chance meeting in Cayman of a rich white woman (*"Dem say uman luck deh a dungle heap, only fowl can 'cratch i' out"*), who had had similar experiences with her husband. After they got to know each other the woman sent for her and initiated her. "Since then, no turnin' back. As she say, 'Only a woman knows how to love another woman!'" Only Dahlia has suffered a setback, because her partner, a female lawyer, who "did a min' mi to the max" found out Dahlia was keeping a matey and left. As a result, her account is now running a deficit. But they all four live like sisters, "If one eat, all a wi eat!"

The level of intolerance of lesbianism, on the part of both males and females, is nowhere as great as that reserved for male homosexuality. But at the same time, there are male prostitutes who informants say have been forced to sell themselves to homosexuals. "Wi no support batty-ism, but me kinda get a understandin'. For if is a uman pussy cause her fi be so lucky, then some man, realizin' se [that] price deh 'pon dem batty, wi' sell it! Das why mi woulda never beat a batty man again!" Dizzy, a Kingston College graduate with seven CXC passes, came to this understanding after pondering the fate of the twenty-five members of the Ludo club. Eighteen of them had passed through high school, but only three graduated. All, including these three, find it difficult to get a job. Dave, with two CXC passes, is a security guard; Roy with four has become a thief. The system makes it easier for girls.

According to informants, homosexuals like "Lady Jane", a male sixteen-year-old high school student, are tolerated in the community. Because they were born and grew up there, people have learned to accept them and do them no harm, provided "dem never iina fuss wid anybody". The only harrassment they get is a "little jeering" or a "tax levy" on those who serve as whores.

Conclusion

At the end of the excerpt introducing this chapter, I asked the question, "How could two boys, one thirteen years old, the other eleven, already know so much?" Asking *how* is in this instance the same as asking *why*, and the foregoing pages suggest the answer. The streets of Joetown act as the principal site where social attitudes of importance to Joetown society are transmitted. The street is in a very real sense a school – it educates, not only trains. It allows the individual the self-discovery and self-confidence needed to survive in a very dangerous, challenging and contested environment. This is why a Mr KC will survive, and maybe a Dizzy make it, if not to medical school, to some tertiary institution. In a community where hunger stalks daily, threatening so many people; where a boy's stomach ought to be tougher than a girl's; where the source of the next day's meal is sometimes uncertain; and where, with survival as the key social value, women and children's survival are predicated on man's survival, but man's survival is predicated entirely on his own, then the earlier boy becomes man, the better.

Yet, Joetown is not without values common to the rest of the society: the respect for *faada*, the human trust and protection of strangers, personal pride and dignity. But at the same time one cannot help feeling that this is frontier land, on the edge of somewhere else that is not yet, where internal and external factors are being processed all the time into new improvisations that have not yet become fixed. Some of what is promised – *press buttons* and *coke heads* and coarse interpersonal relations – is downright frightening. No society can last where these become norms. But in the processors and the processing is a creative vitality that has shifted many of the culture-building impulses of the Africans from the free villages and rural communities of the nineteenth century to the inner city ghettoes of the late twentieth.

8

Conclusion

Anthropologists don't study villages (tribes, towns, neighborhoods . . .);
they study in villages.

                                                    Clifford Geertz

Addressing the concern that structural functionalism has been unable ad-
equately to incorporate change into its theory of society, Geertz (1973)
locates that weakness "in its failure to treat sociological and cultural processes on equal terms", one always being ignored or treated as a reflection
of the other (p. 143). Accordingly he proposes a distinction between culture and social structure, and proposes further that they be treated "as
independently variable yet mutually interdependent factors" (p. 144), although they are really abstractions of one and the same reality.
     Culture is then defined as "an ordered system of meaning", and social
structure "as the pattern of social interaction itself" (p. 144). Saying that they
are mutually independent is the same as saying that they are not identical,
that the form one takes need not imply the form the other will take. Thus
"there is an inherent incongruity and tension between the two and between
both of them and a third element, the pattern of motivational integration
within the individual which we usually call personality structure"(p. 145).
Elsewhere in the same work (p. 250), Geertz goes on to speak of culture as

both a product and a determinant of social interaction and to draw on several analogies to deepen our understanding of the relationship between the two: what the computer program is to its operation, the blueprint to the construction of the bridge, the recipe to the cake, and so on, culture is to social interaction. Yet, as the computer program is itself the product of prior developments in computer technology, the blueprint the product of earlier bridge building experiments, and the recipe the product of prior successful and unsuccessful cakes, so culture is also a product of social interaction.

Among the Caribbean peoples masculinity is both the product and the determinant of the complex interaction of people, each with his or her own attributes and motives, framed in culturally significant ways. The more we understand masculinity, the more we understand that masculinity does not everywhere mean the same thing, that in multicultural societies "there are likely to be multiple definitions of masculinity" (Connell 1996:208). Between the peoples of African and Indian descent in the Caribbean the construction of masculinity does not take the same form nor mean quite the same thing. And the presence of both ethnic groups alongside each other in a country like Guyana, with their histories of inter-ethnic competition and conflict, means that either group will in the course of constructing its identity use the other as measure, in much the same way manhood is constructed in reference to womanhood. Race and ethnicity are very much a part of Indo- and Afro-Guyanese identity, as both groups construct stereotypes about each other which then become boundaries within which identity is framed (Williams 1991). But in this concluding chapter I focus my summary discussion of the concept of *manhood* as it is symbolically linked and constructed in four areas: the fairly consistent pattern of activities and role expectations; spatial differentiation and identity; comparatively early heterosexuality; and a relationship of super-ordination with women. Of course these are not the only arenas, but these I believe stand out quite prominently in our research in the five communities.

Gender Preferences and Roles

Group preference of boys or girls is determined by the place of the particular gender in the overall system of meaning. What does it mean to Indo-Guyanese to have boys or not to have them? What does it mean to the

African population? Gender preferences among the Indians are well established and clearly understood. Preference is for boys, due to the role which males are expected to play in patrilineal succession, authority over and responsibility for females, and in mortuary rites. Female preference is rationalized by the saying that while having a boy fulfils the cultural norms, a man does not become a man until he has fathered a girl. What is meant is that a man is forced to act responsibly by having daughters to marry out.

There is no clear pattern of preference among the Africans of the Caribbean. Choices seem dependent on two factors, the comparative behavioural expectations of the child, and the particular age of the child. On the one hand, girls or boys may be preferred because they are believed to be more dependable, helpful or loving. On the other hand, the preference is determined by the evaluation of the adolescent – boys are preferred because they give no trouble, whereas girls are a source of problems; come puberty, girls are preferred because they give no trouble at all, whereas boys take a lot of talking to. One man's conviction that daughters never abandon their parents in old age is balanced by a woman's experience that it is the sons who always remit material resources for family, friends and community. The experiences are personal and not shaped by any single cultural norm.

Gender divisions of labour, which begin after the toddler stage, somewhere at age five, are uniformly patterned in assigning males mainly outdoor and females mainly indoor chores. I postpone a discussion of this to make two points. The first is that many parents insist on cross-gender work, teaching boys to iron, girls to help in the field. Often, this cannot be helped, as in the case of a family having all boys or all girls, or depending on the birth order of the genders. Boys who have only brothers or who are born before their sisters have no choice but to perform indoor domestic chores. But such activity is rationalized by parents – as men they need to be able to help themselves, or future spouses are impressed by a helpful mate. But they take great care to avoid over-domestication of their sons, since this would make them too soft. Second, the outdoor-indoor dichotomy is often rationalized as a calculation to save the heavier work for the male, since males are supposed to be stronger. Of course, this may not be true at all. A more plausible explanation must take account of two consideration. The first is that there is, as Ortner and Whitehead (1981) pointed out, a prestige system at work, which undervalues female labour and conversely values male labour. It really does not matter who does what, since labour of itself is not gendered. The only exception, and this is based on biological make-up, is that only mothers can suckle, a function that provides one basis for the conclusion that women are therefore predisposed by nature to be confined to nurturing activities. Ortner (1974) in her famous *nature-culture* article shows in fact that when the division of labour is considered from this binary oppositional frame, *culture* is given greater value and a male assignment. The poignant example of this is cooking, which at the domestic level in most cultures is a woman's chore, but once it becomes a cultural (public) matter, as in *haute cuisine,* it is assigned a male role in the person of the chef and sous-chef. A similar point could be made of high fashion: from lowly local seamstress to international trend-setting fashion designer.

The second consideration concerns the notion of purity and pollution. Certain female chores are considered contaminating. In the African-Caribbean communities washing clothes and dishes, cleaning and making up the house are considered by males as demeaning chores. But disposal of night soil, in families without internal domestic running water, and contact with the female underwear either as an item for laundry or already laundered are downright contaminating. The notion of pollution applies, as is well known in the Caribbean, to the female herself experiencing the menstrual flow. In Jamaica, a male child's growth could be impeded if he passes underneath a woman, and her menstrual flow has the power to "tie" a man when added to the food he unknowingly ingests. All Rastafari families observe rituals of confinement during the menstrual flow, with one group establishing a hostel for secluding such women (Chevannes 1994). Mary Douglas's idea that "all margins are dangerous" (1966:121), and that matter issuing from the orifices of the body is marginal and therefore dangerous, provides a clue to explaining the taboo against contact with excrement and urine. Blood is also contaminating for the same reason. If, she says, we avoid treating bodily margins in isolation from other margins, we may understand why some bodily functions, menstrual blood for example, are dangerous in one culture but not in another. Cultures that observe sex pollution, of which menstruation is one aspect, are cultures with a strong "Delilah complex, the belief that women weaken or betray" (p. 154). The female taboo then is a means of protecting male power. I am unable to say to what extent the Delilah complex is strong throughout the Afro-Carib-bean, but of its strength in Jamaican folk culture I am quite sure (see Chevannes 1994).

There is thus a latent but fairly widespread fear of the power that women can exercise over men owing to their closer association with natural bio-logical processes. As essentially marginal beings women are a potential threat to men. But as Ortner (1974) reminds us, the nature-culture dichotomy applies but with some ambiguity, in the sense that woman is also simulta-neously seen as part of culture, allowing then for her to be associated with both feminine subversive symbols (witchcraft, menstrual pollution) and femi-nine transcendental symbols (goddess, justice, fertility and so on). In Afri-can Caribbean culture women, from their position of dominance in the domestic sphere, do play a culture-building role (Besson 1995), as transmit-ters of the repertoires of folk stories and folk traditions to children, and in religious life as symbols of healing (Wedenoja 1980; Chevannes 1989).

The last is directly linked to a woman's nurturing role, which she be-gins training in from the childhood stage when she is assigned to model her mother's role in taking care of younger siblings. The softness and warmth which her nurturing roles is supposed to bestow on the character of a woman directly contrasts with the tough personality the young African Car-ibbean boy is socialized to take on, to avoid a show of tears on every occasion of inward hurt, to learn to suffer deprivation with a self-sacrificing nobility of spirit. This after all is one of the modes of survival all through the holocaust of slavery; it becomes a motif in cultural tradition.

The softness-toughness dichotomy is translated into a biological script to become a guideline for bringing up females and males. Boys, particularly in the urban areas, when they repeatedly deviate from parental instruction have as it were become possessed by malevolent spirits, which can only be exorcised by severe chastisement that only a man (because he is physically stronger than a woman) can administer. The analogy of possession is by no means far-fetched, as flogging is a not uncommon device employed in some African Caribbean religions to drive out evil.

By contrast, Indo-Guyanese manhood is crafted with a greater sense of collective responsibility, which expresses itself in two ways. First, a man's responsibility towards his family of socialization requires at the least lip service to patrilocal residence, which may take the form of an adjacent but independent nuclear household, or brief postmarital residence, in anticipation of moving out shortly. Many families will purchase their son's separate house site prior to the marriage itself as a way of resolving the tension between traditional cultural values of domestic cooperation and the achievement orientation of the wider social system. Second, a man achieves manhood status by extending responsibility to the wider ethnic community, which having girls to marry out enables him to do. As Brackette Williams (1991) painstakingly describes it, this social demand is called *making life* as distinct from *making a living*. Both Indians and Africans in Cockalorum share a common understanding of *making a living*: productive income-generating activity through working for self or working for others; and making life: an individual's "interest in the socioeconomic well-being of others and his inclination to balance work against sociability – the enjoyment of life through participation in organized and casual forms of socializing, on the one hand, and conspicuous consumption, on the other" (p. 56). Both groups, however, diverge in their understanding of what constitutes work, what constitutes socializing and what should be the appropriate balance between them. For the Africans, making life means being in independent control of work, not being a slave to it, and being able to enjoy its fruits in equal measure with the efforts expended. Indians, however, she says, do not draw as clear a line between work and sociability; work is pleasurable activity. Hence what appears stereotypically to others as working for work's sake is a source of fulfilment. In this regard, religious rituals are considered both work and sociability and the sponsor of a ritual activity refers to it as "doing a work". As a result "the East Indian who places too great an emphasis on sociability, *especially individualized forms of socializing*, over work and works may not be considered a true East Indian" (p. 61; my emphasis).

Space and Identity

The identification of indoor activities with females and outdoor with males is a fairly universal pattern, and therefore is also common among Caribbean cultures. But this is in a general sort of way, since cultures will vary as to what constitutes indoor, what outdoor. Among the Africans both rural and urban, the boundaries of the *yard* are clearly demarcated by a fence and gateway or by seclusion within the framework of a dispersed rural settlement pattern. Some outdoor activities will consist of work performed outside the confines of the house itself, such as gardening, tending to animals, farm work and the like, which may extend beyond the yard, and these are considered male work. On the other hand, some "outdoor" activities are not at all gender specific. Among such would be running errands and fetching water. The yard, however, as private space, is identified with the female. As Durant-Gonzalez (1976:39) observed, in Jamaica it is always referred to as belonging to a woman, never to her husband.

In Overflow, because most of the Guyana coastline is below sea level, houses are elevated on piles, leaving underneath a space of eight or more feet in height, thus giving the appearance of a two-storey dwelling. This space below is sometimes used as a car port or laundry area, and is considered outside, where during a wake or other ritual activity, or a project, the men gather to socialize, drinking and eating, while the women retire "inside", that is above.

Outside of the yard or home is public space. Here the binary opposite to *yard* would be *street*, meaning street corner or bar in the urban communities, or the *road*, meaning the square or cluster of bars and shops in the rural village. This is almost entirely a male domain, where it is a sign of manhood to be able to visit without censure. Men of both ethnic groups attach great importance to the activities which centre on this space, as it is the principal means of expressing and solidifying male bonding and enhancing reputation. Identity with this form of public space takes two forms. One is a sense of ownership, as in the kind of activity known in Trinidad as *liming*, which is defined by Allsopp (1996:348) as "To sit, loaf or hang about with others, usually on the sidewalk or other open space, chatting aimlessly, watching passers-by and sometimes making unsolicited remarks about them." Here is where young women are sometimes verbally harassed as they pass. The other is identification with a specific site, such as a bar or street corner, where friends assemble, drink, receive credit, celebrate birthdays, taunt each other, quarrel, plan, and generally carry on a range of social activities that increase their solidarity.

In the communities studies, this space is where the final stages of male socialization are accomplished. In the African and Indian communities alike, an important part of male life takes place on the street, the corners and sports fields, if they are young, the pub if they are older. This is too consistent a pattern to be explained as a result of parental dereliction of duty, though in fact many adults see it that way. As our ethnographic data suggest, the central concern among parents at this stage of male sibling development is the consolidation of a male identity, and as this cannot be accomplished within the yard or house, since domestication is ideologically defined as female, parents give tacit, sometimes verbal, approval of this change in behaviour. This is most marked where the sibling group includes females; girls, no matter their age in relation to their brothers, have to account for unauthorized absence from the yard, whereas their brothers are rarely subject to such demands. Males, young or old, who confine their activities and pastime to the yard or the house run the danger of a confused identity – the sissy, the *maamaman* – unless their confinement inside is focused on activity that is non-female and carries greater value, such as education.

The institution outside the confines of the yard through which male socialization is mediated is the peer group. We can identify two important functions served by the peer group. One is its role in sexual identity, which I will deal with in the next section. Here I wish to comment further on its male bonding role. It is remarkable how little studied this aspect of male social life in the Caribbean is, particularly in the formative adolescent stages. Its forms vary with age. Older males are found mainly at the rum bar, where alcohol consumption is most pronounced, but also in the observance of important ritual occasions such as funerals. Among adolescents and young adults, the village square and the street corner serve as congregating points, where they gamble, listen to music, talk, share jokes, drink, sometimes play games, and organize commensal rituals. They even support one another by sharing job opportunities. Sports, both organized and spontaneous, occupy a very high place in the order of male youth activities. Among Guyanese East Indians both participants and spectators are male, while among Africans females not only participate in their own games but are the supportive fans of their men. I would argue that this form of male socializing has been vital to Caribbean community life as we have known it. Through formal and informal groups males have been sometimes able to mobilize and represent communities. Without it, in fact, a vast section of the male population, those separated from the education system, would be deprived of opportunities to participate in representative sports, the arts and culture.

There is clearly here also a point of representation and politics, which as we know are gendered. Females make up more than half of any community, and are the majority in most formal organizational structures outside of youth clubs. Yet rarely do they see themselves in leadership and representational roles, leaving these to men. Nowhere is this as clearly evident as in religious organizations, where women do assume roles of leadership roles within the church but reserve ultimate authority to men (Toulis 1997; Austin-Broos 1997). Among Jamaican Revivalists a woman may be the founder of a church but still find it necessary to appoint a "pastor", who by virtue of his preaching role is seen as the leading functionary (see Chevannes 1978). Symbolically, the role of pastor is a male one. In drop pan, a Jamaican numbers game of Chinese origin (called *weh-weh* in Trinidad), in which each number is assigned one or more meanings, the number representing pastor or preacher is the same as that for pulpit, the penis, and the male of all animal species, such as bull, ram and so on (Chevannes 1989). People who invest in drop pan are often guided by dreams. This does not mean that a woman cannot become a pastor or a bishop, and indeed there are examples, but these are as rare as a woman becoming prime minister or president of a country, or as infrequent as leaders in representational politics and community and national life in most parts of the world except Scandinavia. There is a need to study such processes at the micro-level.

In theory, then, women are seldom associated with public space, except where such space forms part of their occupational role, as in marketing. Recreational use of the street or square is restricted. But in actual practice, at least in the three Jamaican communities, such rights and privileges are vigorously contested, for as we have seen females do participate in gambling and recreational activities. Notwithstanding the ideal of female identification with private space and male freedom to own public space, and the routine inculcation of this division in growing children, the praxis never achieves universal conformity. The protectiveness over the girl child through confinement, which is generally characteristic throughout the Caribbean, though decisively stronger among East Indians, never fully achieves the ends intended, as girls somehow find room to express their sexuality, to make achievements, and, in the case of the Africans, to begin their childbearing careers. Ironically, pregnancy as deviance reinforces the cultural norm by making parents more determined about the dangers of the external world.

The one exception to cultural norms governing spatial symbolism is the productive activity of women outside the home. These have traditionally been of two sorts, agricultural labour on sugar estates or supportive activities to male farmers and marketing. In more recent years large numbers of women have moved into professional work. As Rhoda Reddock (1994), points out, Caribbean women were always an integral part of the labour force, during and after slavery and indenture. They were brought to the Caribbean to work. The idea then that a woman's proper space is the house is not as old as we think. However, female productive work, precisely because it is female, attracts less value than male productive work. On the estates women are the most lowly paid, and in the professions they do not receive equal pay for equal work. Indeed teaching, which was once a male profession, has everywhere declined in the emoluments it attracts, because, as Miller (1986) shows, it has been systematically feminized. The fate of higglering, however, proves that we cannot move from generalizations to abstract universals. Particularly among the African Caribbean people, higglering has been a female-centred activity, even in its West African provenance. Traditionally, higglers, including those who market their husbands' produce, retain their own accounts. This gives them a source of leverage and power, which, when added to the ability to own land and household headship, help to produce matriarchal authority and leadership at community level. But this is only one route to female leadership. The other is through religious charisma, usually in the form of healing and divination. The spatial focus of these activities is, not surprisingly, the yard. But so powerful at times is the reputation a woman thus acquires that her authority extends beyond the religious realm.

There is yet a third way in which women are able to circumvent male symbolic domination of public space as political space and to acquire representational status. I refer to the recent but increasingly prominent role being provided by formal institutions. The education system has been the main conduit through which women have been able to acquire and display intellectual and professional leadership. But it is also the main means whereby they rise to community, national and even international leadership in the arts and sports, since most schools invest in these activities either because of a philosophy of education which speaks to rounded development or because of self-serving interest in fame, or both. Other formal institutions are the all-women sports clubs paralleling men's clubs, in such all-male areas as football, cricket and, most recently, basketball.

Despite these advances, the spatial symbolisms endure. It might be argued that they do because women's inroads are fairly recent, that culture lags behind social practice. The fact, is, though, that no matter how brilliantly women perform, their performance is still rated below that of men. The differences in sponsorship, pay, media attention and crowd participation, at community, national and international levels are glaring.

Sexuality

I draw attention to three points in relation to the acquisition of manhood status through sexual activity: the early start of it, the licence it gives men, and heterosexuality, under which I comment on the attitudes to homosexuality. My first point is that sexual activity begins early, among East Indians through ritually sanctioned marriage, among Africans casually and through one of the other forms of conjugal bonding common among them. This circumstance, the presence or absence of form ritualized sanction, would seem to determine the divergent paths of the two ethnic groups in relation to the place of sexual activity in the construction and maintenance of a male identity. By arranging marriages early, East Indians in effect give an early start to sexual activity. And while this has been changing dramatically in that marriages are taking place at later ages than previously, owing to the integration of tradition with modern demands of education, the ideal is still to regard it as a state to be assumed while young. The effect is to put sexual relations within marriage rather than outside of it. This parameter is true of females, rather than males, hence the emphasis on female virginity and lack of concern that the bridegroom also be a virgin.

For the African Caribbean peoples, the fact that conjugal bonds are established without formal rituals is not to say that they are not culturally sanctioned. Statistical data from the censuses for all the African Caribbean islands confirm what our ethnography and group discussions reveal, namely that the majority of first children are born to parents in a visiting union, despite its non-recognition by the state and the church. Roberts (1975) found that the incidence of marriage was uniformly lower and the incidence of visiting unions uniformly higher in communities in Trinidad in which people of African descent outnumbered those of Indian descent. M. G. Smith (1962) also made the important observation that visiting unions, or extra-residential, as he termed them, were socially sanctioned, that is recognized and approved by the community as bestowing on a young man the right of sexual access to a particular female. Thus, the early "extra-residential" mating noted by anthropologists from as early as the 1950s is a cultural practice, which moves towards marriage step by step, so to speak, through common law into legally recognized marriages in later life.

In the absence of formal rites of transition, impregnation and pregnancy are the principal means by which a young male and a young female, respectively, announce their claim to adulthood, often not without resistance by the girl's parents, but almost always with their ultimate acquiescence. The ethnographic work of R. T. Smith (1956) in Guyana, Durant-Gonzalez (1976) in Jamaica, and a recent study I conducted (1996) also in Jamaica, make this quite clear. The pregnant adolescent girl in effect undergoes psychological and sometimes physical separation from her immediate family, remains for most or all of the pregnancy in a liminal state before being reintegrated as a young mother. Most of those I interviewed and their mothers confirm that their relations were subsequently better after being reintegrated than before they became pregnant. I interpret this as as good a sign as any of a change of status. In the present study, parents are by no means unclear about the timing of the transition to adult status. For their sons, some express it as the right to stay out late, others as the moment of achieving economic independence, and still others as the establishment of a independent domicile. All these responses are synecdochisms for the freedom to engage in sexual activity, which comes with biological and social maturity. For their daughters this freedom is never won except by pregnancy.

Even with this transition to adulthood the female is restricted in ways her male counterpart is not. I refer to multiple, casual and promiscuous relations. In the context of the Caribbean it is important to recognize the existence of multiple partnerships, including the dual marriage system (R. T. Smith 1996) which spans different social classes. Multiple partnerships refer to a man or a woman having more than one sexual partner. It is the stability of his or her multiple relationships that makes it different from casual and promiscuous relations. Following Roberts and Sinclair (1979) I further distinguish casual from promiscuous relationships. Both are uncommitted relationships, but promiscuity involves not one or two, now and then, but many partners within relatively brief periods of time, with none of them stable. Becoming an African Caribbean man privileges one to engage in all the above forms of sexual relationships, from the promiscuous and casual to multiple partnerships (which in effect is unrecognized polygamy).

A woman has no such licence. Beyond casual relationships, she is stigmatized: whore, prostitute, jammette, mattress, loose. But here again we are beginning to see that in actual practice women do successfully enter multiple relationships – successfully, that is, without attracting negative sanction. Chambers and Chevannes (1994) report that many women will keep a stable outside relationship to satisfy economic or sexual needs where one or the other is not being met by the primary relationship to which they are committed. However, these secondary partnerships are the object of great guardedness and secrecy, for if known their primary relationships would become untenable. But if these are practices whose sustainability require public ignorance, there are those which the community knows about and incorporates in public discourse. A woman who passes off another man's paternity as her husband's is said to have given him a "ready-made" or a "jacket". Ready-mades and jackets are the subject of humorous gossip rather that stigmatization, as the once popular calypso, *Shame and Scandal in the Family*, beautifully captures. A boy wants to marry a girl but his father objects, confessing that the girl is indeed his sister, but "yu mama don't know". The poor boy goes and tells his mother what his father said, whereupon she laughs and encourages him to go ahead, because "yu daddy ain't yu daddy, but yu daddy don't know".

A man is not a real man unless he is sexually active. But his activism must be *hetero*- not *homo*sexual. Peer socialization among children mimic the gender divisions and heterosexual contact of adults, in "dolly house", and encourages their first sexual intercourse shortly after puberty. Among Afro-Caribbean males, first sex takes place on average between fourteen and sixteen, with females following on average two years later. Which suggests that male first sex is generally with older girls. A male heterosexual identity is not only a matter of personal choice, but is also an issue of concern of the wider community. Many parents are therefore quite anxious to confirm their sons heterosexual orientation, and as we have seen, even to encourage it. Where homosexuality is concerned, we should first of all note that whereas the same condition applies to women, in the Caribbean lesbianism does not attract the venom that male homosexuality does, and in fact is treated with much the same kind of humour that "ready-made" generates. Indeed, a homosexual is generally thought of as being a male. Bem (1993:150) cites this difference in attitude as yet another instance of andocentrism, which so devalues everything female that stepping outside the boundary of correct gender behaviour has more negative cultural meaning for men than for women. Quite apart from the more negative sanctions that male homosexuality attracts, homophobia is particularly intense in the anglophone Caribbean, with Jamaica perhaps heading the ranking.

Following Mary Douglas's suggestion (1966:142) that the belief in and practice of sex pollution is directly related to the existence of cultural and social difficulties standing in the way of complete male dominance, I would like to propose that the intensity of homophobia, as the antipathy to homosexuality is now called, is directly related to male difficulty in attaining certain aspects of the culturally defined ideals of manhood. The argument is in some respects a structural-functional one, in the sense that it relates cultural symbolic forms to social structure. But if we bear in mind Geertz's rider of an interactive and mutually influential process between cultural meaning and social interaction, or Collier and Rosaldo's position that the cultural representations of gender are not simply reflections of social reality but are "*functioning* aspects of a cultural system through which actors manipulate, interpret, legitimize and reproduce the patterns of cooperation and conflict that order their social world" (1981:311; my emphasis)., we may be able to get a better angle on Caribbean homophobia, without falling trap to a static equilibrium model unable to incorporate the complexity of a changing and dynamic process.

It is not difficult to agree that to become and remain a man requires certain kinds of interactive relationships with women, several of which we have been discussing and are about to discuss – sexual intercourse; sexual initiative, special understandings about who does what within the household, who is free to go where and when; moral and material control, and so on. If women are in general agreement with this kind of relationship or even if not in agreement nonetheless acquiesce to it, then being able to become and remain a man should not be as difficult in such a society as it would be in another where women are not only not in agreement but either contest the premises on which the whole social understanding is based or say they agree but make it difficult anyway. In other words, achieving manhood and maintaining one's masculinity may be less secure in cultures where women also appropriate the same symbols that men use as signifiers of male identity. Take for example the question of household headship and the place of the male within the family. Indian social structure and symbolic representation are at one on this, producing a coherent system of interaction including rights and privileges and ritual obligations – birth order preference, headship, patriarchal leadership, patrilineality, patrilocality, mortuary duties, and so forth. Among the Africans, however, the meaning of headship as a male privilege is often in contradiction with the actual arrangements within the household. Dorian Powell (1986) found that many Afro-Caribbean women were the *de facto* heads of household, but *thought* their husbands were. Their reasons were all based on the idea that men are the head by virtue of their masculine gender. Here many women fall back on biblical creation myths and injunctions. As for the place of the male there are no particular rights and privileges from which a woman is debarred. She may in fact be called head even with her spouse present, may own and transmit ownership of house and land, and assert her undisputed authority over her spouse to the point of physical aggression (Sistren 1986). In sum, the personal construction of masculinity is not as secure a matter among Afro-Caribbean men as among their Indian counterparts.

In the present research we did not set out to research homosexuality explicitly and systematically. We came upon it indirectly through the concerns of the people we interacted with within the communities. I think that the higher frequency and greater intensity of feeling with which it surfaced in some communities than in others are suggestive of greater anxiety rather than a reflection on the quality of the investigation, though I have no doubt that this was an overall factor, as I mentioned in the discussion of the research methodology. I would therefore argue that the relative lack of anxiety evinced by young men in Overflow, on the one hand, and its presence among Afro-Guyanese and Afro-Caribbean men generally, on the other, may be explained by the lack of ambiguity about the place of the male in East Indian culture and social practice, whereas among Africans a variety of social practices, such as female headship, independence and assertiveness, are in flagrant contradiction with culturally held beliefs and contribute to a sense of male insecurity with respect to manhood. If indeed this is confirmed, then one would expect to find that the chronically unemployed and "unemployables" are more homophobic than the regularly employed. One would also expect to find a correlation between more intense homophobia and increasingly higher concentrations of female single-headed households, or households in which females are the only or main breadwinners. Changing social structures show scant regard for cultural principles, which have always placed man at the helm. On top of this, homosexuality creates a breach, so to speak, in the male ranks, by directing male sexuality, the principal mediating form of inter-gender relations, to other men. The Afro-Guyanese reflect this interpretation when they refer to homosexuals as *anti*man, *against* man.

The issue here is not homosexuality per se, but the intensity of revulsion from it. Homosexuality has always existed, and continues to exist, in its own niche, has always attracted cultural stigmatization, but the hostility towards it has risen in intensity, I believe, with the increased level of ambiguity faced by men, particularly young men, in achieving manhood defined in traditional terms of domination over women. All this may not be so novel a hypothesis, for the most anti-homosexuals are sometimes also the most conservative, those who find greater satisfaction looking back than looking around. But a comment on a homosexual niche in a homophobic society is in order, before going on to discuss some aspects of power relationships that define manhood in the Caribbean. It is instructive that Caribbean societies which are said to be very homophobic do at the same time provide space for homosexuals. Baxter's Road in Bridgetown is known as a night-life strip which is also frequented by homosexuals and transvestites. In Port of Spain and in Kingston there are similar areas of the city where male prostitution may be fairly openly transacted. This is not what I principally mean by "niche", however. I am referring to the normal, everyday ways in which heterosexuals accommodate the presence of and interaction with homosexuals.

It is curious that the Motown youths threatened our research assistant but obviously did nothing about the homosexual members of their community with whom, they allege, he was seen talking. And in Joetown, another intensely homophobic community, homosexuals may be tolerated provided "dem never inna fuss wid anybody", as the following two anecdotes confirm. A young man I knew was for several years known as a homosexual both in the school where he excelled as a teacher in one of the performing arts and in the inner city community in which he grew up and lived. In both school and community he had normal relations with co-workers and neighbours, respectively. He once took a group of boys on a weekend trip, and on return one of them lodged a report with his parents that the young teacher made attempts to molest him. Immediately, the young man was threatened, driven from his community and forced to abandon his job. In the second case a young Sunday school teacher in a working-class community in Kingston was stoned and driven out for an alleged attempt to molest one of his pupils. Both men had got "inna fuss" with their community. They were tolerated provided their sexuality was not an issue. For homosexuals, in effect, this means avoiding sexual indiscretions and maintaining a curtain or privacy around their sexuality. This is the condition for being afforded space.

But there is an additional price they pay. By symbolically reducing them to the status of women and referring to them thus, Jamaicans use ridicule as a mechanism of controlling the sexuality of homosexuals. This is what the Joetown youths did by referring to the high school boy as *Lady Jane*. Two other names common in the culture are *Mada Lashie*, or *man-uman* [man-woman]. A *Mada Lashie* is a man who lashes with the tongue like a woman. Clashes between men usually take a physical form, those between women a verbal form known as *tracing*. A man who is given to *tracing* is a *Mada Lashie*. The description *man-uman* is interesting because by reversing the word order to *uman-man* one also gets the patois form for a *women's man*, that is a man who loves women, a profligate, the furthest possible from a homosexual. This way of reducing homosexuals effectively treats them as people who need not be taken seriously, the objects of behind-the-back jokes ridicule, which are liable to become front-of-face abuse in conflicts conducted in public. Needless to say, it is no joke to be the object of ridicule, to suffer involuntary marginalization or to be the target of culturally sanctioned abuse.

The Provider

A man minds but a woman cares. This simple Caribbean formula sets out the respective responsibilities of father and mother. A man's role is to provide for his spouse and his children – food, clothing, education and shelter. If he is separated from her, he is expected to provide for his children by her – food, clothing and educational expenses. He is responsible for accidental costs also, such as medical and recreational expenses. There is in fact no limit to what minding a child involves. This responsibility is very well understood by men and women alike. Afro-Caribbean boys know that even before they produce children they will be expected to shoulder some responsibility for their sweethearts. The responsibility is a personal but culturally recognized one. Indo-Caribbean boys understand their role within the context of the extended family and affinal relations created through marriage.

In her study of women in Cuba, the Dominican Republic and Puerto Rico, Helen Safa (1995) found that despite their increasing role as providers and consequently greater authority in the household, they still define themselves primarily in terms of their domestic responsibilities and their men in terms of their role as breadwinners. Men's inability to carry out this role in the Dominican Republic and Puerto Rico actually contributes to marital instability by driving them from the home or makes women reluctant to marry them. The *myth* of the male breadwinner persists, Safa concludes, as a means of upholding patriarchy. Safa uses *myth* in its derived meaning, but the definition of the male as a domestic provider is so universal that it does read like a myth which lays out an ethos of domestic roles and responsibilities, based on an ontology of gender. The power of a myth is its self-evident and unquestionable quality. Working women are not simply being clever or materialistic when they make it, as many do, a condition for a stable relationship. Sex is simply not enough.

This raises the question of male strategies of fulfilling the provider role, especially in countries of the region like Guyana and Jamaica where male unemployment, which although not nearly as high as female unemployment, nonetheless has a greater social cost in terms of criminal activity and social disorder. I mention two, the informal sector and education. The informal sector, which by definition (see Hart 1982) also includes the myriad little and not so little *illegal* ways people use to make a living, has since the 1980s taken on enormous proportions as both men and women ply the air routes of the circum-Caribbean, buying and selling consumer goods, smuggling and selling hard drugs, and creating local criminal enclaves. I bear in mind two cautions: one, that the relationship between unemployment and crime is not one-to-one, for some criminal activities, the drug trade, to cite an important example, are so lucrative that they attract anyone willing to take the risks, employed or unemployed; and second, that not every adult male criminal act is somehow the attempt of a provider to meet his obligations. But many criminals are fathers and this is how one met his responsibility. In his MSc research paper, based on fieldwork conducted in Huggleton, a ghetto several miles east of Joetown in Kingston, Herbert Gayle (1996) tracked the activities of a twenty-three-year-old *teka* ["taker", a pickpocket] named *Naba*, one Friday. Naba's target on that day was $3,000 to give the first of his two babymothers to pay his two daughters' school fees. On counting up the day's takings he found himself short $10, which he begged the researcher, plus a bus fare to return to the streets after Gayle had dropped him off to hand over the money. Naba's greatest *"lick"* in a day was $20,000, from an innocent lady coming out of a bank *"looking too happy"*. Three-quarters of that *lick* he used to repair his mother's house, the rest he split between his two babymothers and himself. I borrow this example not to glorify the selfless display of familial loyalty by a thief, but to show that for some men there is a connection between their criminal activities and servicing the social construction of their manhood. In both Joetown and Huggleton, men who do not hustle for their families are stigmatized by their community as *wotlis* [worthless]. In these communities, the survival ethos trips in as rationalization for whatever actions, by hook or by crook, a man deems necessary to meet personal and social obligations. For him the need to survive is far more compelling than the benefit of an education with its future and therefore uncertain promise, for on his survival rests that of his woman and his children. He must survive. There is no greater imperative. In the circumstances of the ghetto it is his *raison d'être*. He cannot maintain his manhood, his pride, in the eyes of his babymother, notwithstanding the contribution she may make, or in the eyes of his children or the wider community. When we put to Dizzy that pride was the reason why many youths had no jobs, Dizzy countered with two rhetorical questions, *"Who teach bwaaipikni to be humble? A man is brought up to be proud and fi look big, then later he must drop the pride him learn and beg fi get a job?"* The imperative to provide is virtually universal (Roopnarine et al. 1993:22).

A second route towards fulfilling the provider role is education. State and society both emphasize the need for all children to equip themselves with the requisite skills for the job market. The Caribbean perspective on education is instrumental rather than moral – the principal means to upward mobility rather than the development of human potential. Two observable trends are the greater proportion of females within the system and the choice by males of more vocational subjects. The first holds true up to university level, except, as already pointed out in chapter 4, in Guyana, where it would appear that there are fewer East Indian female than male students at the country's only university. At the regional University of the West Indies the overall proportion of female to male graduates is 6:4, with proportions as high as 7:3 in Jamaica. These trends have been used to support arguments about male marginalization, meaning not the male as victim of male power, which was how Miller (1986, 1991) who first advanced the hypothesis meant it, but the male as victim of his own moral foundering. But a true picture cannot be obtained by looking only at school attendance. It must also take account of what men are doing inside and outside the schools and colleges. At school, as gender scholars (Bailey 1997; Leo-Rhynie 1989) point out, girls choose the clerical and service areas, but boys choose the technical and vocational, the ones perceived as bringing higher levels of income – both types of choices determined by prevailing gender ideas; outside of it they generally fare better than the girls, when employed, and undertake more own-account businesses and high risk crimes. If the male provider role is one way of maintaining male dominance, even in only symbolic terms, there is little chance that men are simply going to marginalize themselves. Only by challenging male dominance in these and other traditional areas will women destroy a myth they themselves believe in.

Conclusion

The full impact of all the above points of discussion so far, gender divisions of labour, spatial symbolism, heterosexual concepts and practices, the male provider role, is that Caribbean manhood may be seen as an expression of control over women, a matter of relations of power. And in all forms of power relationships, whether political or personal, power is secured on one hand by prevailing ideological concepts, now commonly referred to as *hegemonic* (Connell 1996; Kimmel 1996), and, on the other hand, where these fail, by force. I have already discussed wife-beating in chapter 4, where I noted its presence among both Africans and East Indians, with the main if not the only difference being the greater tendency among African women to hit back. But aside from the completely arbitrary instances of abuse, wife-beating almost always implies a prior challenge to male control. Women do find ways of resisting, and the flow of history is on their side to be recognized and treated as full human beings with equality in rights and respect. Developments in that direction will inevitably force onto the stage of daily life different ways that men relate to women and different meanings they both attach to them.

The earlier study by Brown, Anderson and Chevannes (1993), for example, raised serious questions about the general stereotype of fathers as essentially providers and disciplinarians when it found a majority of them spending nurturing time with their children on a regular basis. But what was also instructive was the existential meaning they attached to being fathers. When asked how they would feel if they had no children, the men waxed eloquent, using metaphors like birds without wings, trees without leaves, frustration and death. And in Jamaica health professionals have for several years now been noticing increasing numbers of fathers in attendance with their children at maternal and child health clinics. While I would be more inclined to attribute this development to the increased labour force participation by women and other changes in the economy which make it difficult if not impossible for a family to survive only on the income of the male breadwinner, the public praxis of a form of nurturing by men could serve to alter by expansion the meaning attached to fatherhood, especially if, as is the case, they suffer no peer censure for it, and instead attract public approbation. Of course it is not as simple as that, for as I have already demonstrated, symbolic representation is not necessarily a reflection of social interaction, but there was a time earlier in the twentieth century in certain societies when a boy looked forward to being able to vote, smoke in public and drive a car, as markers of manhood. Today at the close of the century he may see these same activities only as markers of adulthood since voting, smoking and driving cars are also female adult behaviours. Who, then, is to say for certain what awaits us in the twenty-first?

References

Agar, M. H. 1980. *The Professional Stranger: An Informal Introduction to Ethnography*. New York: Academic Press.

Allsopp, R. (ed.). 1996. *Dictionary of Caribbean English Usage*. New York: Oxford University Press.

Austin-Broos, D. 1997. *Jamaica Genesis*. Chicago: University of Chicago Press.

Bacchus, M. K. 1970. *Education and Socio-Cultural Integration in a Plural Society*. Occasional Paper Series, no. 6, Centre for Developing-Area Studies. Montreal: University of Montreal.

Bailey, B. 1997. "Sexist patterns of formal and non-formal education programmes: The code of Jamaica". In *Gender: A Caribbean Multi-Sisciplinary Perspective*, edited by Elsa Leo-Rhynie, Barbara Bailey and Christine Barrow. Kingston: Ian Randle Publishers.

Bailey, F. G. 1960. *Tribe, Caste, and Nation: A Study of Political Activity and Political Change in Highland Orissa*. Manchester: Manchester University Press.

Bailey, W. C. Branche, G. McGarrity and S. Stewart 1996. *Family and Gender Relationships in the Caribbean*. Kingston: Institute of Social and Economic Research, University of the West Indies, Mona.

Barndt, D. 1981. *Just Getting There: Creating Visual Tools for Collective Analysis in Freirean Education Programmes for Migrant Women in Peru and Canada*. Participatory Research Group, Working Paper no. 7. Toronto: ICAE.

Barry III, H., M. K. Bacon and I. L. Child. 1957. "A cross-cultural survey of some sex differences in socialization". *American Anthropologist* 59.

Barry III, H., I. L. Child, and M. K. Bacon. 1959. "Relation of child-training to subsistence economy". *American Anthropologist* 61.

Bascom, W. 1982. *African Folktales in the New World.* Bloomington: Indiana University Press.

Bem, S. L. 1993. *The Lenses of Gender: Transforming the Debate on Sexual Inequality.* New Haven: Yale University Press.

Benedict, R. 1934. *Patterns of Culture.* Boston: Haughton Mifflin.

Besson, J. 1995. "Religion as resistance in Jamaican peasant life: The Baptist church, Revival cult and Rastafari movement". In *Rastafari and other African-Caribbean Worldviews,* edited by Barry Chevannes. London: Macmillan.

Bisnaut, D. A. B. 1977. "The East Indian immigrant society in British Guiana, 1891–1930". PhD diss. University of the West Indies, Mona.

Brana-Shute, G. 1979. *On the Corner: Male Social Life in a Paramaribo Creole Neighbourhood.* Prospect Heights, Illinois: Waveland Press.

Brodber, E. 1975. "Yards in the city of Kingston". Institute of Social and Economic Research, Working Paper no. 6, University of the West Indies, Mona.

Brown, D. A. V. 1994. "Reassessing and rationalising resources for greater results: a tracer study of graduates of Jamaican secondary schools, 1991–1992". Unpublished report, Education Research Centre, University of the West Indies, Mona.

Brown, J., P. Anderson, and B. Chevannes. 1993. "Report on the contribution of Caribbean men to the family". Unpublished paper, Caribbean Child Development Centre, University of the West Indies, Mona.

Burton, R., and J. W. M. Whiting. 1961. "The absent father and cross-sex identity". *Merrill-Palmer Quarterly* 7.

CARICOM. 1997. *1990–1991 Population and Housing Census of the Commonwealth Caribbean.* Georgetown: Regional Census Office, CARICOM.

Chambers, C., and B. Chevannes. 1994. "Report on six focus group discussions: Sexual Decision-making Project, ISER-UCLA". Institute of Social and Economic Research, University of the West Indies, Mona.

Chevannes, B. 1978. "Revivalism: A disappearing religion". *Caribbean Quarterly* 24, nos. 3 and 4.

_____. 1981. "Rastafari and the urban youth". In *Perspectives on Jamaica in the Seventies,* edited by Carl Stone and Aggrey Brown. Kingston, Jamaica: Publishing House.

_____. 1986. "Sexual attitudes and behaviour of Jamaican men". Report for the Jamaica National Family Planning Association, Kingston.

_____. 1989. "Drop pan and folk consciousness". *Jamaica Journal* 22, no. 2.

_____. 1992. "Sex behaviour of Jamaicans: A literature review". *Social and Economic Studies* 42, no. 1 (March).

_____. 1994. *Rastafari: Roots and Ideology.* Syracuse: Syracuse University Press; and Kingston, The Press, University of the West Indies.

_____. 1996. "An evaluation report of the Women's Centre Foundation of Jamaica". Department of Sociology and Social Work, University of the West Indies, Mona.

Chevannes, B., and H. Ricketts. 1996. "Return migration and small business development in Jamaica". In *Caribbean Circuits*, edited by Patricia Pessar. New York: Centre for Migration Studies.

Chodorow, N. 1971. "Being and doing: A cross-cultural examination of the socialization of males and females". In *Women in Sexist Society: Studies in Power and Powerlessness*, edited by V. Gornick and B. K. Moran. New York: Basic Books.

_____. 1978. *The Reproduction of Mothering: Psychoanalysis and the Sociology of Gender.* Berkeley: University of California Press.

_____. 1995. "Gender as a personal and cultural construction". *SIGNS*, Spring.

Clarke, C. 1975. *Kingston, Jamaica: Urban Development and Social Change, 1692–1962.* Berkeley: University of California Press.

Clarke, E. 1957. *My Mother who Fathered Me: A Study of the Family in Three Selected Communities in Jamaica.* London: George Allen and Unwin.

Clifford, J. 1986. "Introduction: Partial truths". In *Writing Culture: the Poetics and Politics of Ethnography,* edited by James Clifford and George Marcus. Berkeley: University of California Press.

Clifford, J., and G. Marcus (eds.). 1986. *Writing Culture: The Poetics and Politics of Ethnography.* Berkeley: University of California Press.

Collier, J. F., and M. Rosaldo. 1981. "Politics and gender in simple societies". In *Sexual Meanings: The Cultural Construction of Gender and Sexuality,* edited by Sherry Ortner and Harriet Whitehead. Cambridge: Cambridge University Press.

Comaroff, J., and J. Comaroff. 1992. *Ethnography and the Historical Imagination.* Boulder, Colorado: Westview Press.

Comitas, L. 1970. "Occupational multiplicity in rural Jamaica". In *Work and Family Life: West Indian Perspectives*, edited by Lambros Comitas and David Lowenthal. Garden City, New York: Anchor Books.

Connell, R. W. 1996. "Teaching the boys: New research on masculinity, and gender strategies for schools". *Teachers College Record* 98, no. 2.

Corsaro, W. A. 1992. "Interpretive reproduction in children's peer cultures". *Social Psychology Quarterly* 55, no. 2.

Corsaro, W. A., and K. Brown Rosier. 1992. "Documenting productive-reproductive processes in children's lives: Transition narratives of a black family living in poverty". In *Interpretive Approaches to Children's Socialization* edited by William A. Corsaro and Peggy Miller. San Francisco: Jossey-Bass.

Corsaro, W. A., and P. Miller (eds.). 1992. *Interpretive Approaches to Children's Socialization*. San Francisco: Jossey-Bass.

Crapanzano, V. 1986. "Hermes' dilemma: The masking of subversion in ethnographic description". In *Writing Culture: The Poetics and Politics of Ethnography,* edited by James Clifford and George Marcus. London: University of California Press.

Cross, M. 1980. *East Indians of Guyana and Trinidad*. Report no. 13. London: Minority Rights Group.

Danns, G. K. and B. S. Parsad. 1989. "Domestic violence in the Caribbean family: A comparative analysis of conjugal violence within East Indian and Black households in Guyana". Paper presented at the 14th Annual Conference of the Caribbean Studies Association. Bridgetown, Barbados.

Denzin, N. K. 1977. *Childhood Socialization*. San Francisco: Jossey-Bass.

Douglas, M. 1966. *Purity and Danger: An Analysis of Concepts of Pollution and Taboo*. London: Routledge and Kegan Paul.

Durant-Gonzalez, V. 1976. "Role and status of rural Jamaican women: Higglering and mothering". PhD diss. University of California, Berkeley.

Fetterman, D. 1989. *Ethnography Step by Step*. Newberry Park: Sage Publications.

Figueroa, M. 1997. "Gender privileging and socio-economic outcomes: The case of health and education in Jamaica". Paper presented at the Ford Foundation Workshop on Family and the Quality of Gender Relations, University of the West Indies, Mona, 5–6 March.

Gaskins, S., P. J. Miller, and W. A. Corsaro. 1992. "Theoretical and methodological perspectives in the interpretive study of children". In

Interpretive Approaches to Children's Socialization, edited by William A. Corsaro and Peggy Miller. San Francisco: Jossey-Bass.

Gayle, H. 1996. "Hustling and juggling: The art of survival for the urban poor". MSc thesis, University of the West Indies, Mona.

Geertz, C. 1973. *The Interpretation of Cultures: Selected Essays.* New York: Basic Books.

_____. 1983. *Local Knowledge: Further Essays in Interpretive Anthropology.* New York: Basic Books.

Harkness, S., and C. M. Super. 1983. "The cultural construction of child development: A framework for the socialization of affect". *Ethos* 11.

Harrington, C. 1968. "Sexual differentiation in socialization and some male genital mutilations". *American Anthropologist* 70.

Hart, K. 1982. *The Development of Commercial Agriculture in West Africa.* Cambridge: Cambridge University Press.

_____. 1989. "The sexual division of labour". In *Women and the Sexual Division of Labour in the Caribbean,* edited by Keith Hart. Kingston: Consortium Graduate School of Social Sciences, University of the West Indies.

Henriques, F. 1953. *Family and Colour in Jamaica.* London: Eyre and Spottiswoode.

Herskovits, M., and F. Herskovits. 1947. *Trinidad Village.* New York: Alfred Knopf.

Humburg, D. A., and D. T. Lunde. 1966. "Sex hormones in the development of sex differences in human behavior". In *The Development of Sex Differences,* edited by Eleanor E. Maccoby. Stanford: Stanford University Press.

Hutt, C. 1978. "Sex-role differentiation in social development". In *Issues in Childhood Development,* edited by Harry McGurk. London: Methuen.

Jayawardena, C. 1960. "Marital stability in two Guianese sugar estate communities". *Social and Economic Studies* 9.

_____. 1963. *Conflict and Solidarity in a Guianese Plantation.* London School of Economics Monographs on Social Anthropology, no. 25. London: University of London, Athlone Press.

_____. 1965. "Religious belief and social change: Aspects of the development of Hinduism in British Guiana". *Comparative Studies in Society and History 8, no.2.*

Jensen, L. 1985. *Adolescence: Theories, Research and Applications.* St Paul: West Publishing Company.

Jones, H. 1981. *Crime, Race and Culture: A Study in a Developing Country*. New York: John Wiley & Sons.

Kagan, J. 1971. *Understanding Children: Behavior, Motives and Thought*. New York: Harcourt Brace Jovanovich.

Karran, K. 1994. "Indo Caribbean women in Britain: Why did they emigrate? A preliminary investigation". *Indo-Caribbean Review* 1, no. 2.

Kassam, Y., and K. Mustafa (eds.). 1982. *Participatory Research: An Emerging Alternative Methodology in Social Science Research*. New Delhi: Society for Participatory Research in Asia.

Katz, P. A. 1986. "Gender identity: Development and consequences". In *The Social Psychology of Female-Male Relations: A Critical Analysis of Central Concepts*, edited by Richard D. Ashmore and Frances K. Del Boca. New York: Academic Press.

Kerr, M. 1963 [1952]. *Personality and Conflict in Jamaica*. London: Collins.

Kimmel, M. 1996. "Masculinity as homophobia: Fear, shame and silence in the construction of gender identity". Paper delivered at symposium, Construction of Caribbean Masculinity: Towards a Research Agenda. Centre for Gender and Development Studies, University of the West Indies, St Augustine, Trinidad, 12 January.

Klass, M. 1988 [1961]. *East Indians in Trinidad: A Study in Cultural Persistence*. Prospect Heights, Illinois: Waveland Press.

Leichter, H. J. 1974. "Some perspectives on the family as educator". In *The Family as Educator*, edited by Hope Jensen Leichter. New York: Teachers College Press.

Leo-Rhynie, E. 1989. "Gender in education: Labour force implications". In *Women and the Sexual Division of Labour in the Caribbean*, edited by Keith Hart. Kingston: Consortium Graduate School of Social Sciences, University of the West Indies.

_____. 1998. "Socialisation and gender identity". In *Caribbean Portraits: Essays on Gender Ideologies and Identities*, edited by Christine Barrow. Kingston: Ian Randle Publishers.

Lindsey, L. 1994. *Gender Roles: A Sociological Perspective,* 2nd edition. Englewood Cliffs, New Jersey: Prentice Hall.

Massiah, J. (ed.). 1986. "Women in the Caribbean Project". *Social and Economic Studies* 35, nos. 1 and 2.

Matteson, D. 1975. *Adolescence Today: Sex Roles and the Search for Identity.*
Homewood, Illinois: Dorsey Press.

Mead, M. 1961 [1928]. *Coming of Age in Samoa: A Study of Adolescence and Sex in Primitive Societies.* Harmondsworth: Penguin Books.

_____. 1996 [1949]. *Male and Female.* New York: William Morrow.

Miller, E. 1986. *The Marginalization of the Black Jamaican Male: Insights from the Development of the Teaching Profession.* Kingston, Jamaica: Institute of Social and Economic Research, University of the West Indies, Mona.

_____. 1991. *Men at Risk.* Kingston, Jamaica: Jamaica Publishing House.

Miller, P. J., and L. Hoogstra. 1992. "Language as tool in the socialization and apprehension of cultural meanings". In *New Directions in Psychological Anthropology,* edited by Theodor Schwartz, Geoffrey M. White, and Catherine Lutz. Cambridge: Cambridge University Press.

Mischel, J. 1966. "A social learning view of sex differences in behavior". In *The Development of Sex Differences,* edited by E. E. Maccoby. Stanford, California: Stanford University Press.

Mohammed, P. 1993. "Structures of experience: Gender, ethnicity and class in the lives of two East Indian women". In *Trinidad Ethnicity,* edited by Kevin Yelvington. Warwick University Caribbean Studies. London: Macmillan.

_____. 1994. "Gender as primary signifier in the construction of community and state among Indians in Trinidad". *Caribbean Quarterly* 40, nos. 3 and 4:

_____. 1995. "Writing gender into history: The negotiation of gender relations among Indian men and women in post-indenture Trinidad society, 1917–47". In *Engendering History: Caribbean Women in Historical Perspective,* edited by Verene Shepherd, Bridget Brereton, and Barbara Bailey. Kingston: Ian Randle Publishers; London: James Currey Publishers.

Moore, B. 1984. "Sex and marriage among Indian immigrants in British Guiana during the nineteenth century". Paper presented at the Third Conference on East Indians in the Caribbean, University of the West Indies, Mona, 28 August–5 September.

Nanda, S. 1990. *Neither Man nor Woman: The Hijras of India.* Belmont, California: Wadsworth.

Nevadomsky, J. 1985. "Development sequences of domestic groups in an East Indian community in rural Trinidad". *Ethnology* 24, no. 1.

Niehoff, A., and J. Niehoff. 1960. *East Indians in the West Indies.* Publications in Anthropology, no. 6. Milwaukee: Public Museum.

Niranjana, T. 1997. "Left to the imagination: Indian nationalism and female sexuality in Trinidad". *Small Axe,* no. 2.

Ogbu, J. U. 1982. "Socialization: A cultural ecological approach". In *The Social Life of Children in a Changing Society,* edited by Kathryn Borman. Norwood, New Jersey: Ablex Publishing; London: Lawrence Erlbaum Associates Publishers.

Ortner, S. 1974. "Is female to male as nature is to culture?" In *Woman, Culture, and Society,* edited by Michelle Zimbalist Rosaldo and Louise Lamphere. Stanford: Stanford University Press.

Ortner, S., and H. Whitehead. 1981. "Introduction: Accounting for sexual meanings". In *Sexual Meanings: The Cultural Construction of Gender and Sexuality,* edited by Sherry Ortner and Harriet Whitehead, Cambridge: Cambridge University Press.

Parsad, B. S. 1988. "Domestic violence: A study of wife-abuse among East Indians of Guyana". Paper presented at Conference on the Genesis of a Nation: Origins and Development of Indo-Guyanese, Georgetown, 5–7 May.

Parsons, T. 1937. *The Structure of Social Action.* New York: Glencoe Free Press.

Parsons, T., and R. Bales. 1955. *Family: Socialization and Interaction Process.* New York: The Free Press.

Planning Institute of Jamaica. 1998. *Economic and Social Survey of Jamaica, 1997.* Kingston: PIOJ.

Powell, D. 1986. "Caribbean women and their response to familial experience". *Social and Economic Studies* 35, no. 2.

Rauf, M. A. 1974. *Indian Village in Guyana: A Study of Cultural Change and Identity.* Monograph and Theoretical Studies in Sociology and Anthropology in honour of Nels Anderson. Publication no. 6. Leiden: E. J. Brill.

Reddock, R. E. 1980. *Women, Labour and Politics in Trinidad and Tobago: A History.* Kingston: Ian Randle Publishers.

Roberts, G. W. 1975. *Fertility and Mating in Four West Indian Populations.* Kingston: Institute of Social and Economic Research, University of the West Indies, Mona.

———. 1979 [1957]. *The Population of Jamaica.* Millwood, New York: Kraus Reprint Company.

Roberts, G. W., and L. Braithwaite. 1962. *Mating among East Indian and non-East Indian Women in Trinidad.* Kingston: Institute of Social and Economic Research, University of the West Indies, Mona.

Roberts, G. W., and S. Sinclair. 1978. *Women in Jamaica: Patterns of Reproduction* in Jamaica. New York: KTO Press.

Rodman, H. 1971. *Lower Class Families: The Culture of Poverty in Negro Trinidad.* New York: Oxford University Press.

Roopnarine, J. L., and N. S. Mounts. 1987. "Current theoretical issues in sex roles and sex typing". In *Current Conceptions of Sex Roles and Sex Typing: Theory and Research*, edited by D. B. Carter. New York: Praeger.

Roopnarine, J. L., P. Snell-White, N. B. Riegraf, J. Wolfsenberger, Z. Hossain, and S. Mathur. 1997. "Family socialization in an East Indian village in Guyana: A focus on fathers". In *Caribbean Families: Diversity Among Ethnic Groups,* edited by J. L. Roopnarine and J. Brown. Greenwich, Connecticut: Ablex Publishing.

Rosenberg, B. G., and B. Sutton-Smith. 1972. *Sex and Identity.* New York: Holt, Rinehart and Winston.

Safa, H. 1995. *The Myth of the Male Breadwinner: Women and Industrialization in the Caribbean.* Boulder, Colorado: Westview Press.

Schlegel, A., and H. Barry III. 1991. *Adolescence: An Anthropological Inquiry.* New York: The Free Press.

Silverman, M. 1980. *Rich People and Rice: Factional Politics in Rural Guyana.* Monograph and Theoretical Studies in Sociology and Anthropology in Honour of Nels Anderson. Publication no. 16. Leiden: E. J. Brill.

Simey, T. S. 1946. *Welfare Planning in the West Indies.* Oxford: Clarendon Press.

Sistren Theatre Collective and H. Ford-Smith. 1986. *Lionheart Gal.* London: Women's Press.

Slim, H., and P. Thompson. 1993. *Listening for a Change: Oral Testimony and Development.* London: Panos.

Smith, M. G. 1962. *West Indian Family Structure.* Seattle: University of Washington Press.

———. 1965. *The Plural Society in the British West Indies.* Berkeley: University of California Press.

Smith, R. T. 1956. *The Negro Family in British Guiana: Family Structure and Social Status in the Villages.* London: Routledge.

———. 1996. *The Matrifocal Family: Power, Pluralism and Politics.* London: Routledge.

Smith, R. T., and C. Jayawardena. 1958. "Hindu marriage customs in British Guiana". *Social and Economic Studies* 7.

_____. 1959. "Marriage and the family amongst East Indians in British Guiana". *Social and Economic Studies* 8.

_____. 1996 [1967]. "Caste and social status among the Indians of Guyana". In *The Matrifocal Family: Power, Pluralism and Politics,* edited by Raymond T. Smith. New York: Routledge.

Snitow, A., C. Stansell, and S. Thompson. 1983. Introduction. In *Powers of Desire: the Politics of Sexuality,* edited by Ann Snitow, Chistine Stansell and Sharon Thompson. New York: Monthly Review Press.

Stone, C. 1980. *Democracy and Clientelism in Jamaica.* New Brunswick: Transaction Books.

Thakur, A. P. 1978. "The impact of technology on agriculture: A study of the mechanization of Guyana's rice industry". PhD diss. University of Alberta.

Toulis, N. R. 1997. *Believing Identity: Pentecostalism and the Mediation of Jamaican Ethnicity and Gender in England.* Oxford: Berg.

Tyler, S. A. 1986 [1973]. *India: An Anthropological Perspective.* Prospect Heights, Illinois: Waveland Press.

Van Gennep, A. 1960. *The Rites of Passage.* London: Routledge and Kegan Paul.

Wedenoja, W. 1980. "Modernization and the Pentecostal movement in Jamaica". In *Perspectives on Pentecostalism,* edited by Stephen Glazier. Washington, DC: University Press of America.

Whiting, B., and C. Edwards. 1988. *Children of Different Worlds: The Formation of Social Behavior.* Cambridge, Massachusetts: Harvard University Press.

Williams, B. F. 1991. *Stains on My Name, War in my Veins: Guyana and the Politics of Cultural Struggle.* Durham: Duke University Press.

Wilson, P. 1973. *Crab Antics: The Social Anthropology of English-Speaking Negro Societies of the Caribbean.* New Haven: Yale University Press.

Witter, M., and C. Kirton. 1990. "The informal economy in Jamaica: Some empirical exercises". Unpublished paper, Institute of Social and Economic Research, University of the West Indies, Mona.

World Bank. 1997. *World Development Report 1997.* Washington, DC: World Bank.

Index